Automotive SHEET METAL
Forming & Fabrication

Matt Joseph

CarTech®

CarTech®
CarTech®, Inc.
39966 Grand Avenue
North Branch, MN 55056
Phone: 651-277-1200 or 800-551-4754
Fax: 651-277-1203
www.cartechbooks.com

© 2011 by Matt Joseph

All rights reserved. No part of this publication may be reproduced or utilized in any form or by any means, electronic or mechanical, including photocopying, recording, or by any information storage and retrieval system, without prior permission from the Publisher. All text, photographs, and artwork are the property of the Author unless otherwise noted or credited.

The information in this work is true and complete to the best of our knowledge. However, all information is presented without any guarantee on the part of the Author or Publisher, who also disclaim any liability incurred in connection with the use of the information and any implied warranties of merchantability or fitness for a particular purpose. Readers are responsible for taking suitable and appropriate safety measures when performing any of the operations or activities described in this work.

All trademarks, trade names, model names and numbers, and other product designations referred to herein are the property of their respective owners and are used solely for identification purposes. This work is a publication of CarTech, Inc., and has not been licensed, approved, sponsored, or endorsed by any other person or entity. The Publisher is not associated with any product, service, or vendor mentioned in this book, and does not endorse the products or services of any vendor mentioned in this book.

Edit by Paul Johnson
Layout by Connie DeFlorin

ISBN 978-1-61325-171-3
Item No. SA196P

Library of Congress Cataloging-in-Publication Data

Joseph, Matt
  Automotive Sheet metal forming & fabrication / by Matt Joseph.
       p. cm.
   ISBN 978-1-934709-36-8
   1. Automobiles--Bodies--Maintenance and repair. 2. Sheet-metal work. I. Title. II. Title: Sheet metal forming and fabrication.
   TL255.8.J67 2011
   629.2'60288--dc22
                              2010036411

Written, edited, and designed in the U.S.A.
Printed in the U.S.A.

Front Cover:
The English wheel shapes thin gauge sheet metal between its upper and lower wheels. Whether it's aluminum or steel sheet metal, a wondrous variety of parts can formed with this piece of equipment.

Title Page:
To fabricate the outer part of this fender from sheet metal, you would have to shrink the area around the wheel arch opening. When you can see why this is so, you have grasped the essence of what flat metal has to do to assume specific, three-dimensional shapes.

Back Cover Photos

Top Left:
The metal hammer, plastic-clad dolly, and small shot bag are among the most basic metal working tools, and among the most useful. With just these three tools, it is amazing how much can be done to shape metal, particularly aluminum alloys.

Top Right:
This panel seam is being TIG welded between and over tack welds, which are visible to the left of the arc. While TIG is the premier choice for quality thin section fabrication welding, some other methods also work well.

Middle Left:
Riveting panels together, and to substructure, with a pneumatic rivet gun is one of several time-honored ways to join them. Many, but by no means all, of the other ways involve heat.

Middle Right:
As this metal brace part is worked further, it becomes smooth and visually acceptable for what it is supposed to be. This is not a bludgeoning, but an imaginative and carefully calculated way to make a part strong and visually acceptable.

Bottom Left:
The Eckold shrinking heads shown here are performing two operations simultaneously, shrinking and smoothing a panel. The Eckold shrinking device can move plenty of metal, but does it so gently that it does not damage the metal's surface.

Bottom Right:
The cross wheeling pattern, shown here, is usable for some forming and a lot of smoothing at the same time. When you get the hang of it, it's amazing what you can do with an English wheel.

CONTENTS

Acknowledgments 4
Preface 5
Introduction 6

Chapter 1: First Considerations 8
A Wide Range of Possible Projects 11
Limits of Material, Skills and Imagination 12
Subtle Factors to Consider 14

Chapter 2: Auto Body Metal 18
Characteristics of Sheet Metal 19
Alloys: Steel and Aluminum 21
Work Hardening and Strengthening 21
Workability 24
Heating and Annealing 24
Selecting Metals and Their Alloys 27
Acquiring Metal Stock 28

Chapter 3: The Art of Making Sheet Metal Work With You 29
Basic Theories of Metal Forming 31
Bilateralism and Other Tricks 34
The Importance of Good Foundations 36

Chapter 4: Planning and Implementing 38
Choosing Constructions, Materials and Tools 40
Modeling, Patterning and Templating 41
Measuring, Drawing and Laying Out Work 42
Structural vs. Nonstructural Fabrications 46

Chapter 5: Major Forming and Fabricating Processes 47
Cutting 47
Simple Bending 50
Flanging 52
Creating the Correct Crown 53
Wheeling 58
Power Hammer Forming 59
Avoiding Unnecessary Damage 60

Chapter 6: Other Processes and Skills 61
Filing 61
Sanding 62
Edge Deburring 63
Drilling, Piercing and Punching 63
Edge Treatments and Bead Rolling 63
Louvers and Exotic Trim Formations 65
Using Tension 65

Chapter 7: Finishing Processes and Touches 67
Checking Final Dimensions, Contours and Attachments 67
Weld Finishing 68
Metal Finishing 69
Checking Metal Integrity 72

Chapter 8: Filling with Lead and Plastic 73
Four Types of Filler 73
Proper Filler Application 74
Proper Shaping and Smoothing Techniques 75
Proper Surface Preparation 80

Chapter 9: Tools and Equipment 82
Hand and Vise Tools 83
Specialty Tools 84
Clamping and Fixturing Tools 85
Making Special-Purpose Hand Tools 86
Small Equipment 88
Multi-Purpose Devices 91
Power and Hand Tools 92
Blacksmith Tools 92

Chapter 10: The Art of the English Wheel 94
Using an English Wheel 95
Effective versus Harmful Techniques 97

Chapter 11: Power-Operated Machines 99
Power Hammers 100
Big Machine Basics 100
Special Power Hammer Tooling 103

Chapter 12: Methods of Attachment 105
Non-Welding Jointure Techniques 106
Welding 108
Tips for Fabrication Welds 111

Chapter 13: Small Demonstration Project: The Little Black Box 114
Meet the Little Black Box 115
The Basic Plan 115
Preliminaries 117
Forming the Top Piece 119
Making the Skirt 124
Assembling the Two Pieces 125

Chapter 14: Large Demonstration Project: Fender Fabrication 131
Planning and Patterning 132
Fabricating the Side Section 133
Fabricating the Top Section 136
Joining the Two Pieces 138
Wire Edging the Fender Panel 140
Making Support and Base Brackets 141

Appendix 144
Radiated Colors 144
Gauge Specifications 144

DEDICATION

To Herb Statz for helping so much with this book, and for being such a great friend

ACKNOWLEDGMENTS

Three main and very different resources were drawn on extensively to photograph and write this book. All three were essential to its existence.

The first was the extraordinary intelligence, skill, and good humor of Herb Statz of Waunakee, Wisconsin.

It is Herb's skilled hands that you see in many of the photographs in this book that illustrate sheet metal procedures and processes. But Herb did so much more than hand modeling for this book. *Automotive Sheet Metal Forming and Fabrication* is really a collaboration that draws on both of our knowledge, skills, and experience. As a bonus, Herb's outstanding good nature makes it a genuine pleasure to work with him and to be anywhere near him. This is the second book that we have worked on together, and I hope that there will be more.

The second resource that I relied on was L'Cars, Bob Lorkowski's amazing restoration and fabrication enterprise in Cameron, Wisconsin. In this case, "amazing" covers a comprehensively broad range of restoration and fabrication services that are, without exception, delivered at the highest possible levels of quality.

I have toured enough restoration and fabrication shops to know the real thing when I see it. L'Cars is that real thing, because Bob Lorkowski and his workers have the skills, knowledge, tools, and equipment to do sheet metal work, and other work, consistently to world class standards.

Beyond the basics, a spacious, well organized, well lit, and beautifully equipped shop, staffed by knowledgeable and accomplished craftsmen, L'Cars has something else, something that gives them a competitive advantage. The L'Cars workers have enthusiasm and a spirit of inquiry regarding this work that they do so well. Upfront, they don't pretend or claim to know everything about metal fabrication, even though they probably do. That's refreshing.

Wayne, Blaine, and Matt in L'Cars' metal shop are among the best practitioners of sheet metal fabrication in the world, but they never show any pretense or puffery about their extraordinary skills and accomplishments. They always seem to be looking for better ways to plan their projects and perform their tasks. It is that humility and freshness that gives them their terrific edge in this work.

Those who are willing to listen, experiment, and learn, no matter how advanced they already are, will always find ways to improve, because they know that improvement is possible, no matter how good you are. And these guys are good—like no one else I have ever seen doing this work.

Creating an environment where all of this is possible is a great achievement. Bob Lorkowski has succeeded in creating an environment of skilled, cooperating, and growing craftsmen in the metal shop at L'Cars. I know of no other place quite like it.

My thanks to Bob for opening L'Cars to me and letting me photograph and learn from Blaine, Wayne, and Matt, as they routinely performed sheet metal fabrication miracles. At least, they seemed like miracles to me. These men's willingness to share their knowledge and good humor was outstanding and extraordinary. I am greatly in their debt.

Finally, Jim Crews at Tin Man Fabrication graciously let me photograph some of the street rod and restoration work in progress in his shop in Oak Grove, Minnesota. Jim's shop is a wonderfully open and beautifully equipped and organized place. He brings an astounding level of skill and knowledge to his work on street rods and other metal working projects. It was a genuine pleasure to watch and to learn from him as he worked.

PREFACE

As with any other fabrication project, writing a book about sheet metal fabrication should have a purpose, goals, a guiding concept, and methods that will lead to success.

The purpose of this book is simply to communicate to readers as much useful information as possible about the theories and practices that are the basis for high-quality sheet metal fabrication work.

The goal is to communicate this material in ways that are clear and useful to readers. That means that after reading this book, or reading parts of it for reference, readers will know, understand, and retain the material that they have read. The motto for this goal might be, "Here today, with you tomorrow, and part of what you know and understand for the long haul."

The guiding concept for this book is to keep it as simple as possible. This guiding concept mandates *not* including material that is not directly pertinent or important to understanding how to do sheet metal fabrication work. You will *not* find "everything but the kitchen sink" in this book for two reasons.

1) No matter how pretty pictures of it may be, off-topic, extraneous material just clutters a book, obscuring the central points that relate to its topic.

2) Most kitchen sinks are not made out of sheet metal, anyway.

My main method for achieving success, offering material that "sticks to your mind," includes presenting the same material in different contexts until readers are comfortable enough with it to make it their own. Only then can they walk around it and see it in three dimensions, adding depth to their understanding of it.

This method necessarily involves considerable repetition. Many places in this book cover the same projects followed in different contexts, illustrating very different points. I hope that this gives you familiarity with what you see and a sense of comfort with it. You will also read multiple discussions of the same points and issues, which are presented in different contexts. This repetition is intended to help you to internalize these points, so that they become useful and active parts of your working knowledge. Few of us remember much of what we only see or hear once.

The two extensive fabrication projects in this book are a small electrical box cover and a tractor fender. You will see photos of these fabrications throughout the book, used to illustrate many diverse and different topics. Then, Chapter 13 and Chapter 14 cover the projects specifically, from start to finish. By the time you get to those chapters, they should seem like reviews of material that is already somewhat familiar to you. They should seem like old friends.

It is up to you to determine if my chosen method—looking at the same examples and concepts in different contexts—increases the depth of your understanding of this material or just bores you. I hope that it does the former. I also hope that you take the information and concepts in this book to great heights of achievement in sheet metal fabrication work, and to the highest levels of personal satisfaction and pride in those achievements.

Matt Joseph
Honey Creek, Wisconsin

INTRODUCTION

The next time you see an inspiring sheet metal fabrication, a street rod, or a great restoration of original panels, give Englishman Charles Bessemer some of the credit. By inventing a process for reliably and cheaply producing mild steel in the mid 1850s, he made the dream of forming useful and/or beautiful shapes out of hand-crafted, and later stamped, metal a wonderful reality. That changed our world forever.

Bessemer's steel-making process provided the first raw material for metal workers that was easily formable, consistent, and relatively inexpensive. Before that, acquiring good mild steel stock was hit-or-miss, and usually expensive.

By the time of Bessemer's steel-making innovation, many of the tools and processes for hand-forming mild sheet steel were already invented. They had been used for centuries to fashion the likes of jewelry, cooking utensils, and architectural structures and ornaments out of metals such as copper, brass, bronze, and crude steel. With the availability of inexpensive, high-quality sheet metal, they could be yoked to the ingenuity and creativity of designers and craftsmen to make distinctively beautiful metal items. This included the sheet metal in the automobiles that began to appear less than half a century after Besssemer's invention.

That ingenuity and creativity came to the fore very quickly as new forming techniques were added to sheet metal working knowledge. Utilitarian structures, such as fenders, that originally had been fabricated in relatively simple flats and angles, could now include artfully curved shapes with the addition of simple, compound, and reverse-compound formats, sometimes mingled with angular bends and creases. What looked great was added to what simply worked, and the results were often spectacularly beautiful automobiles. Styling now took its place as a critical factor in automotive design.

The pioneer automobiles were hand-built, but that changed in the early twentieth century as the needs of mass production mandated major improvements in the field of metal die stamping. Still, the art form of custom auto body construction continued. It was kept alive by numerous custom "coachbuilders" that supplied distinctive bodies for the upscale chasses of both small and large automakers. It survives today in the shops and factories of several small, limited-production car manufacturers.

At the turn of the twentieth century the process for extracting aluminum from ore (anodizing) was perfected, making it feasible to produce this metal much more cheaply and with vastly greater quality than had been possible before. Suitable alloys for workable aluminum-based sheet stock followed quickly. Within a decade, aluminum joined mild sheet steel and became a material of choice for hand-forming and stamping auto body panels. It had the distinct advantages of being easier to work than steel and possessing better corrosion resistance. However, its high cost and the difficulties of welding or brazing it restricted its use to expensive custom bodies.

The era of custom coachbuilding employed both steel and aluminum fabrications. It reached its zenith in the 1920s and 1930s, and then declined during and after the Depression. By the time of World War II the age of large-scale custom-body building was over, but individuals and small shops kept the art of metal forming and fabrication alive. Some of this effort was directed at automobile restoration, while some of it was used to create one-off "customs" and limited-production "specials."

All of it was driven by a basic human desire to create, own, and drive distinctive vehicles that expressed the originality and creativity of their makers and owners. Terms, such as "automotive art" and "rolling sculpture," are often used to describe this concept.

After World War II, custom panel fabrication quickly found a new purpose in the emerging hot rod movement. A few car owners wanted vehicles that were more distinctive, creative, and expressive than the increasingly similar mass-produced cars sold by the few remaining vehicle companies. These custom-vehicle enthusiasts realized their desires by modifying existing car bodies to personalize them.

As those few became many, the street rod movement was born. While hot rods were mostly about performance, street rodders were often more interested in creating and owning cars that, while exotic in appearance and potent in performance, were also usable on the roads and streets, not just on race tracks. Early practitioners of this emerging art tended to take already beautiful and/or distinctive automobile designs, and modify them into spectacular semi-original creations. In this process, cars such as Lincoln Zephyrs and Continentals, and V-8 Fords and Mercurys, were transformed into more visually exciting transportation. The 1949 Mercury, and many Fords and Hudsons of the postwar period, were particular favorites of the early modifiers. As the movement grew, many other cars became candidates for body modifications.

By the 1960s, the street rod hobby and business had caught fire with a growing number of enthusiasts. Improvements in the availability of high-quality metal-working tools, and particularly of once exotic and expensive welding devices and techniques, brought this hobby within the reach of many more people than had been able to participate in it during its earliest days. These advances also affected the capabilities of small restoration and street rod shops by increasing the affordability and sophistication of their equipment, and, thus, of what they could accomplish.

By now, with the availability of inexpensive and serviceable tools and equipment such as wire welders, metal shears and brakes, planishing hammers, and shrinker/stretchers, it has become possible and affordable for many people who once only dreamt of forming and fabricating metal into the shapes and constructions of their fantasies to actually do this exciting work. For many, this is a dream come true. The art of metal forming long ago ceased to be the exclusive domain of a brotherhood of older craftsmen. Today, young men and women are developing proficiency at it and achieving terrific results.

This book means to be part of the trend that has increased knowledge of the *hows and whys* of sheet metal forming and fabrication. It intends to increase that know-how for people who are working, or want to work, along the nearly endless learning curve of this craft. It is designed to explain and to instruct in most of the common processes and operations in sheet metal fabrication work, the basic ones that you can accomplish with some work and access to fairly modest tools and equipment.

The emphasis here is on how to perform most of the basic operations and tasks used in metal forming and fabrication. I also attempt to explain the reasons for doing things the way that I, and others, suggest that they should be done. Giving those reasons should help you move along that learning curve.

Of course, some of the more exotic tools, equipment, and techniques in this field also get attention in this book, but my focus is largely on the reliable basics of this work. Even with modest equipment, if you have enthusiasm, persistence, and a willingness to learn and to experiment, you can accomplish great things in metal forming and fabrication. Remember, this craft is all about dreams that can come true, and often do.

CHAPTER 1

First Considerations

Every time that you want to fabricate a small bracket to mount an accessory, or repair a rusted out panel, or part of a panel, you bump up against it. Every time that you try to create a new, original feature on an existing sheet metal structure, it happens. Inevitably, you run into the field of sheet metal fabrication, with all of its possibilities, challenges, and limitations. Beyond shaping metal for those obvious and limited purposes, the sheet metal forming and fabrication craft has the potential to take you to heights of imagination and creativity rarely, or never before, reached.

If you can imagine a shape or structure, you can probably find a way to fabricate it in metal, or to build something pretty close to it. At times that means exactly copying an existing piece, such as a rusted-out fender section. Other times, it can mean coming up with something original, such as sheet metal interior panels to replace formerly plastic surfaces for a street rod or motorcycle.

The number of items that you can fabricate with sheet metal is almost limitless, if you have the materials, tools, equipment, knowledge,

Before you soar to sheet metal fabrication heights, remember that much of this work involves mundane tasks, such as making small catches and latches. If you do this work well, it can be very satisfying. This catch was built from the parts and materials behind it.

This cycle footrest is a small detail in an original and dramatic custom bike creation. Details like this contribute much to the success of custom vehicles. This piece was designed and fabricated from scratch. The alloy cover plate will later receive a uniform finish and protective clear coating.

---

8   **AUTOMOTIVE SHEET METAL FORMING & FABRICATION**

FIRST CONSIDERATIONS

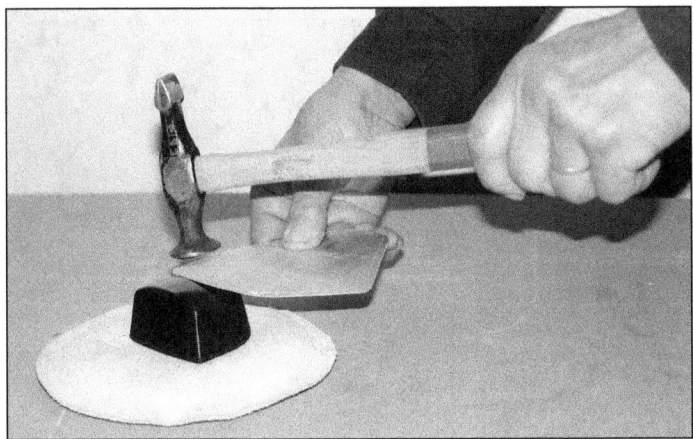

The metal hammer, plastic-clad dolly, and small shot bag are among the most basic metal working tools, and among the most useful. With just these three tools, it is amazing how much can be done to shape metal, particularly aluminum alloys.

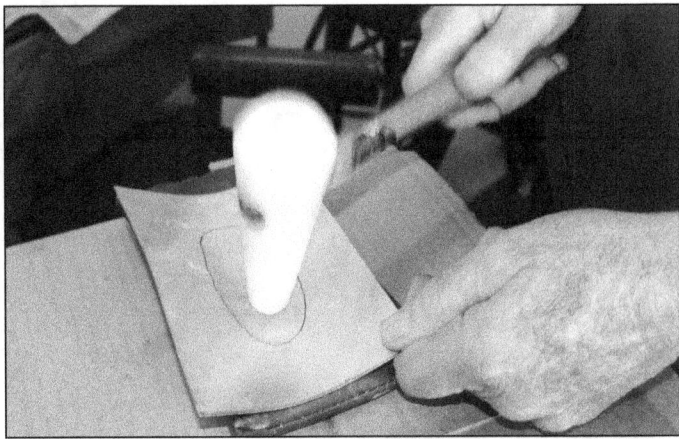

This basic process, hammering thin aluminum section with a plastic mallet into a shot bag, can yield dramatic results. The basic process of shaping and stretching is inherent in hammer forming work and is critical to forming metal into desired shapes.

skill, and determination to make them. What is not endless is the number of basic operations that are employed to form sheet metal into shapes, parts, and assemblies. In fact, that number is surprisingly small.

You can cut sheet stock with a variety of tools and devices such as hand and power shears, nibblers, torches, etc. You can gently bend it in a brake, slip roll, or beader. You can ungently bend it and stretch it between hammers and dollies, anvils and shot bags, etc. Hammering operations can be mechanized, as in power and planishing hammers. You can shrink or stretch it with heat, special hammers, and other devices designed specifically for these purposes. When you combine shrinking and/or stretching with hammering, you can form it into compound curves, that is, domed or bulged shapes. Finally, you can attach it to other sheet metal with techniques such as welding, riveting, and seaming. That is about the extent of what can be done, generally, with sheet metal in terms of basic processes.

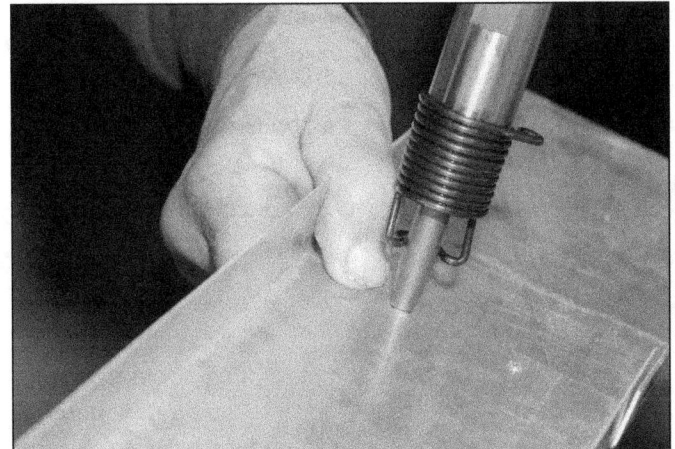

Riveting panels together, and to substructure, with a pneumatic rivet gun is one of several time-honored ways to join them. Many, but by no means all, of the other ways involve heat.

"But wait," as they say on the TV infomercials, "there's more." Read on a bit, before you conclude that all you need to know to progress in this work are the names and natures of those few basic operations that I just mentioned. While there are not all that many things that you can do with or to sheet metal, there are dozens to hundreds of ways of doing each one of them. That allows for thousands of usable combinations and sequences. Some of them work only, or best, in limited circumstances, while some are just plain better than others in terms of efficiency and/or quality. Part of the craft of successful sheet metal forming and fabricating lies in knowing the best procedures to use for specific tasks and jobs, and the best sequences in which to apply them. This may sound simpler than it really is.

In some cases, using one particular approach limits your choice of the approaches that you can use later in a job. For example, if you use a massive power hammer, or just a small planishing hammer, to the point of overworking an area of metal until it becomes dangerously

CHAPTER 1

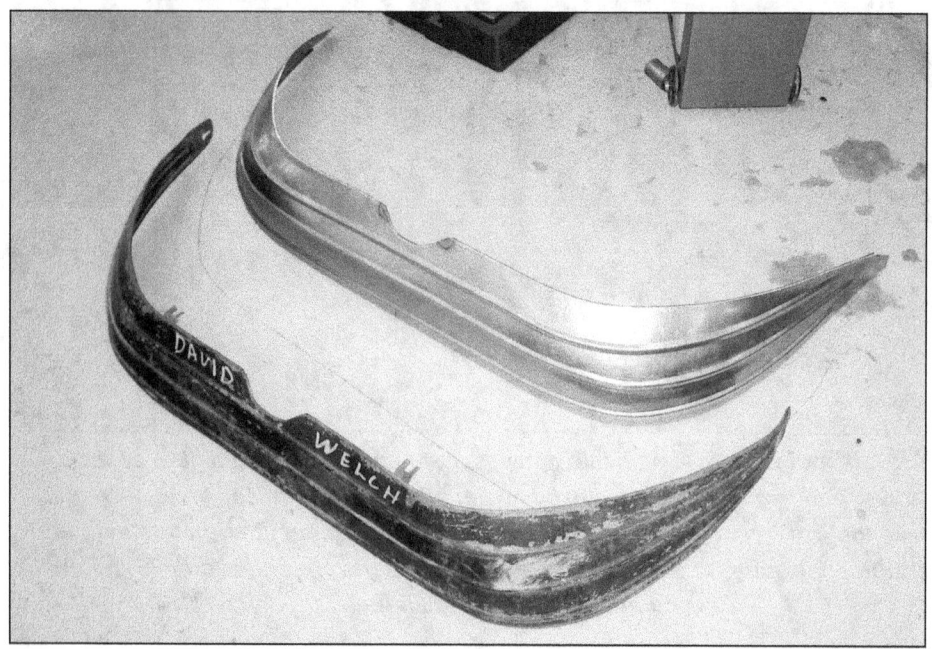

A fabrication like this one (back) uses most of the advanced metal working technology. These include patterning, forming, fitting, welding, and metal finishing. It was reproduced from an original splash shield (front). If you don't have your task sequences in order for a job like this, the outcome is a likely fumble.

The job of fabricating this patch panel for the rusted-out top of this fender requires terrific precision and detailed planning, which includes patterning, bending, welding, metal finishing, and filling. Every move must be calculated to form and locate the patch to exactly duplicate the original metal. You just don't stumble into success on a job like this.

This tragically misshapen attempt at dishing a thin piece of aluminum ended up being too thin to save. When you stretch metal radically, it is best to start with thick enough material to make the stretch without having your material become hopelessly brittle and thin.

thin and brittle, you may quickly run out of options for further forming and smoothing it.

The best way to avoid painting yourself into one of those proverbial corners is to plan your jobs effectively. That means selecting the sequences of tasks and procedures that will work best with each other for your particular purposes. If, for example, it is desirable to have a panel with riveted edges, you need to plan your project so that there is something substantial enough to rivet those edges to at the panel's ends. The key is in having the knowledge to lay effective plans, and then to follow them.

Those few basic types of tasks, or operations, that I noted above—cutting, gently bending, hammering, shrinking, stretching, and attaching—allow for a mind boggling number of possibilities, sequences, and combinations. Few jobs require just one of them. Most jobs require several, or all of them, often with numerous repetitions of many of them. This is likely the case when two or more parts have to fit precisely together.

The reasons for performing automotive sheet metal fabrication are also numerous. I have mentioned the use of this craft in restoration, and in the creation of modified vehicles of several types. Sheet metal fabrication is also widely used in prototyping parts and whole vehicles, and for short-run production of specialty parts in numbers that do not justify the use of stamping dies

FIRST CONSIDERATIONS

or conventional volume manufacturing processes.

There is also the exciting possibility of sheet metal fabricating as an art form, to soar with this material to heights that no one else has ever realized before—to form it into shapes that no one previously thought were possible, or even imagined. The challenges can be considerable, and the rewards for surmounting them can be enormous.

A Wide Range of Possible Projects

Auto body sheet metal forming and fabrication work has possibilities for an incredibly wide range of shapes and uses, from the mostly mundane and functional, to the purely ornamental and artistic, as well as combinations of both.

In restoration work, it is used to form parts that are missing or irreparably damaged by impact and/or corrosion. Sometimes large, complex structures and shapes are built from smaller pieces that are joined together to make the larger item. In restoration work, the premium is on accurately duplicating existing shapes and configurations. Some of this work is wildly impressive; for example, the exact and faithful replication of an entire fender or hood for a vehicle. More often, small but important fabrications are needed to restore or customize cars. Individually they may not seem like much, but it is often impossible to restore or modify a car without them.

When applied to the category of modified vehicles, sheet metal work can be used to make functional items, such as tanks, headers, exhaust systems, brackets, and supports, roll bars, and so on.

While it is sometimes possible to fabricate serious structural items, such as control arms and engine mounts, out of heavy stock metal, those types of items require extensive engineering and validation testing (beyond the scope of this book). However, creating reinforcing fabrications for existing structures is something that is often necessary and sometimes can be noodled out, without extensive engineering and testing.

Remember, just because you can figure out how to make something, that doesn't mean that it is safe to use it. I draw the line at fabricating critical structural items that may have catastrophic failure modes for drivers and passengers. I recommend that line to you for your fabrication endeavors. Up to a point, you may be able to reduce risk to acceptable levels by fabricating items, such as roll bars, headers, and tanks, out of proven materials, with techniques that are verified to produce safe results. However, when it comes to items, such as suspension components and steering and brake linkage, it is best to be very cautious about fabricating new parts.

Before you set out to create exciting metal shapes, you should master the skills to do small fabrications, like this one. It may seem very simple, but it takes dozens of these parts to make cars work. While they inspire little glory, they offer a lot of utility.

The man on the cycle designed and fabricated these handlebars from mild steel tubing. He used good bending equipment and great skill to do it. The handlebars are a proof of concept fabrication. Later, for this job, he will form new handlebars from substantial stainless tubing.

CHAPTER 1

Structural reinforcements, such as this one in a Ford V-8 frame, rely on pretty well-known principles and engineering. This is the kind of fabrication that is safe if you apply common sense to its use. I wouldn't put a 1,000-hp mill in this chassis, but 250 might be okay.

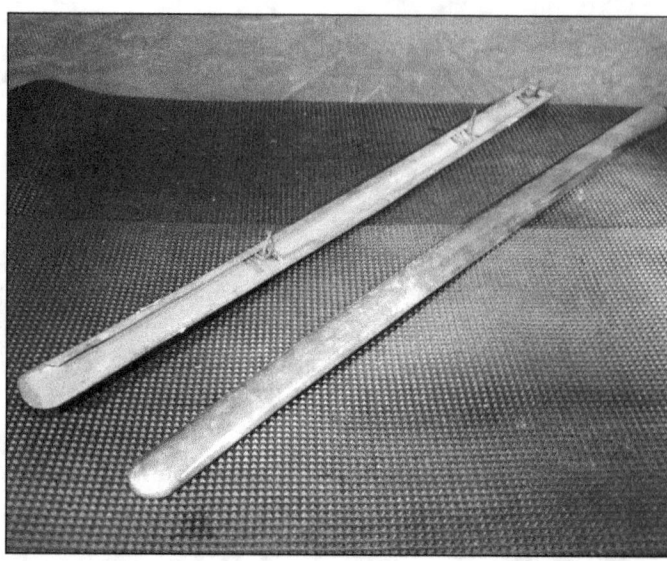

These body side moldings are at about the limit of what it makes sense to fabricate, because they require terrific accuracy to look right. If they were curved or fluted, or both, it would make very little sense to try to duplicate them in most fabrication situations.

Often, the key to fabrications that serve critical purposes is in overbuilding them to create safety factors that are many times any possible adverse condition that these parts will ever encounter. It is fine to do this with a simple structure, such as an oil tank, or a non-structural roll bar, but it can be dangerous to try it with a suspension part. The differences are in the complexity and difficulty of considering and calculating all of the variables, such as the often numerous stresses on a suspension part, and in their potential for causing catastrophic structural failure. My advice: Leave these critical fabrications to the guys with the engineering knowledge, big computers, and advanced structural analysis software.

That still leaves plenty of exciting territory for amateur fabrication work. Fins are a favorite modification of street rodders, as are hoods, particularly louvered hoods. Spoilers, headlight brows, wheel arches, doors, deck lids, quarter panels, roofs, and

This impressively crafted tank rides under the front fork of a wild-looking custom motorcycle. It's safe for amateur fabrication because it's a non-critical item—an air tank for the bike's air horns. However, a fuel tank would best be left to professionals.

fenders are fair game. Interior panels and parts, and most other visible surfaces are open territory for reproduction, modification, or entirely new fabrication. If you can see it as an outer surface, and can imagine a way that you would like it better, it's in-season for you to modify it.

Limits of Material, Skills and Imagination

Safety considerations aside, the limits of what you can accomplish in sheet metal forming and fabrication work are the capabilities of the material, your imagination, your skills, your patience and persistence, your tools, and your equipment. Most people don't favor limitations on anything that they choose to do. In this case, the nice thing about these limits is that like sheet metal itself, they are plastic. When you bump against them, they tend to move.

Those materials—mild steel and aluminum alloy sheet stock—have improved progressively and greatly since their first volume production, between 100 and 150 years ago. And there is every reason to believe that they will continue to improve.

I can't say that your imagination will improve, but I am certain that as you work with sheet metal your ability to imagine what you can do with

FIRST CONSIDERATIONS

it will expand. That is, you will learn to discipline your imagination to think the sheet metal way. Your skills should certainly improve as you gain experience with this material. That goes for novices, intermediates, and advanced professionals, alike. There is always a better way to accomplish tasks and jobs, and you should instinctively search for it. No matter how many times, or how successfully you have done something, there are details, or even major aspects of it, that you can work to improve.

Improvements in tools and equipment are another thing that you can count on. Not only are new tools to ease and advance metal work constantly being invented and released into the marketplace, many tools that may once have been unaffordable often become available at lower and lower prices, and, thus, become affordable.

Sometimes shops and manufacturers sell off older tools or machines to replace them with newer tools or equipment. And while the newest equipment is often marvelous, you may not need features like the laser guides, digital read-outs, and data ports that often come with it. Keep an eye out for good used equipment, like sheet metal brakes, jump shears, and other specialized sheet metal equipment. There are some real bargains out there.

Tools based on new ideas often greatly aid metal fabrication work. Consider items like the auto-dimming welding helmet. How ever did we weld without it? With a great deal more difficulty, that's how. I remember those days of trying to weld what you could see only dimly, or using hoods that dropped when you shook your head a certain way—that one was a real loser. The first safe auto-dim welding helmets cost several hundred dollars thirty years ago. You can buy safe and serviceable versions of these helmets today for a small fraction of that amount.

Or consider new abrasive blasting media, such as soda and PMB (plastic media blasting). The business of cleaning metal quickly and without objectionable warping or distortion has been revolutionized.

Some tools are continuously improved. The original locking pliers device, the Vise-Grip, was a terrific addition to everyone's tool kit. Over the years, it was improved and made wonderfully affordable. As time went by, it became the basis for a myriad of specialized tools, from long-reach locking pliers to the flanging tools that can be so useful in metal forming and fabrication work.

Finally, some tools improve greatly in affordability. Tools, such as plasma arc cutters, shrinker/stretcher devices, hand-held grinders, etc., have become cheaper and cheaper over the last several decades, with little or no loss in capability and durability. In many instances, lower

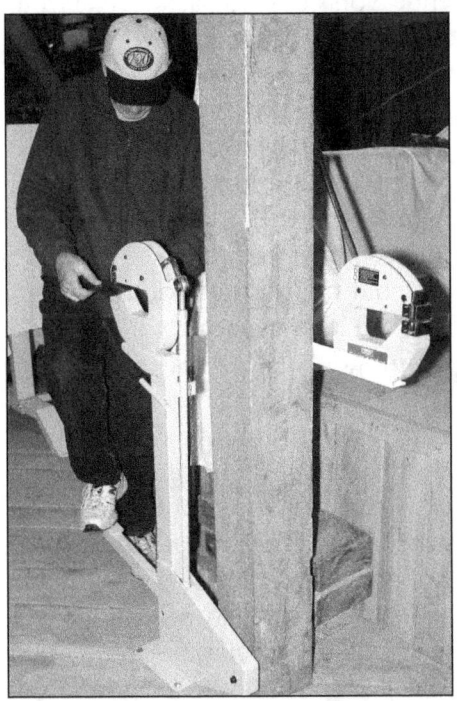

No one will confuse these 8-inch shrinker/stretchers with a Pullmax with good tooling. They fall far short of that mark. Still, for under $200, they represent an affordable way to shrink and stretch beyond panel edges, and at far less cost than just a few years ago.

This old Niagara jump shear would be a delight in any small sheet metal fabricator's shop. It has just the right capabilities for that setting. Items like this can turn up used with rewarding regularity, if you keep an eye out for them.

CHAPTER 1

I wouldn't weld thin-section metal without an auto-dim helmet. The one on the left cost several hundred dollars thirty years ago. The helmet on the right costs well under $50 today and performs admirably. The prices for useful sheet metal tools and equipment often fall over time.

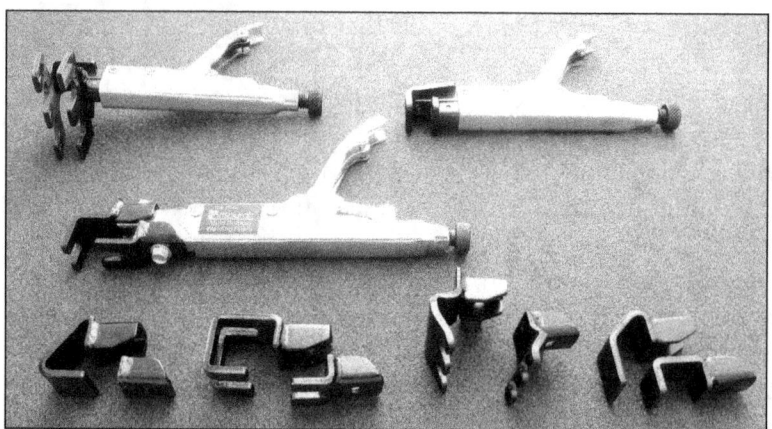

These modern variations on traditional locking pliers are very useful for holding panels together, particularly when they are being welded. The one on the bottom comes with the replaceable jaws just below it.

In its day, the 9-inch Milwaukee grinder (front) was a great tool. It was powerful, rugged, repairable, durable, and heavy. The imported 9-inch grinder (back) is many of those things, but sells for a fraction of what the Milwaukee cost new. For occasional use, the cheaper grinder should serve well.

prices have been accompanied by improvements in durability and performance. If you doubt that, check out the price, heft, and performance of a body grinder from the 1950s or 1960s. You might be amazed.

In fact, you have every reason to anticipate improving the ease, quality, and efficiency of your metal fabrication work, as your imagination becomes accustomed to the possibilities of the sheet metal craft, and as your tool and equipment profiles improve. You may even benefit from improvements in sheet metal itself.

An electro-plating process was invented years ago to plate a thin, protective layer of galvanizing material over the sheet steel used to manufacture parts of vehicle bodies. This was not the then-common hot-dip galvanizing (applied as molten zinc) that was rough and costly to paint in auto production. At the time, the new process was generically known and advertised as "one-side Gal. panels." It revolutionized anti-corrosion protection for automobiles.

Not long after that, one-side Gal. body metal became available to automobile repairers and custom metal fabricators in workable mild steel panel stock. A few years later, "double Gal. panels" (two-sided zinc alloy electro-plated steel panels) were introduced on new cars. Soon afterward, it became possible to acquire this material for repair and fabrication as well, and in a variety of gauges. This gave custom fabricators access to an advanced material with a sacrificial zinc ion coating that was highly corrosion resistant, but also smooth and paintable. It was a great advance in sheet metal.

Subtle Factors to Consider

After reading about the rosy prospects for your progress in sheet metal forming and fabrication endeavors, due to factors like your improving skills and access to better materials, tools, and equipment, I note some of the factors that you will have to consider to keep that progress on the tracks and to avoid having it halted, *pronto*. I'm talking about the things that you need to keep in mind to avoid the not-so-obvious disasters that can lurk menacingly in the background of sheet metal fabrication. This class of things is covered by my statement of Murphy's Law, "Nature always sides with the hidden defect."

Here are some of those potential disasters, the ones that can lead to embarrassing failures. As you observe failures in actual work—I hope not your own—you may be able to add to my list of things to keep in mind, the ones that might come back and bite you.

Shape Changes

The loss of contour or shape is a surprisingly common failure in custom metal work. Initially, a piece fits perfectly, and its contours blend or

FIRST CONSIDERATIONS

contrast with its surroundings, just as planned. However, after a few years and/or thousand miles, the piece has lost its shape and looks out-of-place. The reasons for this may involve forces applied to the piece by adjacent parts and/or substructure, or vibration cycling of the panel itself. These forces act on metal to distort it from its existing shape. If the metal was stressed before, or when, it was installed, the unreleased forces in it may cause it to lose its proper shape, and even to distort adjacent panels. Panels that become wavy are often an example of this problem.

Obviously, if you bend and/or clamp a panel, or part of one, under great pressure to make it fit to another panel and then weld it into place, you are asking for trouble later. Likewise, you court problems when you weld panel edges together with excessive heat, or fail to provide enough space in the fit-up of adjacent edges to allow for expansion during welding. Without adequate room for this expansion, you can initiate contact and pressure that lead to locked-in stress that will sooner or later produce distortion.

The term "oil canning" refers to the tendency of stressed, poorly fitting metal to pop into and out of position. That is necessary in an oil can, but it feels awful in a welded-in replacement floor or door handle area patch panel.

These kinds of mistakes must be avoided if you want the items that you form and fabricate to keep the shapes in which they were installed. When a welded-in piece demonstrates the trait of "oil canning," the tendency to be capable of popping in-and-out like the bottom of an old oil can, you have locked force into the metal structure. This is an open invitation for later distortion.

Support vs. Stress

Some structures are of a size, configuration, and location that require bracing to keep them from gradually twisting and distorting in service. They simply will not fly in formation without supporting structure of some kind. Experience and common sense can identify areas and constructions that are likely to need reinforcement to keep their shapes.

In general, long expanses of unsupported sheet metal are vulnerable to later distortion. If those expanses lack features like crown and creases—features that reinforce them by their very configurations and by the local work hardening the panel that accompanies their creation—they become even more exposed to the ravages of vibration cycling and other stresses, like minor impacts.

The same issues that apply to maintaining desired shapes in metal also apply to keeping attachment points sound. Rivets and welds can succumb to direct force and to vibration cycling; failing as a result. Vibration cycling can also cause cracking in sheet metal fabrications, particularly when it reaches already weakened areas, such as those at and near welds and those under great or changing stresses. Such forces work hardened metal until it becomes brittle and prone to cracking. Vibration

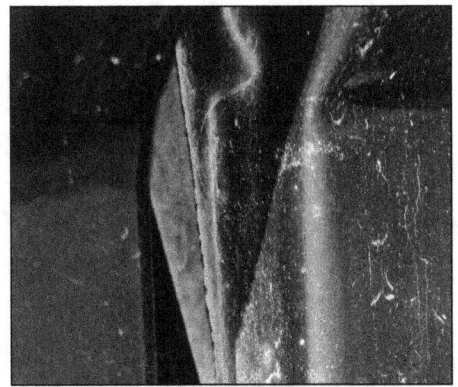

This panel junction is a disaster. It was never properly sealed, allowing moisture and electrolytes into the seam and corroding it. The rust's expansion opened the seam, allowing more moisture and contamination in, and promoting more rust. Avoid situations like this by designing your seams properly and sealing them adequately.

can also result in flexing that causes metal to shed protective coatings, such as paint, primer, and other anti-corrosion measures. That is often followed by corrosion.

Another example of the importance of combating inadequately supported sheet metal's tendency to shape shift is what happens to unsupported panels when you store or work on them. Many years ago, I was involved in the restoration of a 1933 KB Lincoln roadster. It was a major restoration that required almost three years to complete. The body's wood was badly rotted and had to be replaced. However, the fenders looked very good and were stored by draping them over the tops of 55-gallon drums, while the other restoration work progressed.

Since the fenders were a different color from the body, they were dealt with off the car. Minor straightening, metal finishing, and refinishing were applied to them.

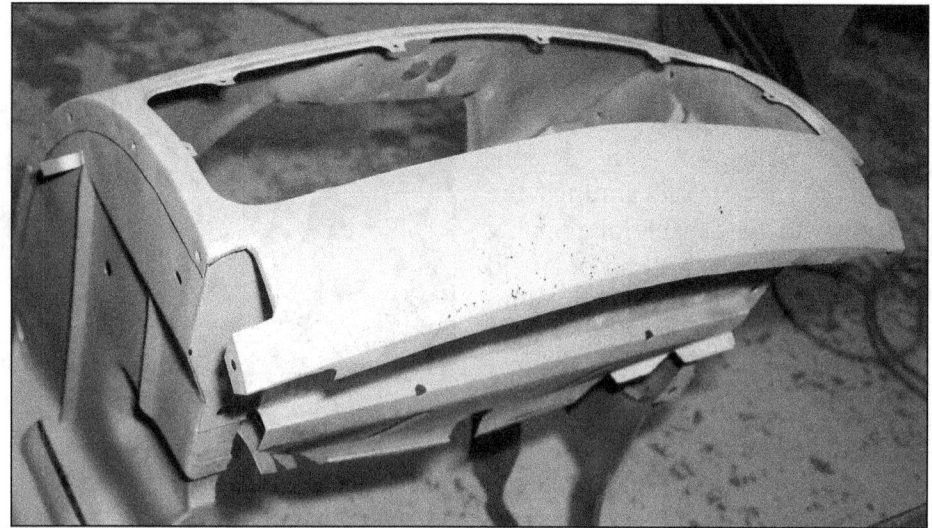

This lower cowling suffered perforation rust due to trapped moisture that lodged behind it. It lacked adequate ventilation to allow moisture to exit. Gravel abrasion against the front of the panel didn't help the situation. Always seek to provide a way out for water that can become trapped behind panels. Strategically placed drain holes and air ventilation holes work best.

Remounting them should have been simple; and it was for the front fenders. But the rears were off by the proverbial "mile." They were the original fenders from the car, and nothing about their mounting points had changed during our work on the body. However, when I attempted to remount them, I found that their mating contours to the body had changed. They were about 3/4-inch too long for their openings.

Sitting and spreading over those steel drum tops for almost three years had caused them to lose curvature, and stretch laterally. They had been designed to be supported by mounting them to the body, not draped over drum tops. This is, of course, an extreme example of what can happen to un-mounted and improperly supported metal.

Corrosion

Another factor that must be considered in all metal fabrication projects is the possibility of trapping and holding moisture, and/or moisture-laden dirt, in contact with metal. You know what happens in these circumstances, *rust!* However, avoiding them is never easy. Clearly, undrained box sections are very vulnerable to this rusting sequence, particularly if they contain folded edges where water can penetrate by capillary action, but where it has little opportunity, access, or incentive to exit.

One obvious solution is to seal everything so tightly that water can never splash into it. However, this doesn't work in practice. Moisture can get into structures indirectly by condensing out of ambient humidity on inner surfaces. This happens when panels cool off, either after shutting down heat-producing mechanical components that are near them, or from normal changes in ambient temperatures; say, day-to-night temperature shifts.

Attempts to absolutely seal constructions, particularly their back sides, from moisture usually create problems as bad, or worse, than those that such measures were intended to solve. They can succeed better at trapping moisture rather than keeping it out. If you doubt this, consider the highly sealed head and taillight covers on modern cars. A lot of work goes into making them impervious to water. Yet many of them show the obvious failure of these measures, in the form of visible condensation behind their lenses.

This rusted-out door bottom had to be cut out, and new metal sectioned in. Trapped moisture was the culprit. Coating the new folded metal seam with an anti-corrosion coating, and then sealing it with a good seam sealer, goes a long way to preventing this from happening again.

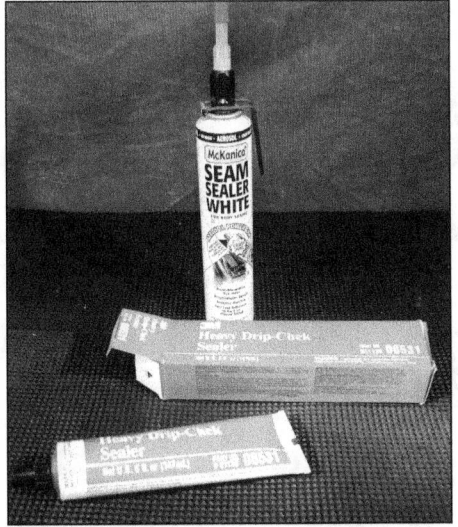

Seam sealers come in many varieties and types. Aerosol dispensers allow forcing them into crevices. Moisture cure urethanes (not shown) tend to dry metal under them as they cure, a definite plus. Traditional seam sealers, such as 3M's Heavy Drip Check Sealer, also work well in many situations.

What happened here is obvious. After vibration cracked the paint under the molding, water lodged there seeped under the door's paint, causing rust. That fractured the paint, allowing more moisture under it to rust and push more paint off. Proper design and better finishes might have avoided this.

You might think the solution is to provide drainage and air circulation behind my hidden structures. That works, up to a point. The trouble is that drain holes and ducts can provide ways for moisture to enter, as well as to leave a structure. They can also clog up with things like dirt, leaf fragments, debris, and flying smut. Then the cavities that you are trying to drain tend to retain the very moisture that you are trying to exhaust. Bigger drain holes may prove to be counterproductive by making it easier for water to enter through them.

What we have here amounts to an endless battle against corrosion. Designs calculated to keep moisture out of structures, and to allow for some drainage and air circulation, have the best chances of success. Avoiding constructions and configurations that are inherently prone to trapping moisture is also a very good strategy. Using anti-corrosion coatings and appropriate sealants, such as automotive seam sealer, at junctions also helps.

Surviving attacks by corrosion on new fabrications goes further than just proper design. It involves details, like providing substrate surfaces with a high potential for good coating adhesion. No matter how good your conversion coating, or other anti-corrosion coating is, it will likely fail if it is applied over any visible traces of oil, grease, or rust. Other contaminants, like soldering flux or improperly cured plastic filler, are just as bad as rust for paint adhesion.

While corners, edges, and lap joints are inevitable in many fabrications, these are the most difficult configurations of sheet metal to reliably coat and protect. Extra care should be taken in preparing them for coatings and in applying those coatings. Other particular corrosion-prone areas are attachment and mounting points. Coating adhesion failure and corrosion are ever-present threats anytime there is a potential for movement between two surfaces. No matter what coatings are applied, or how carefully they are applied, contact between dissimilar metals, such as steel and aluminum, makes corrosion an inevitable outcome. Dissimilar metals must be isolated from each other by nonconducting materials, no matter how clean they are at the time of assembly.

Whatever anticorrosion measures you take in your fabrication design and construction, it is important to visually inspect the structures that you fabricate regularly for early signs of faults like coating cracking and/or lifting. Drains should be inspected routinely, and probed to make sure that they remain open. Any signs of visible rust must be traced to their sources, and the underlying problems must be corrected there.

The best approach is always to keep the potential for attacks by corrosion in mind, and to do everything that you can think of to combat corrosion in every phase of metal fabrication work.

CHAPTER 2

Auto Body Metal

This lovely custom body was largely fabricated from heavy, flat sheet aluminum stock using only hand tools and English wheels. It stands as a monument to what can be accomplished with sheet metal if you have the imagination to think of it and the skill to do it.

We think of auto body metal in different ways. When we view it as finished parts and panels, formed into consistent contours with smooth shapes and accurate creases and coated with shiny finishes, we regard it as something very hard and immoveable. We see it as a rigid, static material, one that yields only to great force by crumpling into chaotic disarray.

There is another way of considering steel and aluminum panel materials—malleable stuff that can be moved and persuaded, incrementally into consistent auto body panel shapes. In this view, these materials are almost endlessly formable by various mechanical processes. Some of those processes are wonderfully automated.

In manufacturing, a stamping or rolling press can take flat sheet stock and force it into door skins, fenders, hoods, and the like, in one (or a few) quick operation(s). What is not seen in that sequence is the great ingenuity and effort that go into designing and fabricating the dies for the stamping or transfer presses that shape the metal. Also unseen are the time and effort spent refining the results of those forming processes to near perfection.

There is also the craft of custom fabrication. This pertains to the forming of sheet metal with hammers, anvils, shot bags, wooden hammer forms, power hammers, English wheels, and numerous other devices used to work individual pieces of panel stock, one panel at a time. This work is an intricate combination of art and science, of applied force and fine judgment. It requires close observation, creativity, ingenuity, daring, restraint, and experience. It is the metal formers' craft.

Success in this craft depends largely on the characteristics of the metal panel stock. If you fight those characteristics, your results probably will look crude, lack durability, and require excessive time to accomplish.

Characteristics of Sheet Metal

To illustrate the importance of those characteristics of sheet metal, consider this: If every time you performed a procedure on metal—say, hitting it with a hammer against a dolly—the outcome was different, you would find those basic tools and operations useless, and the metal, itself, all but unformable into anything but flat objects. It is precisely because the same actions, taken with the same or similar metals, produce very similar results, that we are able to form metal successfully into the often complex and intricate shapes that we desire.

In a large way, learning the craft of effective metal forming and fabrication amounts to learning to *work with the metal*, to respect its characteristics and its limits, and to appreciate its consistency. This approach allows you to leverage these things to assist your progress. If you are successful at this, you are able to anticipate what each action, and combination of actions, with metal is likely to yield. Further down the road, you will be able to plan and sequence your work based on that knowledge.

In the example above, the result of hitting metal between a hammer and dolly makes it harder and thinner. This stretches it where it is impacted. That causes it to assume a dish-like curvature, or "crown," because the stretched metal is bounded by metal that isn't hit and doesn't yield, forcing the impacted area to dish in or out. The curvature of the hammer and dolly faces' impact points also causes specific kinds of curvature to be imparted to an area that is worked this way.

If, on the other hand, metal is hit with a crowned plastic mallet against

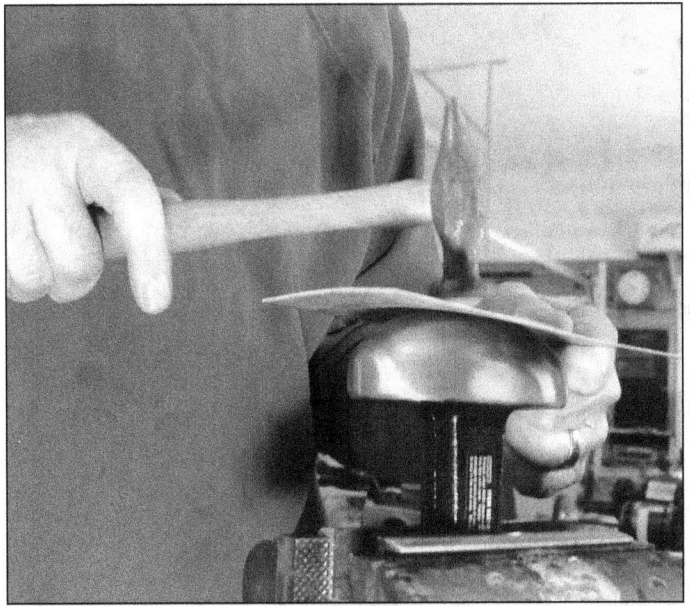

Hitting this .050-inch-thick alloy piece between an iron hammer and dolly both stretches and shapes it. It is the combination of shaping with stretching and/or shrinking that makes forming metal possible.

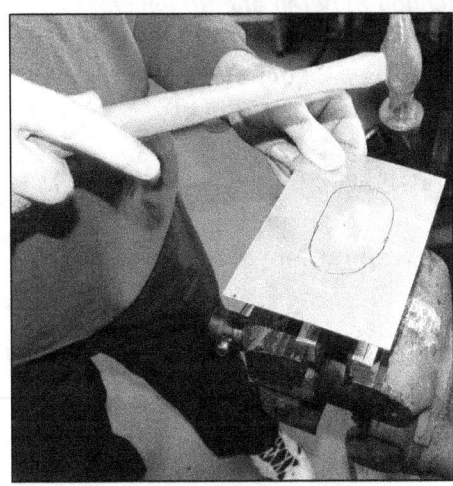

Compare what happens to this aluminum sample piece that is being stretched as it is shaped with a similar piece in the next photograph that is being shaped but hardly stretched. Here, the process of shaping with hard faced tools is stretching the metal as it shapes it.

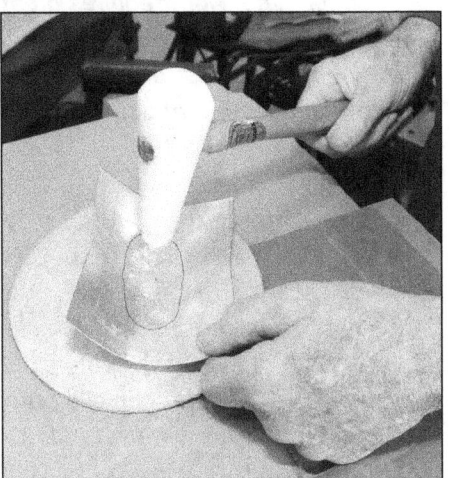

A similar piece to the one shown in the previous photograph is being worked with a plastic hammer over a shot bag, producing shaping without much stretching. You can see the result. The shaping is rough, and the metal around the formed area has become distorted.

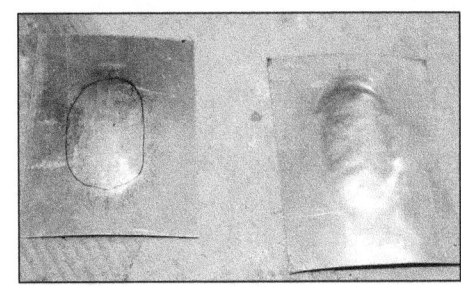

The two pieces shown in the two previous photographs are shown here, side-by-side. The difference that stretching makes is dramatic. The softer tooling has not preserved the metal; it has damaged it, because it failed to stretch it as it was being shaped.

CHAPTER 2

Great sheet metal work requires great attention to detail and an uncanny sense of when to quit while you are ahead. The detail work being done to adjust the final contour of this large fender takes a lot of patience and experience to produce a great outcome.

It took a lot of planning and talent to design and fabricate this elegant aluminum motorcycle battery box. Most of the issues in forming sheet metal were probably encountered along the way.

something softer than a dolly, such as a piece of cardboard or wood, or a leather bag filled with lead shot, it may bend into a slightly rippled dish shape, with less thinning and stretching and more bending. In this case, the metal that is not coerced into stretching into a curvature tends to show distortion that appears as a lack of smoothness, as it is formed.

In these examples, the different outcomes of different procedures occur due to the consistent underlying characteristics of sheet metal, and its responses to those different actions. To understand these different kinds of outcomes, and to predict what they are likely to be, you need to understand some of the basic characteristics of sheet metal. This understanding is both central and critical to this work. Call it knowledge-based informed intuition. When you master this knowledge of likely outcomes, you will be headed toward working *with* sheet metal effectively

and efficiently, and not *against* it. That's good, because very few surprises in forming sheet metal are welcome ones.

A few hours spent watching a talented sheet metal professional should convince you of this point. He or she tends to operate with minimum force to make the metal do what he/she wants it to. At first, this may appear to be some kind of sorcery or magic. However, what is really happening is that the metal's predictable characteristics are being leveraged to produce desired results. If that sounds easy, it isn't.

Even simple operations on sheet metal, such as hitting it between a hammer and dolly, involve several potential variables. For example, the type and condition of the metal affects the result. The amount of rebound by the dolly influences the outcome. The shape of the hammer face, the metal, and the dolly are factors in what happens. Any sliding of

the surfaces relative to each other during impact may be critical. In fact, few seemingly simple actions with metal are really simple, and combinations of actions are always complex.

All of that makes it even more important that you gain a good understanding of the nature and characteristics of sheet metal to work with it effectively. The good news is that what follows in this chapter stops well short of the field of metallurgy. While an interesting and useful study, an understanding of metallurgy is not necessary to work with sheet metals. If you understand their gross characteristics, you know enough to work with them effectively. Understanding why sheet metal does what it does at a granular and/or molecular level is interesting stuff, but not essential to doing great metal forming and fabrication work.

Alloys: Steel and Aluminum

The two materials of choice for custom fabrications are alloys of steel and alloys of aluminum. In this case, "alloy" means mixing a base metal with small amounts of other elements, to give it certain desirable characteristics that are not present (or are present to a limited extent) in the base metal. Steel, for which iron is the base metal, is always alloyed with carbon to give it strength. The amount of carbon added to steel varies from about .25 percent (mild steel, the kind fabricators use to fashion auto body panels) to just under 2.00 percent (incredibly hard, but brittle tool steel range). That is a tiny amount of carbon, but it makes a world of difference.

Interestingly, iron often has a higher carbon content than steel. The key difference is that the carbon in steel is very evenly distributed in steel's granular structure, while in iron it is not so evenly distributed. Other alloying elements, such as manganese, sulfur, phosphorus, silicon, etc., are often added to steel to increase important capabilities, which include formability, corrosion resistance, weldability, and so forth.

Aluminum in its raw form is only somewhat usable for fabrication purposes, but it becomes a marvelously formable material when it is alloyed, work hardened, or heat treated to give it specific properties. In choosing among steel and aluminum alloys, you should consider the superb formability of aluminum alloys, versus the good formability and easy weldability of steel alloys. It's often a trade-off between these factors. Aluminum is easier than steel to form, but more difficult to weld. Steel also has an advantage in strength, measured in panels of similar thickness. Many fabricators end up using both materials, depending on the requirements of the specific items that they are fabricating.

Work Hardening and Strengthening

There are certain important properties of all metals, and their alloys, that fabricators must understand. The most important of these is *work hardening*. Mild steel, the stuff used in most factory body panels and in custom fabrications, starts life as a very soft, formable material. However, as it is stamped, rolled, or otherwise formed, it becomes progressively harder, because deforming sheet metal imparts additional hardness to it. This occurs because as steel (or aluminum) is forced into new shapes, the grains in the metals' structures slide over each other, changing shape as their arrangement changes. As this occurs, these metals become harder and more difficult to work, until they become so hard and brittle that they fracture rather than further deform. The grains simply reach a limit of their rearrangement potential. The correction for this condition of work hardening is to

Aluminum was the obvious metal choice for this beltguard fabrication. It looks great, saves weight, and provides excellent durability. It may also have been easier to form for this application than steel would have been.

Replacements for these fenders must be fabricated from steel to be original. Besides, the strength of steel will be necessary for them to survive in service, if they ever see service. This is not a terribly complex or difficult fabrication in any metal.

CHAPTER 2

Sheet Metal Work Hardening Experiment

To demonstrate the phenomenon of work hardening with a simple experiment, Herb used a pair of sheet metal pliers to bend a 1-inch-wide strip of 22-gauge mild steel as close to 360 degrees as possible. When the metal resisted bending back on itself, Herb placed the hinge area of the strip in the sheet metal pliers' jaws and tried to compress it flat. But that area was so hardened from the previous bending that he never did succeed in flattening it completely.

Next, Herb tried to straighten the strip with his hands, but the strip resisted. The metal on either side of the bend bent back easily, but the original bend resisted straightening despite Herb's best efforts. Even when he moved his hands closer to the bend, and tried to straighten it, the metal in the bend did not yield. Finally, Herb tried using the sheet metal pliers and his hands to straighten the bend, but the best that he could do left the original bend mostly intact.

What had happened was that the initial bend in the strip work hardened the metal in that area, making it very difficult to remove the bend. The strip responded to efforts to straighten the original bend by bending in areas adjacent to it, because they were not work hardened.

Perhaps when you were in grade school you had performed this experiment, yourself. The evidence was probably left on the classroom floor in the form of bent and broken paper clips.

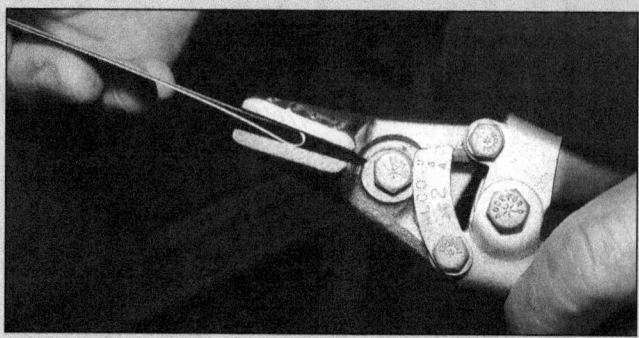

By the time the strip was bent this far, it showed a tendency to bend anywhere but in its existing bend. Work hardening had become an issue. Sheet metal pliers could not overcome it and persuade the piece to lie any flatter than you see it here.

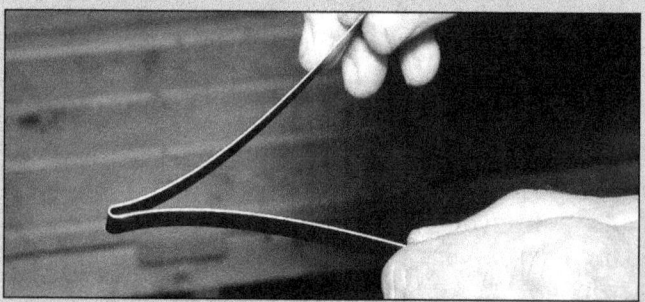

Trying to open the piece with his fingers, Herb confirmed that the bend was much harder than the rest of the strip. It would not yield to finger pressure, but the rest of the strip did.

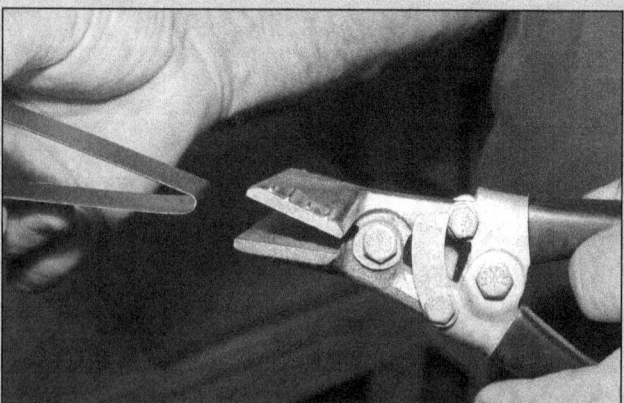

The first step in this work-hardening experiment was to bend our test strip with a pair of sheet metal pliers. So far, nothing unusual is visible.

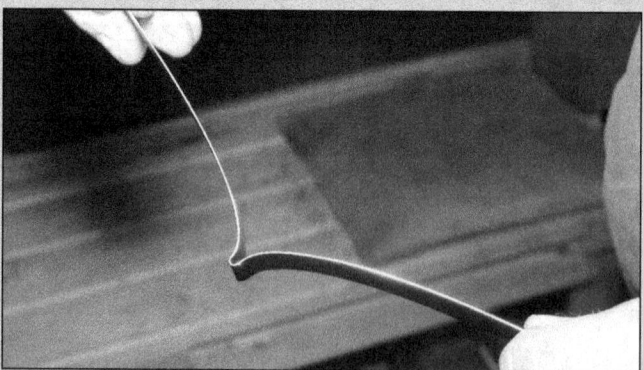

Pulling on the piece to flatten it was futile. You can see everything bending except the work-hardened area. This is the essence of work hardening. Note that only one bend in the strip work hardened it beyond the point that hands or pliers could straighten it.

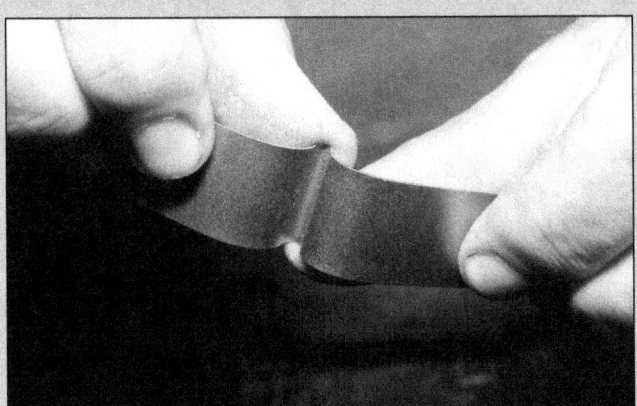

By now, the fabricator was getting serious about straightening the strip by prying against the bend with his thumbs. Of course, I kept egging him on. But it was no use, the original bend could not be opened by hand.

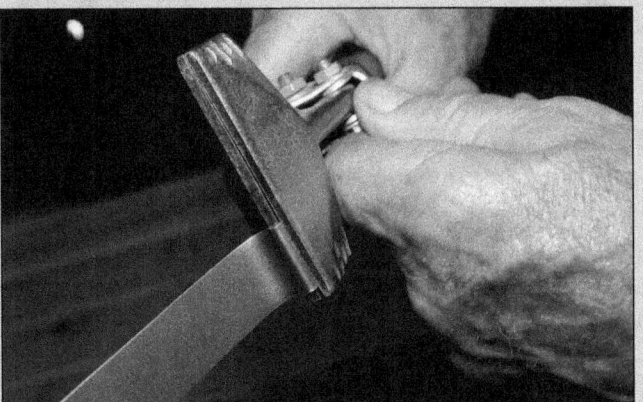

Trying to straighten the strip with pliers and hand pressure did no good either. Herb tried to feed the bend between the pliers' jaws and clamp down on it, but he couldn't put enough pressure on the bend to straighten it.

anneal, or re-soften, the metal (more on that, later in this chapter).

Work hardening is a mixed blessing. It limits what can be done to reshape sheet metal beyond a specific point, without annealing it—that is, re-softening it by applying specific levels of heat to it, and then allowing it to cool slowly. However, it can also be used to impart desirable and/or necessary strength to panels and other structures.

Consider the creases and crowns (domed shapes) in modern production and custom auto bodies. They are there for two main reasons and a number of minor ones. The first reason is to impart strength to them. Flat, unsupported sections of auto body metal have little stiffness, or strength, and tend to move or flutter with wind, or with the application of vibration and/or minor mechanical force. That is unacceptable in auto body panels.

The ledge shoulder and crease lines in this 2010 Lincoln MKT's body are there largely for styling reasons. They also help to strengthen and stabilize its sheet metal by work hardening it in critical areas. This reduces panel flutter and vibration effects. You can use the same strategy in your fabrications.

Styling is also a major reason for giving auto body panels shape. Most people do not want to drive around in vehicles configured like shoe boxes.

Other issues, such as packaging efficiency, aerodynamics, and weight reduction, also factor into the decision to stamp or roll auto body panels into distinctive shapes. But the main reason is to impart strength to them in critical areas by work hardening those areas. That crease along the top of a fender or crown in a deck lid or lift gate work hardens the metal there, making it much stronger than it would be otherwise. As you design and build custom fabrications, it is important to keep in mind the strengthening potential that deforming metal gives your work, not to mention the eye appeal that it will impart.

The downside of work hardening is that metal can fail if you try to form it past its limits. These limits fall into a few important categories. The terms that cover them deal with the ability of metal to be worked up to, and beyond, its *yield point*, or point of permanent deformation.

Workability

The ability of a metal to be bent or deformed and then to spring back to its original shape is called elasticity. Think of a spring. Each time that it is stretched or compressed, up to a point, it returns to almost exactly its original shape when the deforming force is removed. If it is stretched, or compressed, beyond a certain point, it is permanently deformed, because it has reached and exceeded its *elastic limit*. That limit defines the range of its *elasticity*. Elasticity is a critical measure of the sheet metal used in fabrications. It is often referred to as "spring back," because it is the range of deformation from which metal still springs back to its original configuration after a deforming force is removed.

Beyond that elastic limit, metal is said to have reached its *yield point*, which I defined as the limit of deformation by force that metal can sustain without having its shape permanently altered.

Fortunately for metal workers, fabrication metals possess another critical characteristic that allows you to deform them beyond their elastic limits and yield points. This characteristic is called the *plastic limit* of metals, or *plasticity*. It is the limit to which forces of many kinds can be applied to metal to permanently change its shape, without fracturing it. It is what can be done to sheet steel and aluminum to permanently form them into bends, curves, or crowns, and to make the transitions between these basic formats, without fracturing or breaking them.

The reason that it is possible to form metals involves all of the terms that I just defined. To stamp, roll, or hammer metal into a new shape, it is necessary to exceed its elastic limit by deforming it beyond its yield point. As you do this, and modify the metal's grain structure, work hardening occurs, progressively hardening the metal and preventing it from springing back. The deformation then becomes permanent, a crown, a crease, etc. However, you must stay somewhat below the metal's plastic limit, or you will need to soften or repair it before you can continue to form it. Sensing when you are near the plastic limit of metal that you are working is critical to good metal work. That knowledge, or sense, tends to come with experience.

Heating and Annealing

Beyond a certain level of deformation, sheet metal becomes so work hardened that it can no longer be moved (often referred to as "cold working") without breaking it. Most useful shapes can be imparted to good-quality sheet metal well below this point. In these cases, the issue of work hardening may not be a problem. However, there are cases in which the fabrication of extreme shapes is not possible within the plastic range of some metals. In these cases, it becomes necessary to anneal the metal to continue cold working it.

Both steel and aluminum are susceptible to annealing, but aluminum presents some unique problems in applying this process.

Steel

Steel is reasonably easy to anneal, because it gives off all kinds of visible color indications of its temperature as it is heated to progressively higher temperatures. Specifically, beyond a certain point, it changes color as its temperature changes. As steel is brought to temperatures above 400 degrees F its surface scales with oxides, changing its color, first to a light yellow. Underneath that surface scale, the grain structure of the heated steel begins to undergo changes as well.

By about 600 degrees F, the surface of steel will have gone through several shades of brown and blue, arriving at a deep blue. Gray, and then green coloration appear above that temperature, until temperatures reach around 900 degrees F. After 900 degrees F, the scaling colors are

These non-contact pyrometers have many uses, but only very expensive versions of them reach into the range of temperatures that you need to measure to anneal or harden steel. However, they are useful for measuring temperatures in 3003 H14 aluminum's annealing range.

This thermocouple-type "contact" pyrometer reaches handily into the transition temperature range for steel. If you are unsure of your ability to read color temperature indications from steel, this might be just your ticket.

Marks from these temperature-indicating crayons run when their stated temperatures are reached. They are very handy for checking temperatures at the transition range for steel. Also, they leave your hands free to work since you don't have to hold or aim an instrument.

replaced by an array of reds radiated by the heated steel itself. These radiated colors also change with increasing temperature. Each of the reds may have specific importance in terms of when steel is annealed and otherwise treated. In the range of 2,200 degrees F, the reds are replaced by yellow, followed fairly quickly by white, after which, at about 2,600 degrees F, steel makes like the Wicked Witch in the *Wizard of Oz*, and melts.

The "scaling temperatures" below 900 degrees F produce colors that are reflected off the scale (oxidation) that is forming on the steel's surface. These colors look pretty much the same in any light. However, the reds and the other colors above that temperature are generated by the heated steel, and appear in varying shades and intensities, depending on the ambient light in which they are viewed. Keep this in mind when you try to distinguish

This photo shows a range of temperatures in steel. The dark blue scale occurred at 700 to 800 degrees F. The cherry and bright reds are much hotter than that. The salmon spot (above and right of center) is in the magical 1,550 to 1,600 degrees F range.

between shades like red, bright red, cherry red, and salmon red. Low light gives the best and truest color indications of the radiated colors in heated steel.

Although changes in mild steel's grain structure begin to occur at very low heating temperatures, these changes reach their maximum useful potential for annealing and heat

The first step in torch annealing aluminum is to cover it with soot from an acetylene-rich (carburizing) oxy-acetylene flame. Then use a mildly oxidizing flame (shown) to remove the soot from the aluminum at the lowest temperature that does the job. That should anneal it.

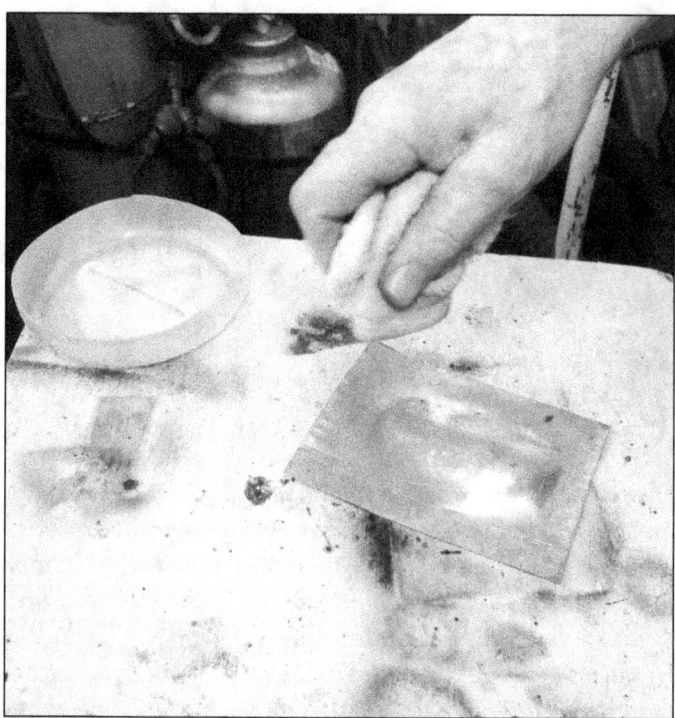
In some situations, it is desirable to lightly quench annealed aluminum after it cools below 500 degrees F, to give it some hardness. This is particularly desirable if you don't plan to work it much after annealing it, but want to leave it hard enough to withstand life's traumas.

treating at between 1,550 and 1,600 degrees F, the point at which steel changes from bright red to salmon red. At that temperature there is a complete reconstitution of grain structure, rendering mild steel fully annealed and soft.

The annealing sequence is important, because as you cold work steel and harden it, it may become necessary to anneal it to bring it back to a workable state. The easiest way to do this is to use an oxy-acetylene torch, adjusted just a little acetylene rich (indicated by a slight feather on the flame's inner cone), and heat the area that you want to anneal slightly above bright red, and into the salmon red range. It is good practice to employ torch movement that blurs the line between the annealed area and the surrounding metal. After heating to annealing temperature, let the annealed area air cool, and you have workable metal again. Avoid heating steel that you anneal any hotter than salmon red, or you may end up with a large, weak grain structure.

Aluminum

Proper procedure for annealing aluminum panel materials varies from one alloy to another. Some require holding the aluminum alloy at a specific temperature for minutes or hours, and then cooling it at a specific rate. This can only be accomplished in an industrial oven. The most common aluminum custom fabrication material, alloy 3003 H14, can be annealed using an old panel beater's trick. It works like this.

First, set your torch for a strong acetylene flame, the one that is short of the flame that sends carbon shard fluff all over the place. Apply this flame to the alloy panel surface and coat that surface as evenly as possible with a thin layer of carbon soot from the flame.

Then set your torch for a neutral or slightly oxidizing flame (slightly oxygen rich) and use the outer flame envelope to remove the carbon that you have deposited on the panel's surface. This brings it to between 700 and 775 degrees F, the temperature range at which 3003 H14 is successfully annealed. Let the annealed area air cool, or quench it with air from a blow gun, splashed water, or a wet rag *after* its temperature has cooled to below 500 degrees F, and you have soft, workable metal again.

As you work annealed metal (steel or aluminum), it becomes progressively harder and may require re-annealing in hard areas to make it workable again. Try arranging your annealing and working sequences so that when the metal reaches its finished shape it is in a condition that is hard but not brittle. It takes some planning and experience to accomplish this. What you don't want to do is anneal, and then make only minor adjustments, because that leaves your metal in a soft condition that may compromise its ability to hold its shape in service. In the same vein, don't finish your shaping operations with the metal in an excessively hard and brittle condition, because that makes it prone to cracking in service, under the stress of vibration, and even minor impacts.

When you use a torch to anneal a small panel, or parts of a small panel, you may experience some distortion in the metal. This is because the area that is heated may be bounded by unheated metal, causing the heated area to bulge as it expands, because it is restricted from moving laterally by the unheated metal around it. Uneven heating can also produce minor distortion, and it is difficult, or impossible, to heat sheet metal perfectly evenly with a torch. In some configurations, this is not a problem, but in others it is. The best way around having difficulties with local expansion is to heat the entire area on which you are working, or at least to taper your heating into adjacent areas.

Selecting Metals and Their Alloys

Different metals have different characteristics. Within the broad classifications of "steel" and "aluminum," there are major differences. Specific alloys of these metals have particular advantages and drawbacks that mandate trade-offs in selecting among them. Some may be stronger or harder than others, while some may have better weldability, formability, or corrosion resistance than others. The selection of the correct metal for a specific job is a matter of utility and personal preference.

Steels used for panel fabrications are always described as "mild," meaning that they have very low carbon content and are soft and formable. The most common and usable steels of this type are 1018 and 1020 cold-rolled (CR) stock. They contain a basic alloying package of several elements in small amounts with .18 percent and .20 percent carbon, respectively. They are rolled from cold blanks, rather than heated blanks, which makes them much tougher and more precisely dimensioned than hot-rolled steel (HR). For their strength, purity, workability, and weldability, these steels are, pardon me, the "gold standard" for panel forming and fabrication.

There are hundreds of varieties of sheet steel, including HSS (High Strength Steel), DDS (Deep Draw Steel), etc. Specific parts of the steel making process are often described as part of the name of a specific steel. For example "killing" (or deoxidizing) steel in its processing can be accomplished in several ways. Using aluminum- or silicon-killed steel (designated "AK" and "SK," respectively) is considered desirable and is used to designate some steels by a suffix to their names.

For most sheet steel used for fabrications, an ideal steel is 1018 CR or 1020 CR. If you go for the suffix AK or SK it costs more, but may be worth it, depending on what you are forming and how you are forming it.

The thickness of the steel panel material that you choose for your work is dictated, of course, mostly by the performance needs of the item that you are fabricating. The method that you use to form it and your ability to employ that method factors into your choice of material thickness.

In general, formable steel exists between 18- and 22-gauge. Steel of 18-gauge (0.048 inch) is very thick and difficult to form, while 22-gauge (.030 inch) is at the thin end of formable steel. My preference for most projects is 20- or 21-gauge (.036 inch and .033 inch, respectively). You will find that 1018 CR and 1020 CR in these thicknesses are nicely workable and very stable after they are formed. (Please note that I have rounded off the last digits of the gauge dimensions given in decimals of inches.) It is always best to specify sheet metal thickness by decimal dimension, rather than by gauge.

Notice that in the examples above, the higher the gauge number, the thinner the material that it describes. The arcane formula for determining panel gauge thickness involves a weight- and dimension-based formula. Actually, several different formulae are used for different metals and for different formats of metal. Don't worry about this; just try to avoid the whole issue of gauge numbers and their attendant confusion. When possible, buy your sheet metal by its dimensional measure in thousandths of an inch. Otherwise, use a good gauge table, like the one in the Appendix.

CHAPTER 2

Instead of rummaging around for fabrication steel, stainless steel, and aluminum in scattered boxes, Jim Crews of Tin Man Fabrication keeps his metal stock neatly on a rack. Useful structural pieces are in front. Sheet metal is kept in back.

There are about half a dozen aluminum alloys used by custom automotive fabricators for specific jobs. These are 3003 H14, 1100 H14, 6061 T6, and 5250 H32 series alloys. The 1100 series of aluminum is pretty close to pure aluminum and has many desirable characteristics, but lacks strength. By far, the most universally preferred and used alloy for most panel jobs is the semi-hard, non-heat-treatable 3003 H14. This alloy work hardens and can be annealed using the acetylene torch trick described earlier. It is very weldable, for aluminum, and is relatively easy to acquire. It is commonly used to form panels in .040-, 0.050-, and .0625-inch thicknesses. Other aluminum alloys, some of them pretty exotic, have some application in automotive work, but are often reserved for the specific requirements of aviation and other unforgiving, high-stress, critical applications.

Acquiring Metal Stock

Finding sources of metal working materials is as difficult as you decide to make it. Body shop supply outfits usually have a limited stock of usable steel panel materials and, sometimes, aluminum panel materials. Local specialty metal suppliers, particularly in or near cities, often have or can get common sheet stocks, such as 1020 CR steel and 3003 H 14 aluminum, in a narrow but useful variety of thicknesses. In some cases, steel panel stock from these suppliers can be specified as "one-side Gal." or "double Gal." This feature adds to their cost, but is a good measure against corrosion.

Obviously, acquiring sheet metal one or two sheets at a time is considerably more expensive than procuring it in industrial quantities. Some Internet suppliers may offer better prices than local suppliers, but by the time you add the cost of handling and shipping, those price advantages often disappear.

One great advantage to acquiring panel materials locally is that you can inspect them before paying for them. Scratched, dented, warped, rusted, scored, inconsistent, or miss-specified materials can be difficult or costly to deal with and can cause serious delays in your work. However, if you find a reliable catalog supplier for panel stock, shipping is not out of the question. It is always a good idea to keep a considerable stock of varied materials on hand but not so much that it rusts or gets damaged before you can use it. I find that a good working relationship with a local specialty supplier or suppliers is the best approach to sheet metal materials acquisition.

CHAPTER 3

THE ART OF MAKING SHEET METAL WORK WITH YOU

There are some amazing demonstrations out there of what can be done to form sheet metal. The best of them rely on the innate characteristics of this material that respond to carefully planned force. In one of them, a piece of metal is worked through several shapes, and then hit once in a strategic location, causing it to return to one of the shapes from which it had been worked. I've never seen this dramatic demonstration but have heard about it many times. Maybe you will be lucky enough to see it yourself someday. It involves a sheet metal phenomenon called "memory."

What I have experienced is the good and forgiving nature of high-quality sheet metal. I have noticed that if you plan and sequence your work properly, the metal responds to your actions consistently and almost helpfully. Bend it in a good brake, and it bends consistently into any angle that you choose. Reposition it in several small increments, laterally in the brake, between bending applications, and you can produce almost any kind of loose radius that your work requires. This

These radical shrinking heads, mounted in a Pullmax, have revolutionized metal forming. By massively upsetting metal in a fast, automated procedure, they do in minutes what could take hours with conventional sheet metal-working hand tools.

A good sheet metal brake can bend a uniform radius if you run the metal through it in small increments. This works if you don't have a slip-roll, or your slip-roll is too narrow to bend what you need to shape. Using a brake also allows easy creation of non-uniform radii.

CHAPTER 3

Slip-rolling is an easy way to create a consistent curve. However, it is difficult to make accurate enough adjustments to slip-roll an inconsistent radius bend. The best choice of tools and methods for jobs often depends on exactly what you are trying to accomplish, and at what level of accuracy.

At first glance, forming this side member for a brace with a powerful air hammer over thick steel dies looks barbaric. However, this procedure makes the brace part very strong because it work hardens the metal in a critical area by massively deforming it.

becomes a very handy way to create long, gradual curves, such as the ones in rocker panels.

Of course, there are many other, and often better, ways to form sheet metal into loose radii formats, and most of them may be preferable to doing it in a brake. But the point remains that it is the consistent response of metal to certain actions, like braking it, that makes it possible, and often easy, to form it. Different thicknesses and specifications of metal react in somewhat different ways to similar applications of force. Therefore, to work effectively, you need to know which metal does what, specifically. An example of this would be mild steel that carries the designation "AK" or "SK" after its numerical designation, such as 1018 or 1020. These grades of mild steel are softer than grades that do not carry those suffixes (discussed in Chapter 2). They can be very useful for forming items that require very deep contours or "draws," but have the drawback of not holding adjacent flat areas very well as you form them, because they are so soft. This causes problems when you try to form a high crown in one area of a panel, while holding a nearby area flat.

While you might think that the softer metal is easier to form, this is not true. Metal can be too soft for certain kinds of forming operations, causing it to draw too easily and too far. There is a balance of how soft you want the panel material to be. As you begin to get a feel for what steel does in areas that you form, and in adjacent areas, you need to note that it tends to be specific to the grade of steel that you are using. What works well on regular 1018 or 1020 mild steel may not work as well on AK or SK versions of these materials and *vice versa*. If you have an intuitive sense of what 1018 22-gauge will do, you can probably carry it over to 1020 20-gauge material, but don't expect it to work exactly the same way on 16-gauge materials. It won't.

The real professionals in metal forming never seem to fight with the metal, because they respect its basically good and cooperative nature. It is at the low and nasty end of sheet metal work where extreme force, often accompanied by considerable foul language, is employed in the futile endeavor to bludgeon it into

*As the metal brace part is worked further, it becomes smooth and visually acceptable. This is **not** a bludgeoning, but an imaginative and carefully calculated way to make a part strong and visually acceptable.*

desired results. As you might expect, the results of that method look as crude as that approach does.

THE ART OF MAKING METAL WORK WITH YOU

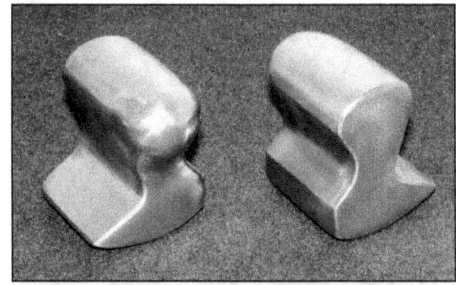

Here is one of the most amazingly useful and carefully worked out items in all of tooldom, a pretty common version of a body dolly. This one has about a dozen useful surfaces for forming metal. I'm not sure of the exact number, because I keep discovering new ones.

If you employ the "bigger hammer" mentality of metal work, you will never achieve much that is desirable. The nugget of good metal work is to leverage the right moves and sequences of moves into desired results. Think of it as persuasion rather than blunt force tyranny. This requires knowledge of the material and of your tools and equipment, and the patience and experience to plan your moves in advance. It is rarely necessary to damage metal in the course of working it. The trick is to work with as little collateral damage as possible.

If you know the metal, know and calibrate the results of each move with it, and plan your sequences for the results that you are seeking, then what at first looks difficult becomes easy. With experience and analysis, the metal ceases to seem unforgivingly rigid and becomes a plastic medium for you.

The great advantage that you have working with and for you is that metal really wants to form into consistent curves, crowns, and other shapes—with the emphasis on the word *consistent*. Bring knowledge, experience, and respect for the metal to your work, and it will cooperate. Treat it as an adversary, and it will fight your every move.

This applies to good-quality metal in the right specification for what you are trying to do with it. It does not apply to metal that is too hard or too soft, too thick or too thin, too rusty, too work hardened, or too damaged for what you are trying to accomplish with it. That may seem obvious, but in the heat of attempting to form metal, it is sometimes forgotten.

Basic Theories of Metal Forming

The most basic theory of metal forming involves the application of close observation and logic to what you are doing. These steps become second nature to seasoned metal workers, to the point that they no longer have to process them consciously. They just know, seemingly intuitively, what steps to take and in what sequences to take them. If they don't know what to do instinctively in a particular situation, their imaginations are guided by knowledge and experience to sense what will work and what will work well.

The most basic theory of metal forming was suggested in Chapter 2, when we looked at forming crown in a piece of flat aluminum sheet stock 1) with "hard," iron tooling, and 2) with "soft" tooling, a plastic mallet and a shot bag. I noted that the hard tooling both stretched and shaped the metal when it was pounded over a teardrop dolly with a slightly crowned iron hammer, making for a relatively smooth and even forming process. It did this by thinning the metal where it was pounded and making it laterally larger as it got thinner. Both of these outcomes accommodated forming a dish shape with more lateral area of metal and shaped metal.

However, when we tried to do the same thing with soft tooling, a plastic mallet, and a shot bag, the

This slip-rolled sheet is beginning its journey to becoming part of a fender. Its next stop will be radical shrinking heads (see top photo on page 29). The grid marks on the metal and notations on the pad contain the plan for shrinking and shaping it toward becoming part of a fender.

AUTOMOTIVE SHEET METAL FORMING & FABRICATION

It took about five minutes to form a smooth, consistent crown in this piece of aluminum with a planishing hammer—a pneumatic percussion device fitted with two anvils to stretch and form metal. The key was to stretch and form it in one operation.

To get the shape required for the crown, it was necessary to shrink the outer edge of the panel. The Eckold shrinking heads are shown doing just that, by way of fine tuning its outer crown.

This inexpensive English wheel has most of the basic features of the breed: a large rolling wheel, a selection of smaller anvil wheels, and a device for adjusting the tension between the wheels. Note that this wheel is adjustable by turning the three-lever adjustment with your hand, knee, or foot.

This high-quality English wheel has stability and consistency that the inexpensive one lacks. Note its much heavier construction. This wheel is adjustable in fine increments with foot levers.

results were warped, rough, and distorted. That was because the soft tooling didn't stretch the metal enough to create the lateral dimensions necessary to form the dish shape that we were trying to create.

In the more successful hard tooling approach, the metal naturally accommodated its new crowned shape, without much distortion in or around the worked area.

The major point to be taken from this experiment is that when you form metal into a crown, you have to stretch it as well as bend it. If the finished shape requires more lateral area, you must thin it as it is being bent. The first approach, forming with hard tools, accomplishes both necessary functions—bending and stretching. The second approach does not.

This is not to say that soft tools do not have a place in panel forming. They do. But it does demonstrate the basic theory of metal forming: To create more than mild crown, it is necessary to stretch and sometimes shrink metal as well as to bend it.

Had we started to create a crown at the edge of a panel, the regimen would have been to shrink that area radically to force the metal into the desired shape. That is because in that situation it has to have less lateral area at its edge, and thus, the metal must be made thicker there. Knowing when to shrink and when to stretch metal takes some experience but is not really very difficult to master.

In many configurations, it becomes necessary to shrink or upset metal to make it take on desired contours. Shrinking is the opposite of stretching. Instead of thinning metal to make it laterally larger, shrinking gives metal smaller surface dimensions by laterally compacting it to force it to become thicker and to assume less lateral area.

Shrinking and stretching are basic to forming metal into anything beyond simple bends.

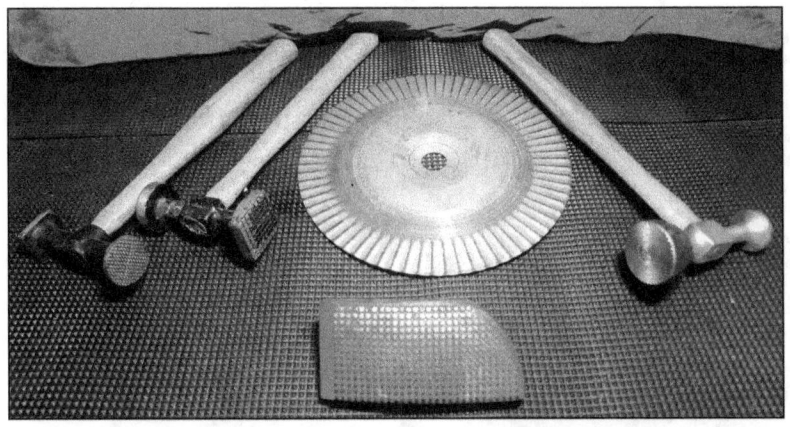

The serrated shrinking disc in the center mounts in a disc sander or grinder and heats and pounds metal to upset it and shrink it. I find this a clumsy approach to shrinking. Various shrinking hammers and a shrinking dolly, are shown around the disc. These work for small shrinks.

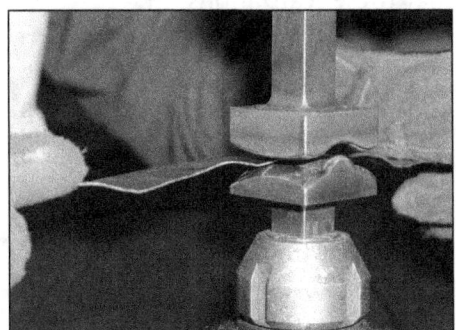

These Cook dies produce radical shrinks by V-shaping metal pushed through their deforming section, and then flattening and upsetting it as it is withdrawn through the dies' flats. This compacts the metal, making it thicker and laterally smaller. This technique can do a lot of shrinking in a big hurry.

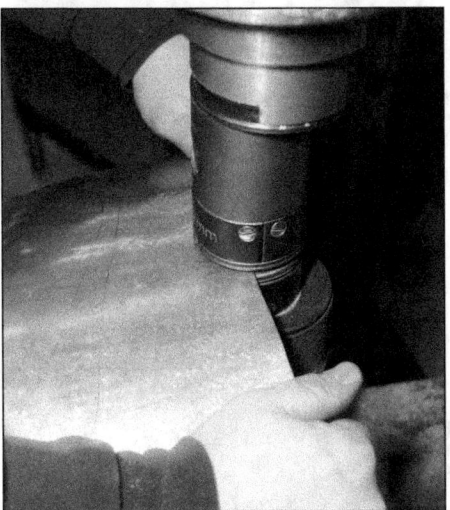

These Eckold shrinking heads operate on a different principle than the Cook dies, and produce a milder result. The heads grip metal, and then come together to gather it. The result is minor, uniform shrinks that are great for creating or adjusting final shapes.

There are many ways to shrink and stretch metal. One comes automatically with some operations, such as hammering metal with a hard hammer face against a hard backup surface. The hammering may be directed at the purpose of shaping metal, but inevitably it also thins and stretches it. Sometimes this is desirable, and sometimes it is not, at least to the extent that it occurs. English wheels are used to smooth and/or form metal, but these tools inevitably also stretch it as they form it and tend to do this in consistent curves when they are used properly. They are basic to panel forming, because the operator can select the outcome of their use by adjusting such variables as the contour of the wheels that are used, the pressure with which they are applied to the panel, and the ways in which the metal is moved through them.

Shrinking tends to be a more deliberate and single-purpose endeavor. It can be done manually with an acetylene torch or arc welder or shrinking attachment. It can be accomplished mechanically with a serrated disc mounted on a body grinder. Special shrinking hammers and dollies can be employed to shrink metal. Edge-type shrinkers can be used to work on or near edges. Or you can go at it big time with the likes of Cook shrinking heads in a Pullmax-type power hammer, or milder Eckold shrinking heads.

There are numerous approaches to stretching and shrinking metal and plenty of hardware available for these purposes. What is harder to come by is knowing in what situations, and where, to perform these operations on the trail to create desired shapes. It takes a particular eye, and some experience, to figure it out. Some cases are relatively simple, such as a crowned 1940s fender. If you visualize what has to happen to a flat sheet of metal to form the crowned section from the top of the fender to its wheel arch areas, you easily can see that the metal nearest to the opening must shrink. In fact, as you move from the center of the crown to the outer edge of the fender the dominant feature of the sheet metal is that it shrinks progressively to form the wheel arch. This shrinking is consistent with the crown in both directions, and it is easy to eyeball what is happening.

Other, more complex shapes take more difficult figuring to see where shrinking and stretching must occur. After a while, you will get the knack of thinking in terms of lateral dimensional change to accommodate the creation of different shapes in three

CHAPTER 3

To fabricate the outer part of this fender from sheet metal, you would have to shrink the area around the wheel arch opening. When you can see why this is so, you have grasped the essence of what flat metal has to do to assume specific, three-dimensional shapes.

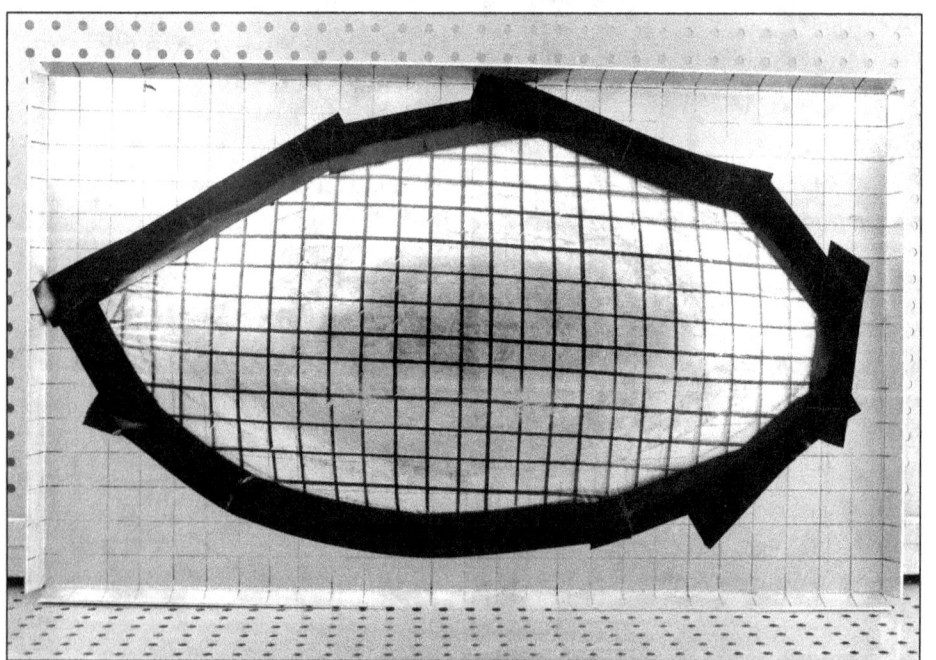

After forming this dish shape on a planishing hammer, its grid lines indicated where it had stretched. Unfortunately, the planishing hammer eradicated those grid lines in the worked area. Stretching a grid-lined piece of flexible plastic over the dish shows what happened to it as it assumed its new shape.

dimensions. I call it "thinking the sheet metal way."

Bilateralism and Other Tricks

There are numerous tricks and "shop kinks" that may aid your sheet metal work. Some are obvious, while others are only obvious when they are pointed out to you or when you think of them for yourself. In both cases, it is permissible to mutter "uh huh," shrug your shoulders, and slap your forehead at exactly the moment that these realizations hit.

Here's a biggie. For the most part, cars are bilateral. In plain English, that means that their right sides and left sides are mirror images of each other. The importance of this fact is not completely obvious. Certainly, it means that if you need to fabricate a missing or badly damaged left something-or-other and have the right something-or-other in good condition (and in-hand) you can transfer measurements in reverse to get dimensions and a model of the missing or damaged part.

Beyond that, let's say that you are doing a fabrication from scratch. In most cases, you would strive to perfectly replicate the reversed dimensions of one side of your creation to the other to preserve its basic bilateral integrity. Right? Well, it's not really necessary, since you cannot see both sides of a car at the same time, except in the unusual circumstance of its being parked next to a reflecting surface.

Slight differences in crown or feature positions are usually difficult to detect if they are not adjacent to other features that make those differences obvious. This is not meant as a blanket authorization to do shoddy,

Walk around a custom-built body, like this one, and try to determine if the left door or front fender exactly mirror those items on its right side in dimensions and shape. Chances are, they don't, and that no one will ever notice that in everyday use.

Is this fender skirt the exact same length as the one on the left? Without measuring both of them it would be difficult to judge that point visually, as long as both skirts fit their openings.

inaccurate work, but it does suggest that absolute dimensional accuracy and fidelity are not as critical as you might think for the sides of a car.

I know of several custom and production vehicles that had substantial left-to-right dimensional discrepancies *when they were new*. One custom-bodied Rolls-Royce that I encountered had a left fender skirt that was 3/4-inch longer than its right fender skirt. This became obvious when the right-side fender skirt was severely damaged, and the left-side skirt was patterned and reversed to fabricate the right-side skirt.

In an ideal world, all dimensions in metal fabrication work would be perfect. In the real world, this is not always possible or practical. It is critical to know where dimensions must be perfect and where they can deviate. For example, if you are dealing with stretched metal that you cannot shrink back to original format and do not want to replace, there are ways of hiding it. If it is in or near a crowned area and not too extensive, sometimes it can be hidden in the crown, particularly if there is a lot of crown. I wouldn't try that on the door of a 1960s slab-sided Lincoln Continental because it would be visually obvious when it failed to match the crown in the other door on the same side. The reflections off it would make the crown discrepancy immediately apparent.

However, extra metal in many fender tops can be expressed as extra crown height and will never be noticed. Extra metal in a flat area below that can be worked into the crown above it, and hidden there. The trick is in how and where you can hide it, without giving this scam away. If you do it near the edge of a panel, it probably will look wrong. If you do it in the body of a crown, it will likely go unnoticed. Admittedly, it is better not to get into situations where visual tricks like this become necessary.

The human eye usually sees what it expects and/or wants to see. It scans for pigment mismatches at the edges of painted panels, because that is where they are obvious, and where they are most often noticed. That is why a good painter knows that in the absence of a perfect pigment match, the best strategy is to blend a color change in a wavy area in the middle of a panel.

That way, the human eye may mistake it for a reflection off clouds or from the ground. If there is a lack of dimensional perfection, it should be placed where it is least likely to be noticed. It may be seen but not register in the conscious mind of an observer. Do not place it in a position that calls attention to it, like a large, gnarly wart on the head of a bald man.

We should all work to levels of dimensional perfection that negate the need for tricking human perception with a bunch of dirty little visual deceptions. Right. Please tell me when you get there. In the meantime, it is a good idea to know just a little larceny in matters of tricking the eye in the sheet metal medium.

The Importance of Good Foundations

One place where visual tricks are a bad idea and do not work is in the foundations under and behind sheet metal fabrications. Most fabrications are built on their own supporting hardware or made to attach to existing supporting features and/or to other sheet metal structures. It is these foundations that cannot be fudged or forced to make new metal work. If you are 1/2-degree or 1/16-inch off at the origin of a panel, you will be much farther off by its middle, and probably, wildly off by its end. That means that it is unlikely that it will match or fit where it belongs and will have to be remade or reworked.

If a fabrication involves creating a panel section piece that fits into an opening, you should have the opening for it in perfect dimensional condition *before* the new piece is planned and patterned to fit. In the case of custom fabrications, issues of exactly how and where they will be attached must largely be solved before they are fabricated and completely solved before you attempt to install them. These are not matters that you should try to figure out on-the-fly. The sidebar "Checking Frame Level" is an extreme example of the importance of having sound foundations—a chassis—for your work.

Checking Frame Level

Here is a relatively simple way to check the dimensions of a frame before a body is bolted to it. It relies on a simple, homemade portable frame-leveling jig that is based on using point-to-point measurements and spirit levels. Lasers and rotating laser devices can also be employed. The measurements must be correct in terms of symmetry and in comparison to known and published factory data.

Jim Crews of Tin Man Fabrication bolts together the nifty, portable frame-checking and aligning rack that he fabricated from I-beam sections. The corners of this rack are scrupulously level and right angled.

A Ford V-8 frame is mounted on Jim's rack and positioned laterally symmetrically to it. The measurements from the frame to the rack also should be symmetrical in terms of issues such as height at the same measuring positions from side-to-side.

Jim looks at factory-supplied data that indicates proper elevations, mounting point positions, and diagonal measurements. Since this frame has been modified in the past, it is critical to use factory data to see if the modifications compromised its dimensional integrity.

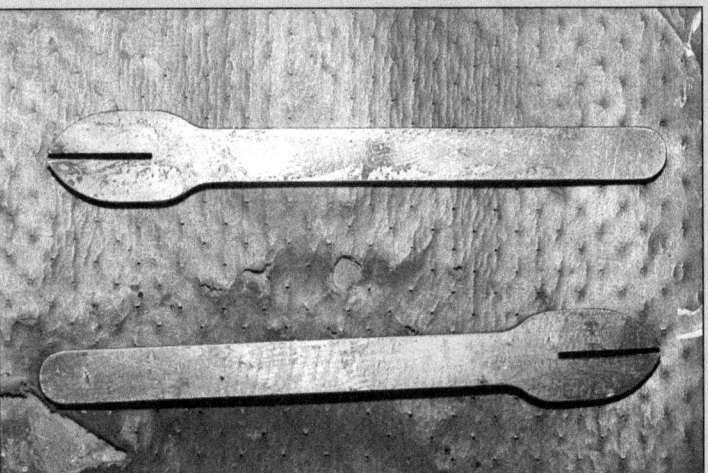

If Jim needs to adjust the edges of this U-channel frame to straighten it, these handy wrenches will be just the tools for that job. Using both wrenches on the sides of the frame members, he is able to effect considerable adjustments to it in four planes.

Since the rack has been leveled and the frame now sits on a level and flat surface, spirit levels indicate any frame position deviations from true, specifically racking or warping. If Jim discovers such deviations, he will be able to figure out their origins and correct them.

CHAPTER 4

PLANNING AND IMPLEMENTING

All metal fabrication projects begin with figuring out how to do them. If you have done the same, or a similar project successfully before, the conceptualizing process is to figure out how to do it with better results, and more efficiently and economically until, of course, you reach perfection. When you reach that perfection, please send me a post card and tell me about it.

First-time projects that present entirely new problems, and combinations of problems, are the most interesting sheet metal undertakings, because they involve the greatest challenges and offer the richest rewards. They hold the excitement of conquering new territory.

While it is possible to attack a new project without a plan—to just sort of start and keep going—I know very few metal workers who try to make this approach work on complex jobs. More often, this approach is taken in desperation, when a worker can't come up with a good plan. It usually follows a cascading course from problems into bigger problems and on to disasters. Eventually, the disasters become dead

When these two fuel tanks are finished, polished, coated, and have their cowling installed, they will be functional adornments of great utility and beauty. One key to the success of this part of this project is in conceiving and planning it. Fabrications like this don't just happen.

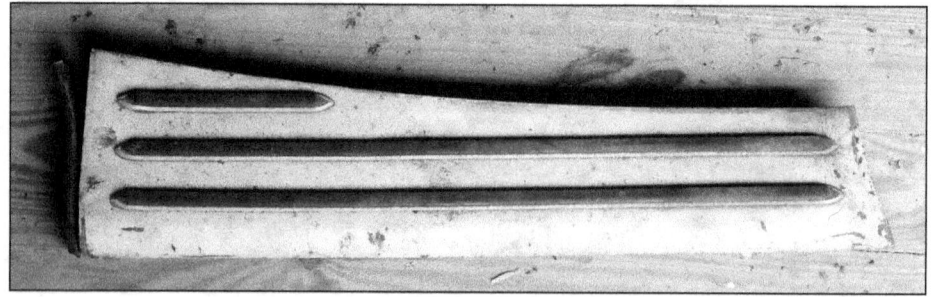

This running board looks simple enough, but to reproduce or modify it you need to make complete patterns and templates of its shape and features. Then you need a plan of attack for the methods that you will use and the sequences in which you will employ them.

PLANNING AND IMPLEMENTING

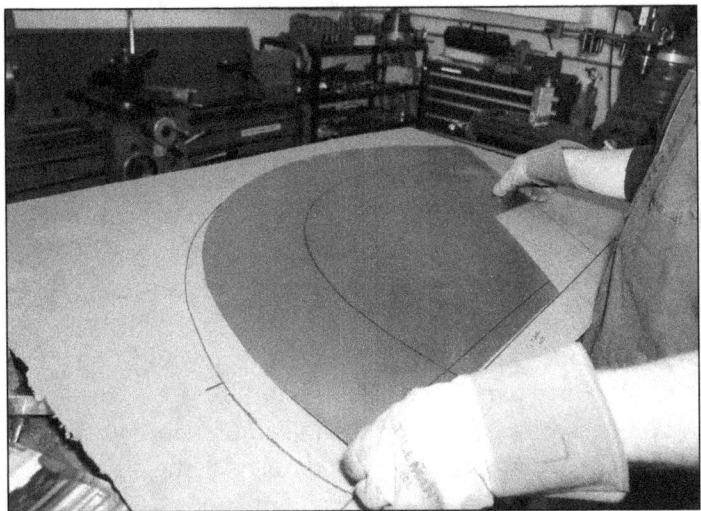

This flat metal is about to begin its transition into a major part of a tractor fender. It takes great skill and planning to get it to that result. You don't just randomly pound out a complex job like this one. (Chapter 14 describes this project in detail.)

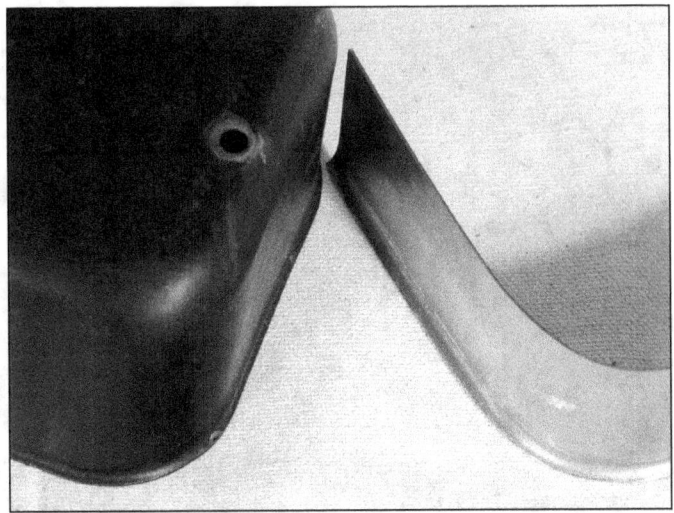

The most difficult aspect of duplicating the electrical box cover on the left was forming its bottom flange. The proof piece on the right confirmed how to do it. (Chapter 13 completely details the project of replicating this electrical junction box.)

The right side of the fender on the left started its fabrication life as the flat metal in the photo above. On the right is an original factory fender. The fabricated fender reflects the overhead fluorescent lights more accurately than the original, and it hasn't even been sanded and painted yet.

ends, from which there is no return or escape. Then the work that has been done has to be discarded and the project restarted. Some may consider this a learning experience, but it's mostly frustrating, and a complete waste of time, energy, and materials.

The best way to start a sheet metal project is to conceptualize and plan the job from beginning to end. Every task should be identified, and each move should be planned and visualized until you are sure how to proceed and are comfortable with your plan. Then, all of the tasks have to be sequenced in the order that will yield the best and most efficient results possible. This is the order that will cause the individual tasks to flow certainly into each other and into the finished job. When you have done this, you have a plan. If you do it well, you will have a good and workable plan.

No matter how good your plan is, sheet metal fabrication sometimes presents unexpected turns and difficulties. One operation may create an unanticipated situation that makes the next planned action undesirable or impossible. Then you have to regroup and try something else. You may have to go back several steps or even to the beginning and try again. As you gain experience with which approaches work best, and in what order, these failures should become rare or almost extinct.

One technique that makes projects easier and more successful is to test any difficult new procedures, and the tasks that they present, *before* you start a job. This may prevent destroying the work leading up to a new procedure by determining that a particular approach will not work. If you get a proof of concept for a new procedure or task before you apply it to a job, you will save time and frustration. Put simply, when you have a new or bright idea, test it out on scrap metal.

CHAPTER 4

Creating hammer forms takes time, but they can ensure accurately reproduced fabrications. The edge opposite the one shown here has the necessary side curve to form this cowling piece. A plastic-clad dolly is being pressed against and run along the aluminum as the first step in forming it.

This kind of procedure testing often begins with patterning and/or templating a project's specific tasks. This process helps you to focus on where problems may exist, particularly problems caused by combinations of procedures applied to the same area of metal. You should always make patterns and templates *before* you start actual work with metal.

While having a good plan before you begin any project is always a sound idea, you should be willing and ready to deviate from your plan if things don't progress as you hoped that they would. Be flexible and ready to adjust to changed circumstances and conditions, if and when, they occur. Your plan is there to help guide you, not to act as a straightjacket. When outcomes change, your plan may have to change to accommodate them.

Choosing Constructions, Materials and Tools

Key parts of any valid sheet metal fabrication plan involve choosing a method of construction, material(s), tools, and equipment. Of course, these items are largely interdependent. If a project requires welding and you lack a method of welding aluminum, then aluminum is out as your construction material. On the other hand, if riveting is acceptable, aluminum may still be your best material choice. Metal gauge is another choice that you have to make. Some projects dictate heavy-gauge metal, such as 18-gauge steel. Others can be done in steel as light as 22-gauge. Most projects in steel fall between these two thicknesses. Aluminum constructions are typically formed in .040-, .050-, and .063-inch alloy materials.

Some projects benefit from creating such aids as wooden hammer forms and other simple "tooling," particularly if you expect to repeat the same fabrication several times. In other cases, it is desirable to do fabrications without any forms or other structural aids. Still, other projects benefit from advanced equipment such as power hammers, shrinkers, stretchers, etc. As critical as the choice of construction methods, materials, and tools is, your ability to work with them is equally—or more—important. For example, if you have considerable skill with a planishing hammer, but have always wanted to form a project entirely by hand on a shot bag with plastic mallets, the best place to learn new shot-bag forming skills is probably not a complex shape involving considerable deformation.

The choices described here are simple or complex. Some of them are dictated by situations. If you are authentically reproducing an original part that was formed out of aluminum, then steel is probably not the right material to use for its reproduction. But if you are working up an entirely new, custom fabrication, then the advantages of aluminum for forming extreme shapes may be desirable.

In some cases you may go around and around, comparing the advantages and disadvantages of some combinations of constructions, materials, and tools with those of other combinations. With experience you gain an instinctive sense of what combinations work best for you for specific jobs.

Before you work with the materials that you have selected for a sheet metal fabrication project, it is possible to divide your work into several discrete tasks, such as bending, crowning, stretching, trimming, welding, etc. It is important to make this division of tasks because it helps you clarify your thinking about how best to proceed.

These propositions tend to be *either/or* choices, where one approach may preclude others. Only when tasks are clearly identified, separated, and sequenced will the significant advantages of the choices that you make be clear.

Modeling, Patterning and Templating

It can take a lot of time to model a project and to work up necessary items, such as patterns and templates for it, but this time is rarely wasted. Whether it is an existing part that you are repairing or duplicating or a new custom part that you are fabricating, work almost always goes more smoothly and comes out better if you have standards by which to check and measure your work as you go along. In jobs where you have to make several copies of the same item, having patterns and templates makes great economies of your efforts possible. This is particularly true if, as you go along, you take the time to modify your patterns and templates to improve their accuracy and utility. Even with the repair or fabrication of a single part, panel, or body shell, patterns and templates can be critical aids.

Without patterns, you have to rely mostly or entirely on your eye. That may work for the simplest jobs but will likely fail in any complex work. There are just too many variables to keep in your head. Work that is completed without using patterns to guide it may look fine on first inspection, but when looked at from many angles, or over time, it usually presents visible dimensional inaccuracies and inconsistencies.

There are hundreds, maybe thousands, of approaches to patterning. Some of them attempt to capture a single aspect of a form, while others

The corner pattern wire is very useful for checking the contour of the new piece's corners. It took all of about 20 seconds to bend it.

This is how the top side-to-side template is used to check the reproduced piece for dimensional accuracy. It is actually much easier to get useful information from this template than by directly comparing the new piece to the original one.

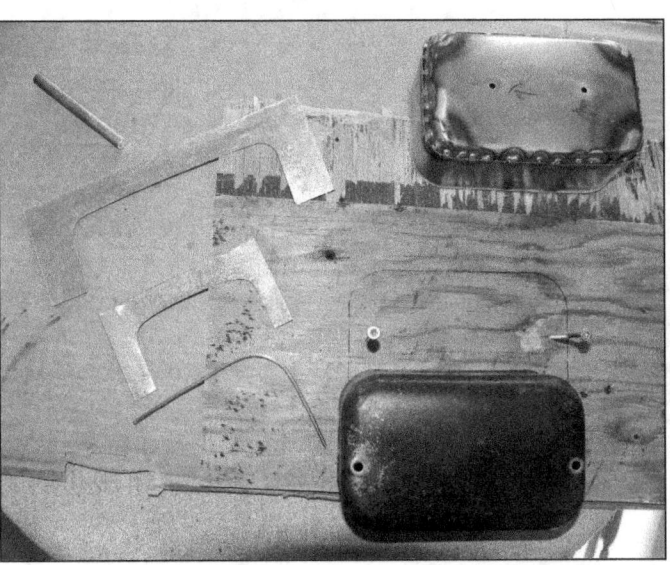

Five templates from the original part (bottom) will guide in reproducing a new part (top). From the top, left, a brass pattern for the hold-down hole bosses, a diagonal top template, a side-to-side top template, a bent wire that captures the box's corner. The two screws are the template that represents the hold-down hole positions.

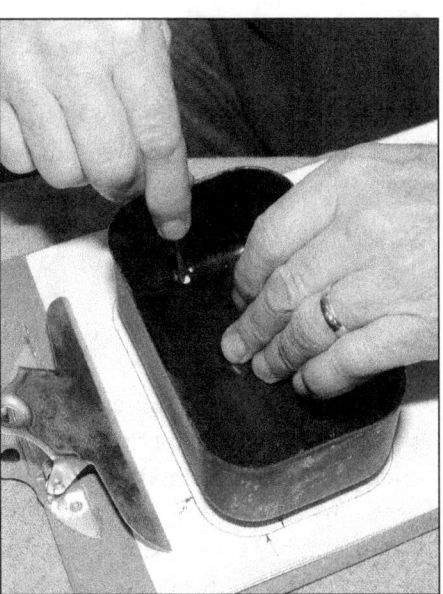

While physical patterns are very useful, it is also good practice to make paper patterns that note dimensions, shapes, and positions. Tracing the hold-down holes on a dimensionally accurate pattern preserves this information. However, in the actual fabrication, I found a better way to transfer these positions to the new piece.

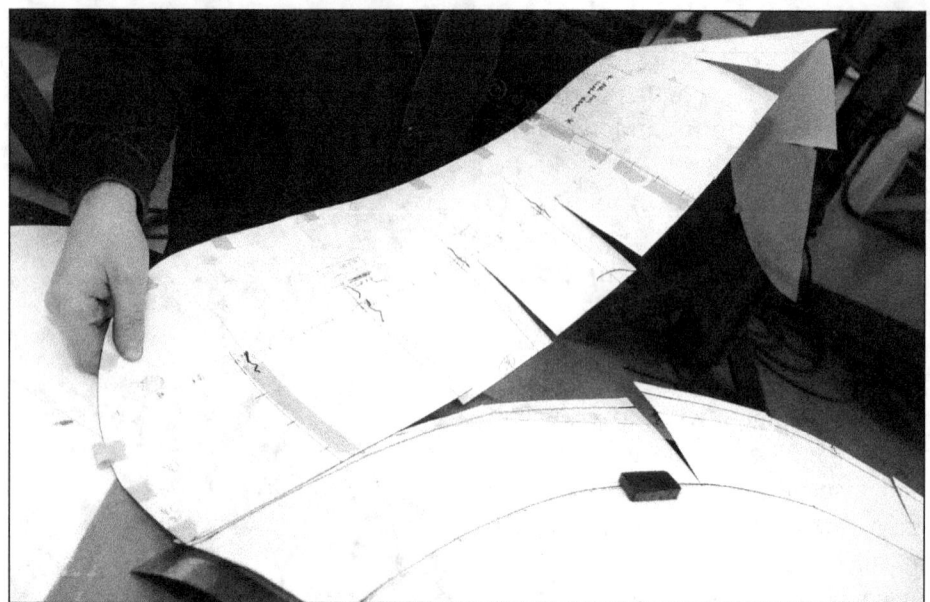

Paper flap patterns are a gold standard for patterning sheet metal. These two mating flap patterns compress accurately into a three-dimensional representation of this part. The flaps overlap to the positions marked on them when they are in the right shape. They also indicate registration to each other.

In the end, you will use the patterning techniques that work best for you, sometimes several different techniques. There is no one correct or best technique for all tasks or all fabricators. It is a good idea to experiment with many patterning approaches to see which ones work best for you, and in which situations they excel. Most good sheet metal fabricators end up using several standard patterning techniques and developing a few unique ones of their own.

Measuring, Drawing and Laying Out Work

One of the most basic ways to usefully capture a shape or contour is to measure and draw it. Representations can be made 1:1 or in any other ratios that are useful. An accurate drawing of a shape, part, or panel simplifies it, using fixed reference points that can be measured and reproduced. A complex part can often be broken into a few easily reproduced shapes and then reassembled in a drawing or other representation of it. For example, are almost comprehensive in capturing its details. Some patterns are wonderfully accurate but not terribly useful. Others strike a medium of both accuracy and usefulness. You might think that the best pattern for a part or panel is the part or panel itself. In fact, these are often only the best place to start capturing detail in a pattern or template.

It often is cumbersome to transfer specific measurements and dimensions from a part or panel directly to your work piece. A contour or profile in a specific area is much more useful for checking accuracy and determining how to proceed in your fabrication. Of course, one profile of a single aspect of something may provide much less information than you need. It may take many pattern approaches and patterns to do that.

Some tried-and-true patterning techniques, such as paper flap patterns, capture a lot of useful information but do not take a tremendous amount of skill or time to create. Physical patterns that capture key aspects of a shape or contour may take more time to create but have the advantage of providing detailed, three-dimensional information to guide fabrication. Wire patterns are very useful in this regard.

This commercial profile taker can capture and reproduce faithful records of the details of many different shapes. It has the advantage of making it easy to transfer these shapes to paper or templates to aid fabrication.

PLANNING AND IMPLEMENTING

Effective Patterning Approaches

The patterning approaches shown here are the most standard and useful ways of patterning parts for both new creations and reproduction of old parts.

Whether you employ the patterning approaches shown here or elsewhere, or invent new techniques for specific situations, the importance of patterning is always paramount to good metal forming.

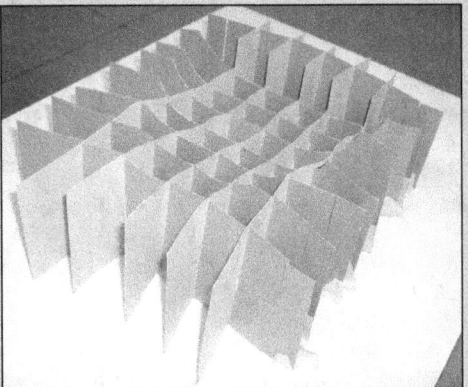

"Egg crate" patterns used to be very popular in sheet metal fabrication work. They can be made very accurately, but are time consuming to construct and somewhat difficult to use. Still, they have their place for some fabrications.

You have already seen the paper-flap-type pattern. It is being used here to check a new fabrication, and to guide work on it. It takes some practice to get the hang of this approach, but it is well worth it. This is a very basic and useful technique.

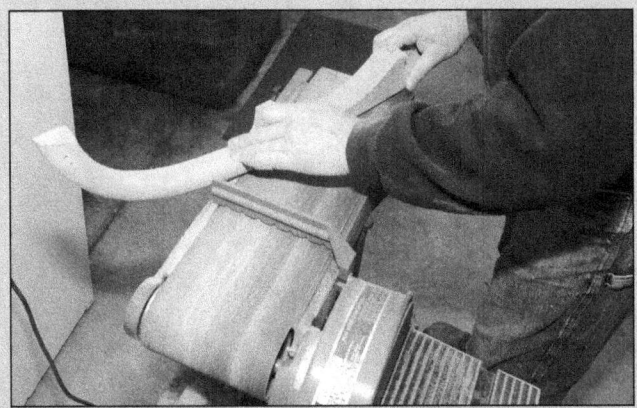

Jim Crews of Tin Man Fabrication refines a wooden hammer form on a belt sander. The form is for the edge of a piece of cowling. This hammer form ensures the new part's accuracy. It can also be used to fabricate several copies of the original part.

Profile templates are basic to any sheet metal fabrication. They guide work by telling you where and how far metal has to be moved. Things like paper, plywood, plastic, and metal can be used to make them.

Here is a really advanced patterning setup. The fenders of this modified Prowler were patterned in wire (note right fender). Then, paper flap patterns were fitted over the wire. The paper flap patterns guided the fabrications that created new custom fenders. (Photo courtesy of Bob Lorkowski of L'Cars)

AUTOMOTIVE SHEET METAL FORMING & FABRICATION

CHAPTER 4

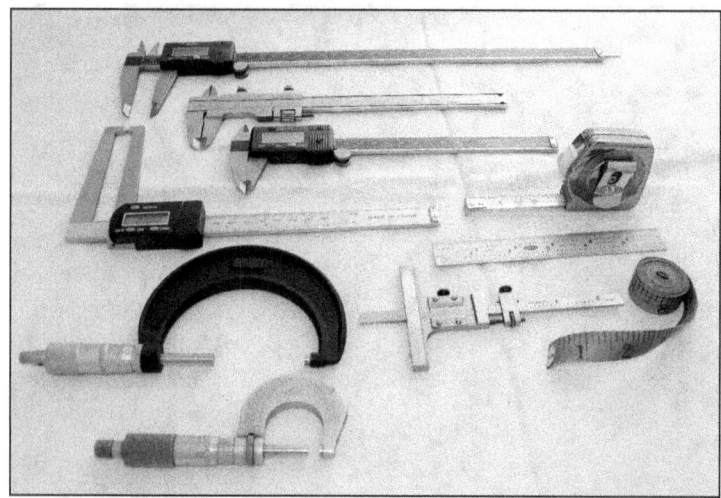

These well-known measuring devices—from simple scales and tape measures to micrometers and depth micrometers and on to digital calipers and micrometers—can be used to collect a lot of dimensional data very quickly.

Determining angles between various aspects of a part or panel can be critical to patterning it and later reproducing it. These devices enable the capture of angle data. The instrument on the right (a machinist's combination square) can be used to find the centers of round objects, often critical points to locate for patterning.

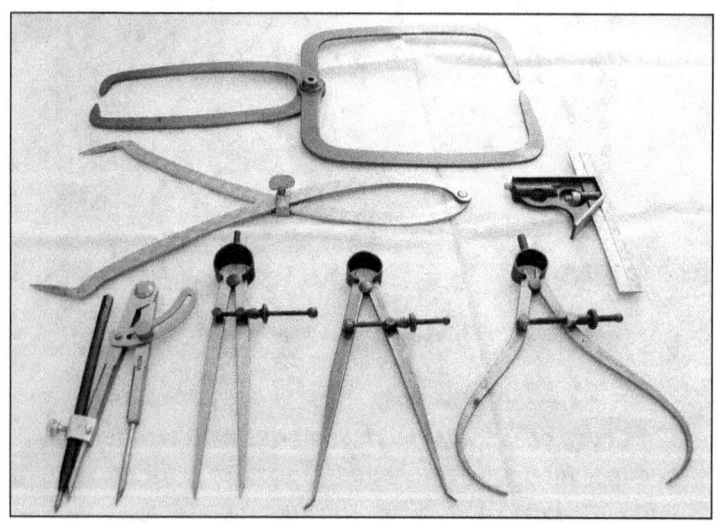

Calipers and squares are sometimes very useful for measuring critical dimensions of three-dimensional objects and for translating specific points from one side of objects to the other. The calipers at the top can be read while still measuring an object. The set below them works for inside and outside measurements.

profiles of individual sections of a part, or of a shape, can be taken and combined into your pattern, model, or template. At the low, but useful, end, this can be accomplished with a profile gauge, a piece of soft copper wire, or many other tools that can capture and retain a shape. At the high end, various forms of digital sensing and photography can be used in conjunction CAD (Computer Aided Design) software can be used to capture and reproduce various shapes. These advanced methods, however, are beyond the scope of this book.

All patterning begins with some very accurate measurements of specific dimensions. Calipers, dividers, micrometers, scales, angle finders, and various other standard measuring devices are the basis of this work. Even simple rules, tape measures, and cloth measuring tapes (used commonly in sewing), are often useful for taking measurements for sheet metal projects. Many of these devices come in a variety of configurations and sizes.

With any patterning technique, measurements taken by various means are transferred to a paper or physical model that is used as a basis for fabrication in metal. Such models are most useful if they yield a variety of the possible readings of specific shapes and contours. This requires the use of hard reference points from the original shape or conception of a shape, which are the basis for transferring all other measurements. Whenever possible, measurements should be used to confirm each other. Some of this is common sense. For instance, if you have a format that is roughly circular, and your pattern has yielded its diameter as 22 inches, then its circumference should be about 3.141 times 22 inches, or about 69 inches. (That is, according to the formula $C = \pi D$,

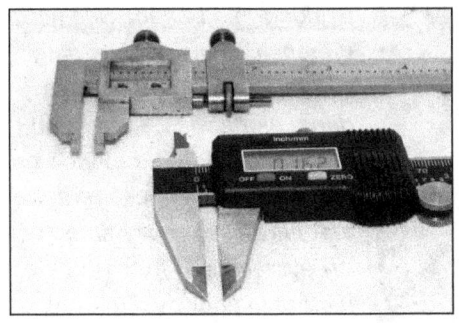

The caliper on top uses an old-style vernier scale. It requires good eyes and knowing how to read that scale. Theoretically, it can be accurate up to a ten-thousandth of an inch. The inexpensive digital caliper (botom) reads out directly, with accuracy as high as half a thousandth.

where C is the circumference, π [pi] is 3.141, and D is the diameter. (Remember that one from school?) In this case, if your pattern drawing designates the circumference as closer to 50 or 100 inches, then there is an error somewhere in your measurements or calculations, and it is time to recheck them.

An accurate profile of a particular curve or contour of something is only useful if you can identify its exact position. This is done with precisely identified reference points, a.k.a. "registration points." The key to good patterning is maintaining these two attributes: an accurate representation of shape or contour, and a way of accurately positioning it.

Every measuring- and position-finding device has a very specific method of recording its data. To use measuring devices effectively, be sure that you understand how to read and interpret their readout scales. If you don't know how to use a vernier micrometer scale, either learn to use one or use a digital device that doesn't require the arcane skill of reading a vernier scale. Both can be equally accurate.

Some measuring devices require using senses like feel, while others put a premium on eye alignment with the scale and the thing or area that is being measured. "Parallax" error, the result of failing to properly align your eye with the item measured and the part of a measuring scale that you are using, is a common source of mistakes in making accurate measurements. Note that as you move your eye from one side to the other of the straight line that intersects a measuring scale and its measurement target, the scale's denominations seem to shift to one side or the other. Scales are only accurate when you view them in direct, center alignment with the thing measured.

A similar problem occurs when you use a straightedge to guide a scored or drawn line. The point of your pencil, pen, or scribe is slightly beyond the edge of the straight edge against which you are drawing. Therefore, if the straightedge is in dead-on position, your mark is slightly offset away from the straightedge. Keep this in mind when you mark critical lines for cutting and bending and compensate by allowing for the offset that occurs with the straightedge and marking device.

When you have collected the dimensional data needed to guide a job and transferred it to patterns, models, and templates, you can move the data that you need to the job metal. This is often the magical phase of patterning and templating, because information that may have been gathered in two dimensions now can be represented in three dimensions.

Transferring and checking measurements is one place in fabrication work where cleverness is a great asset. There are many little tips and tricks that can aid this work. Some are fairly obvious, while others are obscure, but can be found in many books and articles on measurement techniques. And you will discover some for yourself.

One of the most basic of these tricks involves using symmetries to your advantage. If you spot an element of what you are doing that is symmetrical, you can leverage that symmetry by doing things like using diagonal measurements of square and rectangular forms to confirm your patterning data on them. Some-

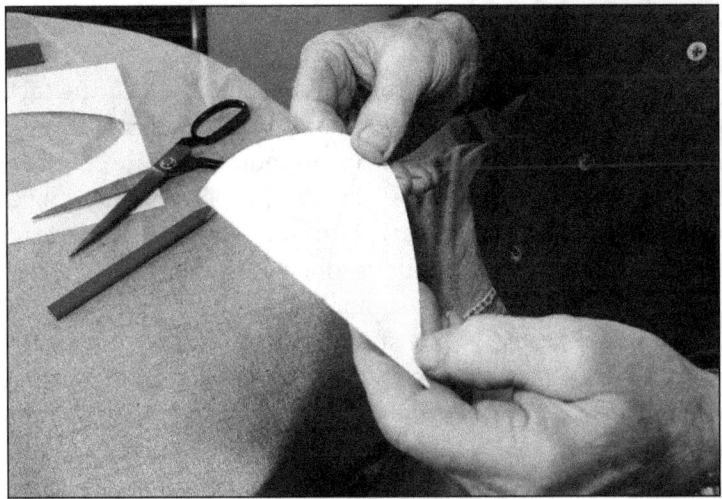

Folding a pattern of a symmetrical shape in half either confirms that symmetry has been captured and preserved by the pattern, or it shows where and by how much symmetry has been lost.

times, just folding a pattern in half confirms that symmetry has been preserved or informs you when it has not, and where any deviation occurs.

I hope that you paid attention to plane geometry in high school. Much of what you were supposed to learn there about forms, such as circles and triangles, can be very useful in patterning work. Alas, if you (like me) never learned or forgot most of that stuff, try enlisting the aid of a teenager who is studying it now, and may be able to help you.

When you transfer dimensions for things like bend lines and indications of crown from your pattern to your work metal, it is important to do it in a non-destructive way and in a way that remains legible as you work the metal. Permanent markers work for some of this marking. Score lines made with a scribe are often okay, but can become starting points for fractures in the metal as you work it. (This is particularly true with aluminum.) In some cases, you may have to periodically retrace your original markings to bring them back up to easy visibility.

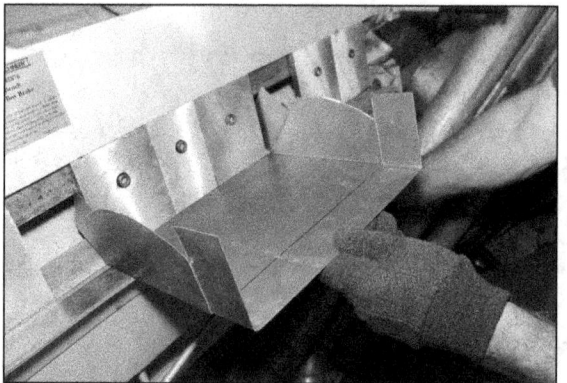

Braking this box to specific dimensions means knowing what its inside and outside dimensions will be after you brake it, and that depends on the metal's thickness and the actual radii of your bends. Always account for these factors in your design of metal parts and panels.

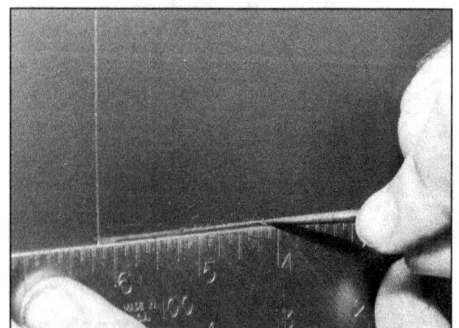

When you score metal to indicate positions, be careful that your score lines don't damage it. Also, remember the problem of the distance between your scribing tool and the scale that guides it. Lines that indicate bend points must account for bend radius and the thickness of the metal.

Here is a small but important point, one that has brought grief to many metal workers: Every time you change one dimension of the metal that you are forming, it changes other dimensional hard points. Here is an example: Say that you want to construct a simple 6-inch-square box out of 22-gauge mild steel. You mark off a 6-inch square and then the sides beyond it, however high you want them to be. You cut the corners out of your work piece, and bend the sides up at 90 degrees on the bend lines. Mission accomplished. You have a box. But it isn't a 6-inch-square box on its outside. If you bent the sides at score lines that were 6 inches apart, then the inside is likely to be a bit more than 6 inches, while the outside is even larger. No way can you call this a 6-inch box.

So, what happened to cause this grievous failure? You forgot to include the thickness of the metal or the fact that your 90-degree bends, made on a brake, have radii that are a little under, or over, a perfect right-angle radius. If it was critically important that the outside dimensions of that box be no larger than 6 x 6 inches, you should have included the thicknesses of both of its sides in your calculations, in this case 2 x .0299 inch for 22-gauge metal. The radius of the bend may make it a bit larger than that, but not much. Actual calculation of these factors depends on the metal and on the equipment. Just remember that changing metal shape can involve some complex calculations, like those that account for its thickness when it is bent. Any actions that shrink or stretch metal should be accounted for when you plan your work.

Structural vs. Nonstructural Fabrications

Many other factors influence the planning stages of your sheet metal fabrication work. I have already noted that the demands of structural fabrications are very different from those of non-structural items. Structural fabrications require engineering, validation, and testing. The primary factor for them is their performance under varying conditions. Appearance may be important, but it is secondary to performance. For non-structural fabrications, the prime directive is that they look good for a long time.

Each sheet metal job or creation has its own logic and its own imperatives and mandates. Be sensitive to these and incorporate them into every aspect of your work, from design and patterning, through fabrication and finishing.

CHAPTER 5

MAJOR FORMING AND FABRICATING PROCESSES

There are hundreds, maybe thousands, of basic operations that you can do to, and with, sheet metal to fabricate it into useful and/or ornamental objects. Some involve big, expensive machines, while a lot of sheet metal work relies on simple hand tools. Much of it falls between those two extremes. It is important to note that equipment of greatly differing complexity and expense often performs the same operations, frequently with equally good results. Usually the difference is in the speed, efficiency, and sometimes accuracy, with which the operation is done. Required skill levels may also differ.

The important thing to remember is that you can often do the same work with hand tools that you can do with the most sophisticated power tools and equipment. In fact, there are places and situations where simple hand tools perform functions better than the exotic stuff. On the other hand, if you are working on an advanced project, say constructing a complex fender or cowl from scratch, the advantages of exotic and/or powered metal forming equipment are unquestionable.

As you read this chapter's account of basic sheet metal forming operations, and the tools and equipment used to perform them, don't be intimidated by the more sophisticated equipment that is shown and discussed. No matter how well equipped you are, there will always be times when a good pair of tin snips or flanging pliers is your best friend.

Cutting

Cutting and trimming sheet metal is very basic, a starting point for most projects. There are many methods of severing thin sections of metal, each with its own advantages and limitations.

Hand shears and snips, often called "tin snips," are the starting point for cutting sheet metal. They are great for accurate cutting operations in thin sheet sections. Don't try to cut 16-gauge metal with them, because the effort will be too great, and, used that way, even the best shears won't last long. Very accurate cutting in both thin and thicker sections is best accomplished with a stationary hand shear, often called a "Beverly Shear," after the most famous maker of this type of device. Long runs of sheet metal can be cut with power shears, both pneumatic and electric. If you have to cut more than a foot or two of metal, power shears will serve well. However, they may not work well for cutting intricate shapes or very contoured sections.

Air nibblers work well to sever both long and short sections of metal. Their drawbacks are that they consume a relatively wide cut line, and they produce a terrible mess of spat-out little metal crescents. On the good side, they steer easily in tight turns, and, hey, if you find some valid use for those little metal crescents, you could become famous and wealthy.

Small, air-driven grinders, such as muffler grinders, are very useful for severing short cut lines, and for making entryways into sheet metal for other cutting devices, like jig saws. They do not work well for long cuts, and tend to produce excessive heat if you try to move them too fast through material. Still, they are useful in some situations.

Jump shears are endlessly useful and allow the cutting of pretty stout stock in dead-straight lines with great ease and accuracy. Hand-powered stationary shears aren't as slick as jump shears, but are usually inexpensive and work well with thin sections. Hydraulic stationary shears are very useful, but very expensive.

Metal cutting band saws are terrific for doing very accurate work reasonably quickly. They don't make really tight turns and tend to leave ragged-cut line surfaces. Those surfaces often require cleaning up before they can be used. The same is true of hand-held air and electric reciprocating ("jig") saw devices. One strong point for band and jig sawing is that it allows very good visibility of intricate cut lines as cutting progresses.

In recent years, plasma arc cutting outfits have come way down in

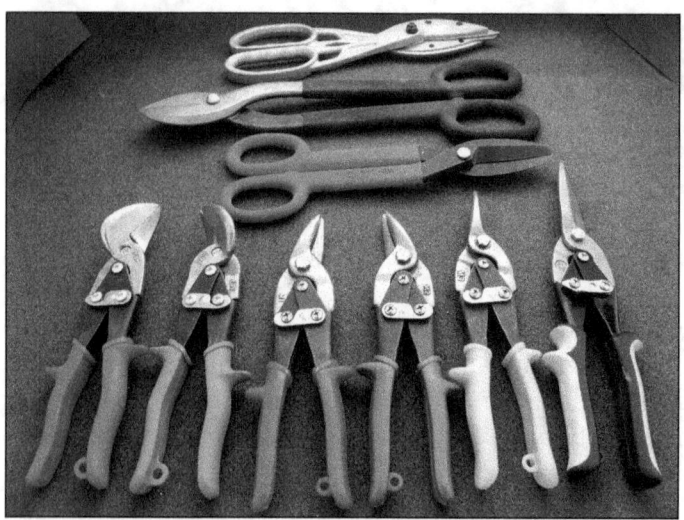
These metal shears (top) are terrific for cutting in straight lines, but awkward for intricate shapes or rounding tight radii. Tin snips are great for detail cutting. The duck bills (left) keep metal nicely out of your jaws way. The far right set has extended-length jaws.

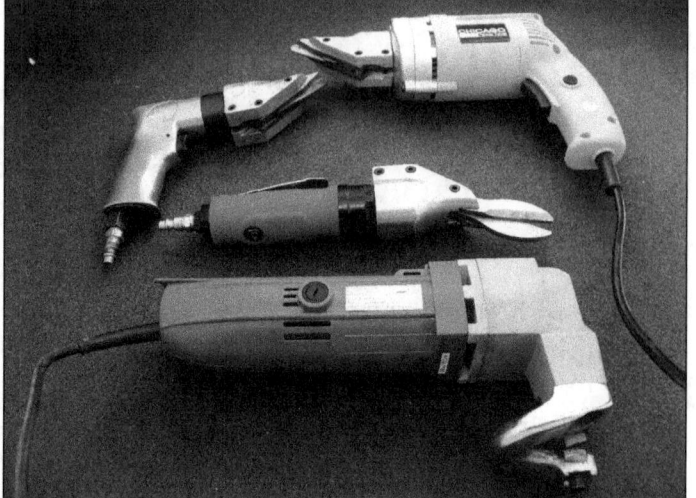
Both electric and pneumatic strip shears (top) remove a 3/16-inch strip of metal, a problem for some uses. This style of electric shear works better than pneumatic versions (top left). These oddball scissor shears (center) work surprisingly well. This type of electric shear can be difficult to guide (bottom).

This throatless Beverly-type shear is terrific for following intricate patterns or straight lines, with great fidelity. Because its leverage makes its hand lever easy to operate, you can concentrate on your cut line.

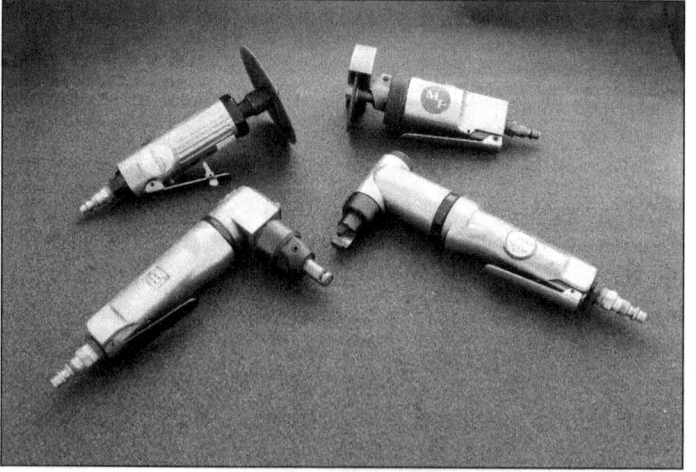
Two small grinding wheels (top) mounted on a die grinder (left) and a muffler cutter (right). These work for cutting entries, but overheat metal if you cut very far with them. These two air nibblers (bottom) remove a strip but are fine for cutting straight lines and non-intricate shapes.

MAJOR FORMING AND FABRICATING PROCESSES

price, while improving greatly in capability, durability, and the quality of their results. The learning curve for using plasma cutters is relatively shallow. Smaller units can quickly go through 1/4-inch ferrous, and many non-ferrous, metals, leaving a clean and weldable edge with almost no distortion. Larger units can sever bridge girders. The main drawback of plasma arc cutting is that it is impossible to see the cut line that you are making clearly. That makes following intricate, detailed cut lines, as you cut with them, difficult or impossible.

Hacksaws are at the other end of the metal cutting technology spectrum

This old jump shear is capable of cutting metal straight, while leaving a clean, undamaged edge. Its performance depends on maintaining its alignment and keeping its blades sharp. Note the guide stop grooves in the table for accurately cutting the same width piece repeatedly.

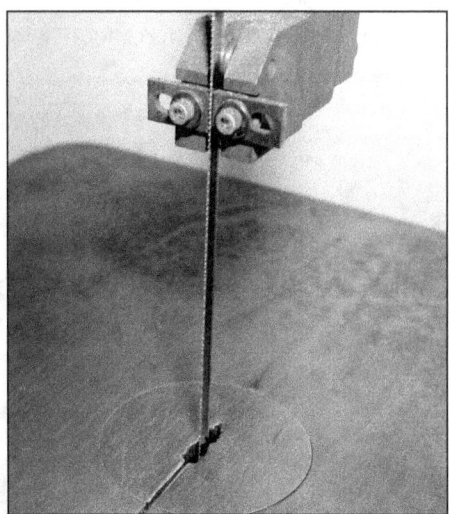

Band saws work for cutting both thin and thick sections of metal, making them very useful in sheet metal shops. They cut with good accuracy and can follow moderately radiused curves.

The bottom section of this 52-inch combination slip roll/finger brake/shear tool is capable of severing 20-gauge mild steel. Operated by hand levers, it takes considerable effort to cut long strips and/or thick material.

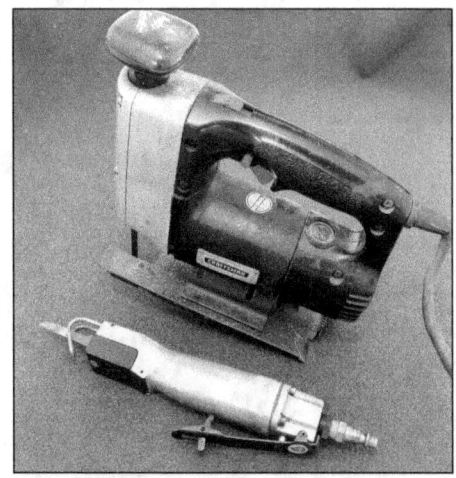

Electric (top) and air reciprocating (bottom) saws work well for cutting short distances and following moderately intricate cut lines. They also serve well where you have to make an entryway into a panel's interior to cut with a reciprocating saw.

from plasma arc cutters. Although they are extremely low tech, they are endlessly handy for making short, accurate cuts in metal. Maybe, if they had a more impressive sounding name, they would get greater respect. How about "Hand Guided, Manual, Toothed Metal Severing Device" (HGMTMSD)? Yes, that definitely sounds better.

Simple Bending

Many jobs and parts of jobs require simple bending. This is the consistent bending of metal into a particular angle along a straight line, or lines, or bending metal into a curve, or curves, in parallel planes. Simple bending is distinguished from other bending in that it produces creases or curves in parallel planes. It does not produce crown or compound, three-dimensional curves.

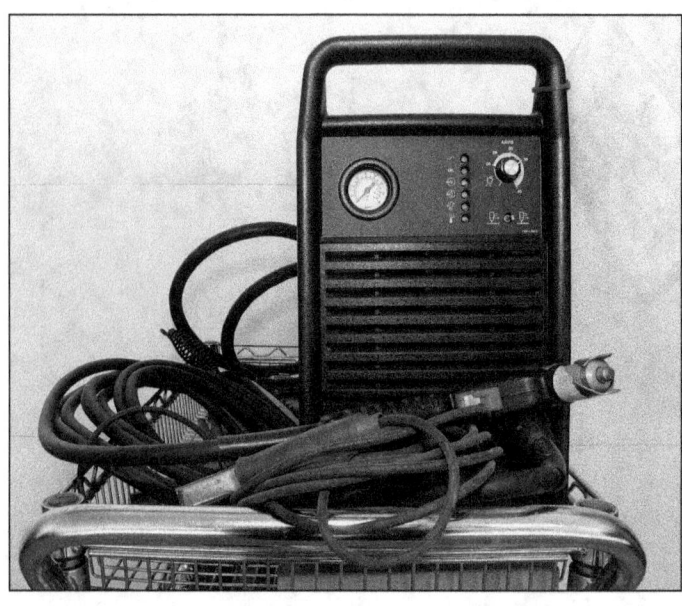

This plasma arc cutter unit uses compressed air and electricity to slice through metal. The homemade stand-off legs around the torch head makes it possible to get some view of the actual cut area. Plasma arc cutters work particularly well for cutting along and around templates.

With the right amp setting for the type and thickness metal that you are cutting, and a steady hand, you can produce smooth, high-quality cuts in many different metals with the plasma arc process.

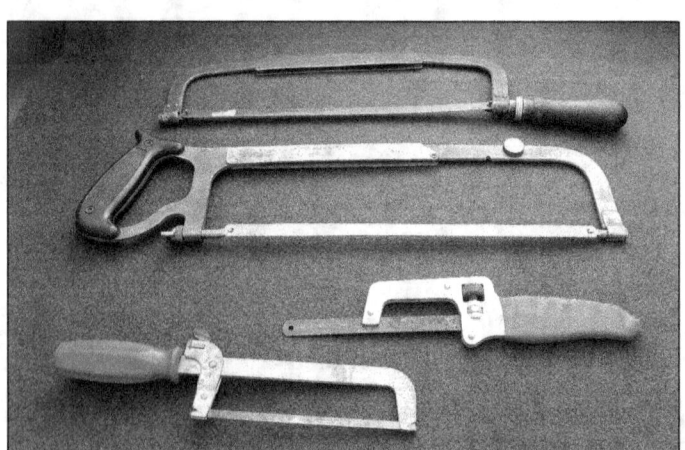

Hacksaws are simple, low-tech metal cutters of almost endless utility. A key to loving your hacksaw is to treat it to a high-quality blade of the right tooth count for what you are asking it to cut. Low-quality blades are a waste of your time and money.

Using this 16-foot brake might seem like overkill for bending this small piece of thin aluminum material, but it makes an important point. Brakes work best when they operate well below their limits. When your brake groans and racks on a job, you know that you need a sturdier machine.

(The topic of crown is discussed extensively later in this chapter.)

The sheet metal brake is the basic tool for making crease-type bends, and occasionally, simple curves. A crease-type bend is made with a single motion of the brake against the metal clamped in it. Curves can be made on a brake by moving the metal in small increments out of the brake's locking surface, and bending each increment slightly. The result is a fairly fluid curve.

Finger brakes, also called "box and pan" brakes, feature removable fingers that allow making bends and forming radii of varying lengths between areas of standing metal, up to the depth of the brake's fingers. Think of a box or pan, where you have to form one or both sides or ends between standing sections of metal that you have already bent.

Slip rolls are used to make simple curves in metal. Two gear-driven

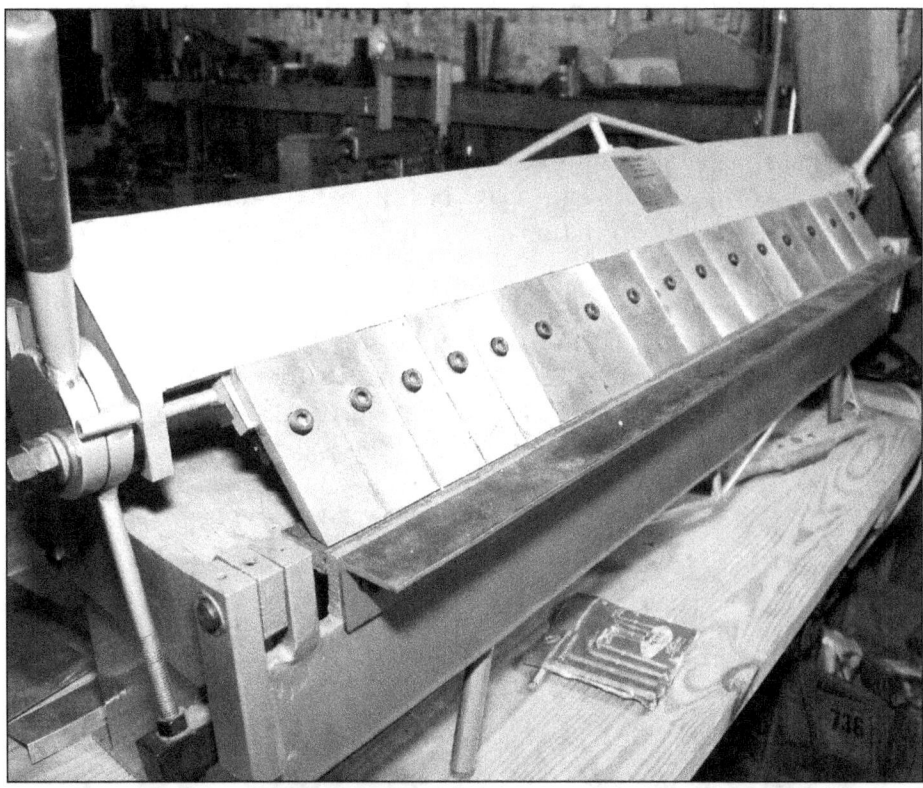

This light-duty (up to 20-gauge) finger brake is an essential tool for a lot of what goes on in sheet metal fabrication. It makes it possible to bend in tight spaces and around low obstructions.

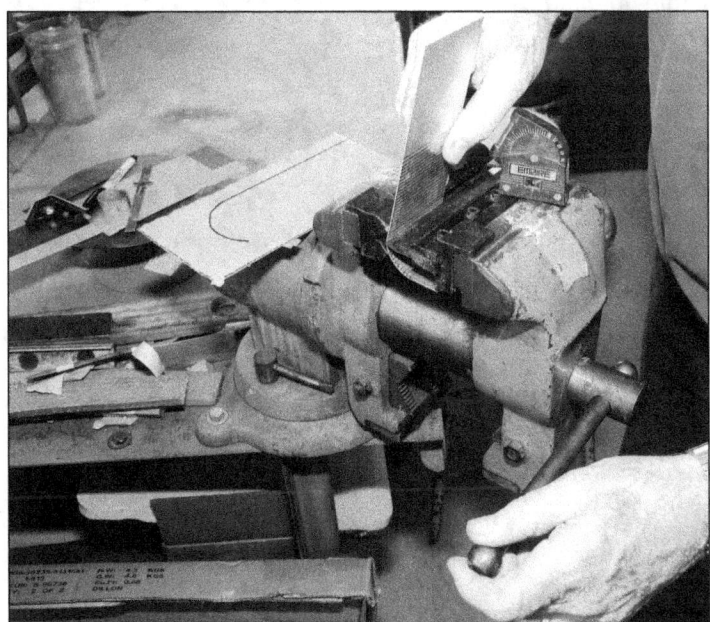

This magnetic, vise-mounted finger brake is handy for bending small parts. Here, it is being used to incrementally bend a radius into a small section of thin aluminum. The lines show bend points, and the magnetic protractor indicates bend distance. Note the bend pattern to the left.

Slip rolls are another must-have device for a lot of sheet metal fabrications. This one is part of a combined slip roll/finger brake/shear device. Self-standing slip rolls are more convenient to use. By adjusting its moveable end roll's position, a slip roll can bend cone shapes and rounds.

rollers force the metal fed between them to deflect into a curve around a third (sometimes also gear-driven) roll. The amount of curve that is imparted to the metal is adjusted by varying the position of the movable roller, relative to the two stationary rollers. There is always some springback in metal fed through a slip roll, because the slip roll is shrinking one side (the inside of the curve) of the metal and stretching the other (the outside of the curve). The metal's memory will fight both of these processes, resulting in spring back. This must be accounted for in adjusting this device. The amount of spring back in any situation can be estimated from experience, or tested on a sample strip of the same metal, or of similar metal, fed into the slip roll at the same settings. By adjusting the movable roll's ends differently from each other, you can produce consistent, conical shapes on a slip roll.

Bead rollers are incredibly versatile tools that impart specialty curves to small areas of metal. They are used on the edges of metal sections or on the sections' interiors to dress them up and/or to impart strength to them. A variety of dies is available for bead rollers. This allows rolling beads of many different widths, and in many specialized formats.

Flanging

It is sometimes necessary to flange the edges of metal. An offset flanged edge is often created to accommodate lap welding the edges of two pieces of sheet metal together. Some jobs require right-angle flanged edges. Right-angle and offset flanging can be done with flanging dies mounted on a bead roller, or with special air and air-over-hydraulic tools that are specifically

Bead rollers are multi-talented performers. They can lay down creases in many different sizes and formats. Note that this metal will require some flattening after it is bead rolled. (Hint: A little imaginative edge shrinking and stretching will do wonders to flatten this piece, and to keep it that way.)

Just hammering the edge of this strip of mild sheet metal over a piece of angle iron accurately formed a radiused, flanged part that was essential to a complex, small fabrication.

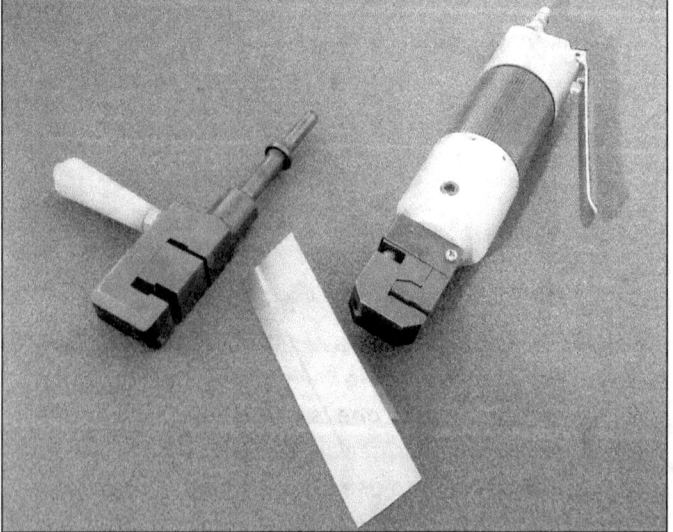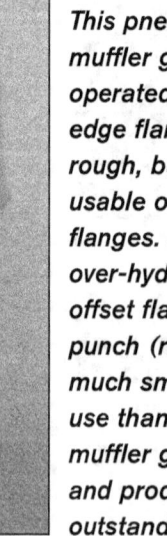

This pneumatic muffler gun (left) operated offset edge flanger looks rough, but makes usable offset flanges. An air-over-hydraulic offset flanger/punch (right) is much smoother to use than the muffler gun outfit, and produces outstanding results. The strip of metal (center) was flanged with the offset flanger.

MAJOR FORMING AND FABRICATING PROCESSES

This flanged metal material required very precise corner bends to form a small box. The simple expedient of hand bending it around a wooden form went a long way to completing the required flanged corner bends.

designed to flange sheet metal. Flanging can also be accomplished by hammering an edge down over a custom die, or over something as simple as a piece of angle iron. Curved flanged edges present their own particular problems.

Creating the Correct Crown

Creating crown is basic to many sheet metal fabrications. It is discussed briefly in Chapters 2 and 3 in this book. Creating crown is also covered in several different contexts in Chapters 10 and 14 because it is a critically important and basic operation in sheet metal fabrication work.

While many structures can be constructed in flats and simple bends, say items as simple as battery boxes or as tricky as some rocker panels, most auto body panels have some crown.

Crown describes a format in which metal falls away from a point in more than two planes or directions. Think of it as a three-dimensional compound curve. Reverse crown is the opposite, or other side, of a crowned structure. If a closed end of a bowl faces you, this is an example of a crowned structure; the other end, which is open, is reverse crowned, as opposed to an eaves trough or downspout, both of which are composed of several simple bends and curves, but that have no crown.

One way to impart crown to metal is by bending it, and causing it to stretch at the same time. This is done, with decreasing efficiency, by striking the metal between two hard surfaces (think of a hammer and an anvil), or one hard and one soft surface, or two soft surfaces. The reason that efficiency decreases in that progression is that while striking metal with soft surfaces deforms it, it lacks the stretching potential of hits between two hard surfaces, and that limits the ability to create crown. Hitting metal against a dolly with a hammer is an easy way to create crown, sometimes more than you want to create.

Crown can also be created by shrinking (upsetting), or stretching metal around part or all of the area to be crowned, causing the metal to bulge. In both approaches (stretching and shrinking), the creation of crown depends on an exchange of thickness for lateral panel dimension in the area being crowned. Understanding this exchange of dimensions is crucial to working with

The part mounted upside down on this wooden hammer form is having its crown adjusted—sounds a bit like psychiatry for royalty—by stretching and closing its corners by hammering the metal against a tube dolly. Crowned areas of metal come in sizes from tiny to huge.

CHAPTER 5

These Cook forming heads on a Pullmax make one mean shrinking, crown-forming machine. This setup shrinks metal and creates a basis for forming crown almost as fast as you would pull your thumb out of its dies, if you suffered the misfortune of getting it in there.

crown, no matter what method you employ to create it.

While there is big, sophisticated equipment around that can move and shape a lot of metal into crowned formats in a big hurry, you can accomplish the same end with simple hand tools and some skill, albeit much more slowly. In most cases, for most people, hammering metal remains the mainstay of shaping it.

Not all hammering to create crown is done with steel or iron hammers. Wooden and plastic mallets are often useful for fine tuning the shape of crown, as are lead-, copper-, and brass-faced mallets. Hammer backups of rubber, corrugated cardboard, leather, wood, copper, and aluminum are often useful. In fact, almost any non-brittle material that you can think of may have some application as a hammering backup for steel and aluminum panel materials.

Shot bags are particularly helpful in some crown-forming operations. Steel or lead shot can be used to fill these leather bags. Shot bags allow metal to move and deform incrementally under impact with less than maximum stretching. Steel and iron dollies of many different shapes and facings are essential in numerous operations, as are hammers and hammering backups.

At the low end of power forming metal to create crown is the planishing hammer, a pneumatically driven percussion device. These hammers tend to be fast, violent, and noisy. While they lack the precision of more senior and sophisticated power hammers, they can move metal quickly. They are relatively inexpensive compared to those machines and are very

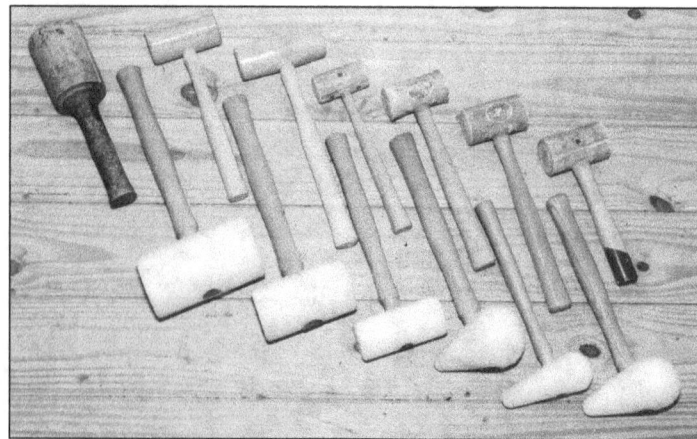

These wood (three top left), rawhide (four top right), and plastic (bottom) mallets are very useful for modifying crown. The three teardrop plastic mallets are particularly handy for this purpose. The rawhide mallet on the far right is shot filled, which makes for very decisive persuasion.

Non-ferrous metal hammers are great for moving metal, while stretching it less than conventional iron hammers would. At the top from left to right are two lead hammers, an aluminum mallet, and a copper mallet. The hammers in the bottom row are all brass.

MAJOR FORMING AND FABRICATING PROCESSES

useful if you want to stretch and deform a lot of metal quickly.

One sure way to create very specific crowned shapes is to hammer them out over, or into, bucks that are detailed to, or close to, the exact shape that is desired. Wood is often the material of choice for creating forms and bucks. This approach to fabrication is different from hammering over dollies or into shot bags to attain specific shapes. With rigid, general hammering backups, like tear dollies, you attain desired shapes by generally working toward them. With a hammering buck, there is nothing general about your backup; it is roughly or exactly the shape that you are seeking to create. In some cases, complex parts may require transitional hammering bucks before they can be formed into one that reflects their exact, final shape.

The main advantage of hammering bucks or forms is that they guide you exactly toward the finished shape, so there is less need to calibrate what you are doing as you work. Consequently, there is less room for error that will require time-consuming correction(s) later. The main drawback is that it can be time consuming and skill intensive to create the form to hammer metal over, or into.

These lead-shot-filled shot bags weigh from 2½ to 120 pounds. The two in the center are hand held. The piece of cardboard mounted on wood (bottom left) is a terrific backup for many jobs, like picking high spots out of flat and crowned panel areas.

You can't own too many dollies. The ones shown here are pretty basic for metal forming operations. The plastic-clad dolly (bottom, right) makes a terrific semi-rigid backup when you want to move metal a little bit, without stretching it much.

This old planishing hammer came with six floating dollies and three hammer heads. When it was new, it was sold as a "fender bender." It is capable of smoothing metal, at the expense of stretching it considerably.

CHAPTER 5

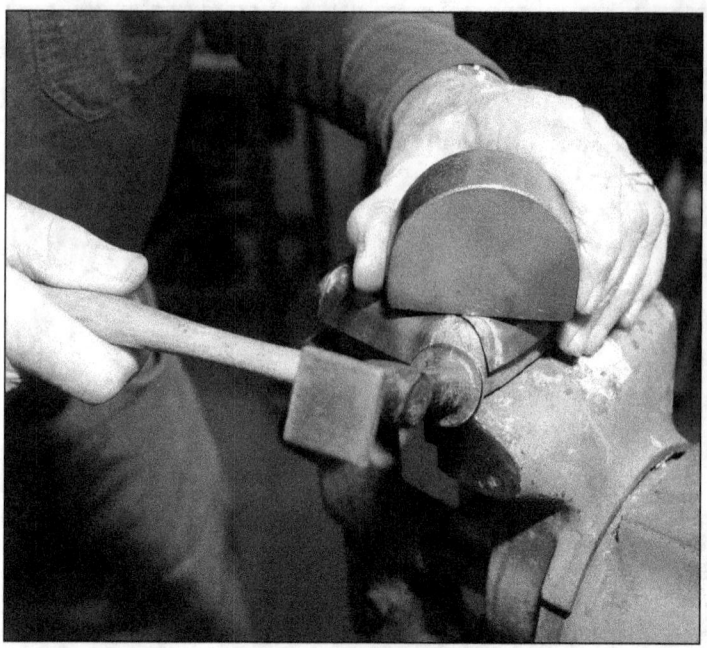

Hammering metal over wooden forms is a time-honored way to form it. Here, crown is being imparted to the corner of this piece by hammering it over a wooden buck. Note the dolly held against the top of the piece to prevent it from warping upward.

The wooden buck under this piece of aluminum cowling helps to guarantee the accuracy of the finished item. Note the use of a plastic mallet on this soft metal part.

In any job that involves creating crown, there is often the need to shrink or stretch areas of metal, locally. Local stretching is no more difficult than hitting metal between two hard surfaces, like a hammer and a dolly, to make it thinner and broader. The trick is often in knowing exactly where to stretch metal and how much.

Shrinking is a bit more complicated to perform than stretching, but also requires knowing exactly where, and to what extent, to apply it. It can be accomplished in several ways. In the past, it was done with an acetylene torch by heating a quarter-size area of metal to cherry red, until it bulges up from its expansion in the unheated and unyielding metal that surrounds the hot spot. Once it bulges, a low crown hammer is used to gently hit down the bulge, so it is level to the surrounding metal. Sometimes a dolly is used to support the shrink spot as it is hammered, to prevent depressing the whole heated area. However, this is not done if there is any chance of hitting the hot spot between the hammer and the dolly, causing it to stretch. After the shrink spot has cooled to about 1,000 degrees F, it can be quenched with a wet rag, or sponge, to stop its contraction, and to "set the shrink into the metal." This step is optional. In this process, the metal is upset, literally compressing into itself, making the shrink spot thicker, and reducing its lateral area, amounting to an area of slightly reduced lateral dimensions, a "shrink spot." Multiple shrink spots of this type are usually needed to produce a worthwhile result.

The raised hot spot method of shrinking can also be performed with a shrinking attachment on a MIG welder or by several mechanical means. Among these are serrated and waffled format hammers and dollies, and contracting contact patch metal gathering hammers. These approaches work with varying results but rarely produce more than very mild shrinking, which is often all that is required. Spinning shrinking discs use heat generated by friction and impact to upset metal and shrink it. They can produce dramatic results, but it is difficult, or impossible, to make them work in some metal contours. It is also difficult to

MAJOR FORMING AND FABRICATING PROCESSES

control the amount of shrinking that they do, or exactly where they do it.

Small mechanical edge shrinker/stretcher devices and small mechanical shrinker/stretchers that work beyond the edges of panels are inexpensive, easy to use, and easy to control.

Mechanical shrinkers work by gathering metal mechanically. This is done by grasping it between two sets of toothed jaws that are separated by a small distance. After the metal is grasped firmly between the jaws, they are moved toward each other, compressing the metal laterally, and causing it to become thicker, and laterally smaller. Small mechanical shrinkers are operated by hand levers, foot pedals, and sometimes, air and/or hydraulic means.

The torch or electric welder method of shrinking involves heating a small spot of metal until its expansion against the unyielding metal surrounding it causes it to pop up. Then, it is gently hammered back, flat, to the panel, sometimes over a loosely held dolly, compacting it.

As a shrink spot cools, the shrinkage of the metal in it can be controlled somewhat by applying compressed air, or a water-soaked sponge or rag to it. This reduces further shrinking and imparts increased hardness to the metal in the shrink spot.

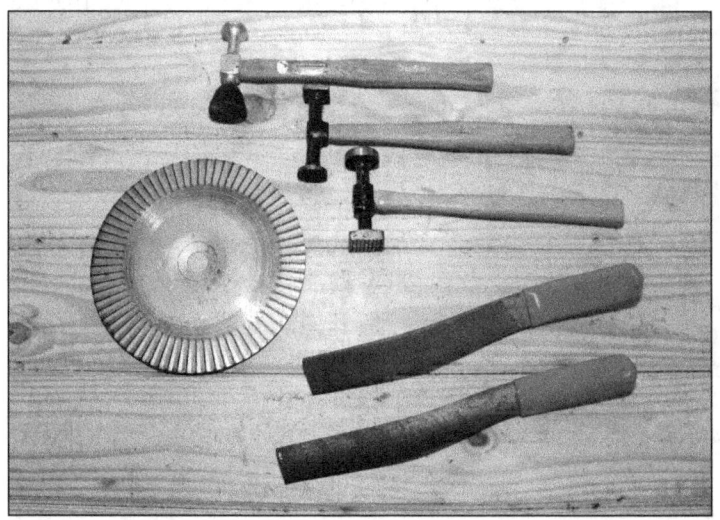
On impact, the hammer at the top counter-rotates inner and outer faces to gather metal, shrinking it. The waffle-pattern hammers and slapping files below it are used with sideways, glancing blows to slightly gather and compact metal. The shrinking disk (left) rotates fast to heat and impact high spots, shrinking them.

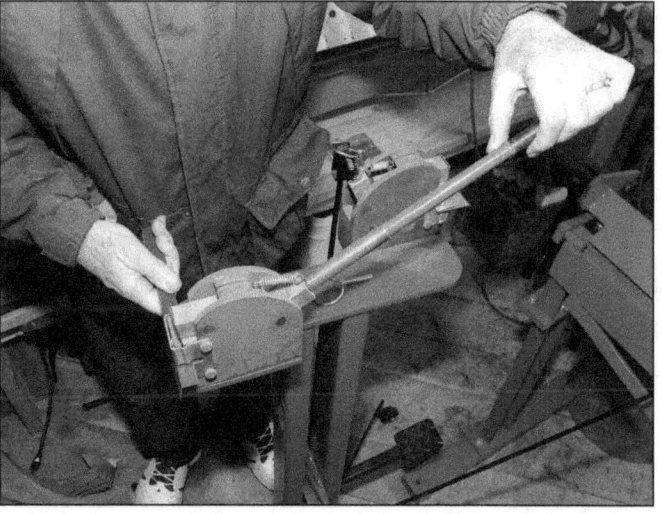
This shrinker/stretcher combination setup operates by hand or foot. Both methods give you some feedback as to what the metal is doing. You don't get that with more advanced mechanical metal forming devices, such as planishing hammers (stretching only) and power hammers.

CHAPTER 5

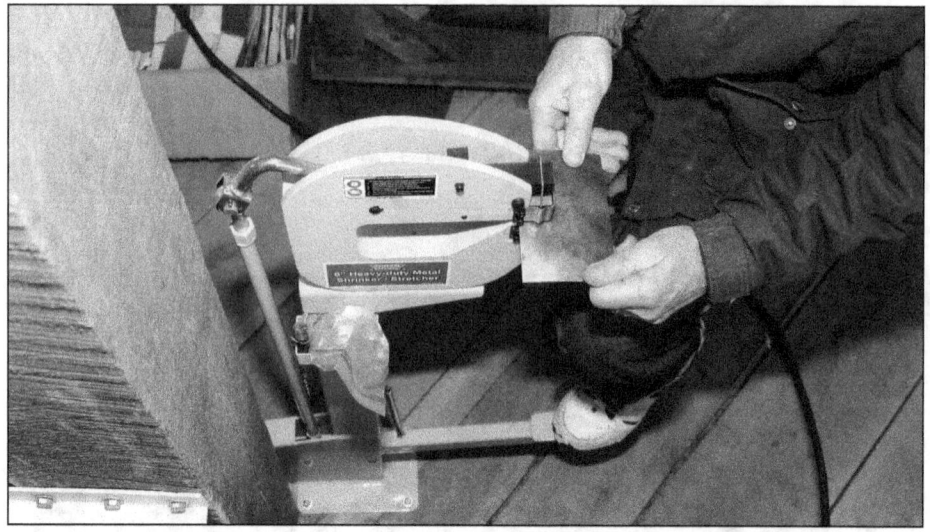

This shrinker has interchangeable jaws for stretching and allows working up to 8 inches inside of the edges of metal sections. The key to using this kind of device is to go slowly and to make changes in metal incrementally, not violently.

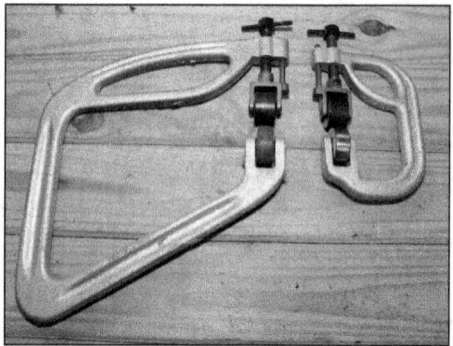

These old, cast-iron, Model T-era fender rollers were designed to straighten out lumps and bumps on fenders. Their flat wheels were supposed to limit stretching, but did not fully succeed at that. Surprisingly, they are still useful for smoothing metal in remote panel areas today.

This robustly constructed English wheel is a nice size for most jobs. Its construction guarantees accuracy and adjustable linear tension between its wheels. Basically, a good English wheel needs to be able to store a lot of torque in varying amounts without allowing much sideways movement of its wheels.

Stretchers work in a similar manner, except that after clamping metal, the jaw pairs move apart, stretching it between them. With both devices, a single motion (of foot or hand) performs the complete clamping and shrinking or stretching operation.

Wheeling

Much has been written about English wheels. They are one of the sexiest and most useful sheet metal forming devices on the planet. They are also one of the most difficult to learn to use effectively. Versions of English wheels range in price from a few hundred to several thousand dollars. In an age that tends to favor complex and automated equipment, I find the popularity of English wheels quite refreshing because they are simplicity itself.

The easiest way to comprehend English wheels is to understand that they do three fairly simple and predictable things. They stretch metal, they form it into mild curves, and they smooth it. That may not sound like much, but it represents a majority of what is required for many metal forming jobs.

Using English wheels involves properly adjusting a few variables to get the results that you want. First, there is the selection of wheels, their surfaces, sizes, and curvatures. Top

The fender top at the right is a reproduction of the rust-thinned and perforated piece on the left that was cut out of the original fender. The new part was formed largely on an English wheel. This kind of smoothly flowing shape lends itself to English wheel forming.

wheels are usually large, flat, and hard, or sometimes soft. Bottom wheels ("anvil wheels") are usually hard, and vary from flat to very radiused. The more rounded a wheel is, the higher the pressure that it applies to the metal worked through it, and the more stretching and deforming the wheeling operation produces. I sometimes think of English wheels as huge stretching machines.

The second variable is wheel pressure, which is operator adjustable via a threaded tensioning device. Again, more wheel pressure translates into more stretching and faster deformation.

Finally, there are the placement, number, and length of stroke through the wheel. Placement involves the distance on a panel between strokes, their distance from each other, and their orientation to the work piece. Repeated wheeling in the same area produces very different results from cross, or diagonal, wheeling at a 90-degree angle. The length of strokes affects where deformation becomes pronounced and where you want to taper it. Number, length, and placement of stroke are all interrelated. It takes quite a bit of practice to get a feeling for how to adjust these variables, and to mesh them with your choices of wheel configuration and pressure.

Suddenly, this very simple device, the English wheel, becomes pretty complex to operate. But the results of using a wheel effectively are worth the effort to learn how to use one. Beyond simple smoothing, an English wheel is capable of producing some astounding panel contours.

Wheeling technique is something that can be approached scientifically or intuitively. It's like playing pool. There are some players who know and analyze the physics of the thing, while there are others who just play, and seem to know, intuitively, how to make their shots. Great pool players can be found in both groups. I wonder if great pool players have a subset, great English wheel operators. (Chapter 10 discusses English wheel theory and practice in added detail.)

Power Hammer Forming

Power hammers originated mostly in aviation and prototyping work. They automate the forming of metal by striking it repeatedly, quickly, and forcefully, often with specialized heads that shrink, stretch, and shape it. Early power hammers used spring escapements and were large, noisy, and often clumsy devices. For all of that, they got the job done far more quickly than it could be done manually. Extensive specialized tooling was available for the early power hammers and made

The design for these power hammer heads has been kicking around the metal forming industries for decades. They are designed to radically shrink metal by deforming it, and then flattening it in a way that causes the upsetting that shrinks metal.

These Eckold shrinking heads mechanically grip and gather metal by closing the gap between the halves of the upper and lower heads, once metal is gripped firmly between them. This produces a definite shrink. Repeated applications in the same places increase the amount of shrink there.

CHAPTER 5

This louvering tooling, fitted to a Pullmax, allows the complete cutting and forming of louvers of one depth and format, but of any length. The device's halves both cut and form the body of the louver. The adjustable bottom die terminates and forms the louvers' ends.

them quite versatile. The best known of these pioneer hammers are the Yoder and the Pettingell devices. Some of these hammers are still in use today.

More modern power hammers and formers, with names such as Pullmax and Kraftformer, tend to be much quieter and less violent than the old metal forming machines. They can be outfitted with specific tooling for particular jobs, or with general tooling for operations like shrinking, stretching, louvering, etc.

Power hammers are beyond the needs of most fabricating tasks. However, they are all but essential for some very advanced tasks. Even for tasks where they are not necessary, they can usually speed work up greatly, particularly where forming crown and making it mesh with specific surroundings is essential. (Power forming equipment is covered in more detail in Chapter 11.)

Avoiding Unnecessary Damage

While there are many ways to work metal effectively, there are just as many ways to damage it in the process of working it. In some situations, some damage is inevitable and can be fixed later. Other damage goes beyond that and becomes very time consuming to repair, or worse, impossible to fix. In these cases, the job must be restarted, often with the waste of considerable time and effort, or even the loss of a valuable panel.

The key to prevent damaging metal is in knowing its limits and being observant and sensitive to when it is reaching those limits. Plastic and elastic limits are obvious danger points. So is just hammering metal too thin for the service in which it is intended. To avoid damaging metal, you need to use common sense and try not to make it do things that it cannot do. In some cases, there are simple precautions to avoid this kind of damage. For example, if you sense that the metal that you are working is hardening to the point that it will fracture if you attempt to work it further, annealing it is a very good strategic step.

Avoid scoring metal too deeply when you mark it, because you may be creating the perfect place for a crack to start. In fact, all jagged edges, stray file marks, saw gauges, etc., should be smoothed out to deprive cracks of one of their favorite birthplaces.

When you use heat with metal, particularly welding heat, always plan for expansion of the area that you are heating, so that there is a place for the expanding metal to go, without needlessly stressing and/or deforming adjacent areas.

There are many ways to avoid damaging your work as it progresses. Most of them involve informed observation and sensitivity to what you are doing. Always consider the possibilities of unintentional damage as you work with sheet metal.

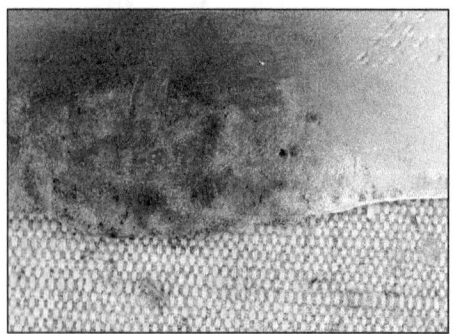

This .050-inch-thick aluminum material has been pounded so thin and cold worked so hard in this area that it is beyond the simple remedy of annealing it to work it further. Experience and close observation saves you from reaching this point in your work.

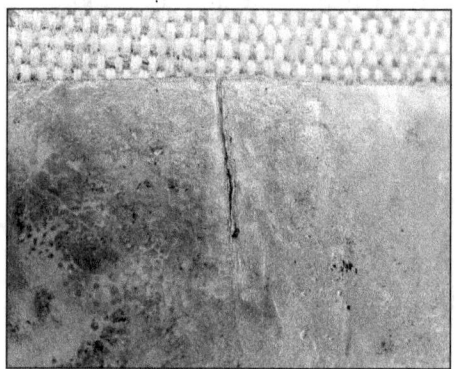

This crack is propagating along a too deep score line in badly overworked 3003 H14 aluminum. The problem is at crisis level, a visible fracture. There is no point in welding this crack shut and continuing to work this part; it is too thin and must be rejected.

CHAPTER 6

OTHER PROCESSES AND SKILLS

There are many small skills that will win no accolades from your adoring public, but still must be mastered to do great sheet metal fabrication work. While no one is going to praise you for mastering them, they can be critical to getting the results that do win praise. I guarantee that the fabricator of a terrific rod or custom never heard an admirer say, "Wow! That's terrific! You really went to the limit in your filing, sanding, and edge deburring on that one!" Still, those skills and others are critical to success in this work.

Filing is properly accomplished with moderate pressure and a sideways slip-sliding motion of the file against your work. Filing should occur on the forward stroke only. Files should be dragged only lightly back across the work for the next forward stroke.

Filing

For too many people, filing metal seems like an automatic task about which nothing need be known or learned. After all, you just drag a file across the metal that you want to remove, and the rest follows, right? Well, no, that isn't right. Properly done, filing is a precision process that can flatten or remove metal in increments of less than one thousandth of an inch. Filing can, and should, be raised to the level of an art.

The choice of the right file for the job is critical. Files differ in coarseness and in configuration. Some are straight-cut, some are cross-cut, spooned, or nibbed. Straight-cut files are generally best for precisely filing metal. Files also differ in shape, including: flat, square, triangular, round, domed, etc. Choosing the right size and shape of file is critical to the success of this procedure. As a general rule, this decision involves choosing the file that will remove the least metal to get you to the shape in the metal that you want.

Files should be kept clean and sharp. You clean them with "file" cards, very short bristled wire brushes designed for that specific purpose. To keep them sharp, you should store them separately from one another in a clean, dry place and discard them when they become too

AUTOMOTIVE SHEET METAL FORMING & FABRICATION   61

Abrasive paper should almost always be backed up with something more uniform than your fingers. This allows the material-removal potential of abrasive papers to be realized. And that creates smooth, uniform, flowing surfaces.

dull to cut. I find that lubricating them with turpentine makes them glide more smoothly and reduces the chance of rusting.

Finally, there is the correct filing motion: forward, away from you. Only a few specialty "pull" files have a different filing motion. All files require a little side slip as you file. The amount of slide slip depends on how much area you are filing and the need to keep that area level. Files require steady, firm pressure, but not King Kong pressure. They should not be dragged back across work, because this does no good, and can dull them. In most cases, files should be run flat to your work, or rocked, toe-to-heel, across areas of metal that you want to remove or smooth. The choice of rocking motion direction depends on the contour of what you are filing, your orientation to it, and where you want to remove or smooth metal.

Sanding

Sanding is a smoothing or blending operation that often follows filing. It should not precede filing, because it is a much finer operation. In large part, like filing, its accuracy comes from its randomness—no two file or sanding strokes are exactly the same, and this averages their action on your work—and because it is slower than most other metal removal processes.

Many of the considerations in sanding are similar to those in filing. You need to choose the right abrasive paper for the job. Some sanding is done with "wet or dry" abrasives that can be used with water to lubricate the sanding operation. Some papers are "open coat," making them less likely to clog with debris if you are sanding something that produces a lot of residue. Sandpaper grits progress from about 40 (boulders!) to near atomic sizes in the micron grit range. In some cases exotic abrasive papers are guaranteed to have no cutting particles larger than a certain grit grade. In other cases, they average their stated grade, with some particles coarser, and some finer, than that. However, most metal sanding employs much coarser papers than those in that range.

Sanding ranges from coarser abrasive grits to finer ones. This allows each grade to remove the scratches made by the previous grade used. For this reason, it is important to remove all debris from sanding with each grade, before moving on to the next, finer grade. If you fail to perform this cleanup thoroughly, you run the risk of getting abrasive cross-contamination scratches, which can be very time consuming to remove, with the finer grit grades that you will use as sanding progresses.

Abrasive papers and cloths can be coated with abrasives made of flint, silica, aluminum oxide, tungsten carbide, ceramic, rouge, etc. Your choice of abrasive is a matter of personal preference and cost. In my opinion, very inexpensive abrasive papers tend not to be bargains.

Sanding should almost always be done with a pad or other backing for your abrasive paper. This prevents the uneven sanding that the pressure points made by your fingers can produce. Backings can range from foam rubber pads to paint sticks, and even files wrapped in abrasive paper. The choice of backing depends on what you are trying to accomplish. Straight sanding motions that go with the contours that you are

Because a straight radius is being sanded here, it makes sense to use a somewhat hard, concave backup for the emery cloth abrasive. A warped paint stick is used to back the emery cloth with its concave side under the paper and against the surface.

OTHER PROCESSES AND SKILLS

This edge deburrer quickly cleans up the edges of metal that have been roughened by cutting and other processes. It is worth taking the time to use this inexpensive tool to smooth the edges of the metal, whether or not they will be hidden or welded later.

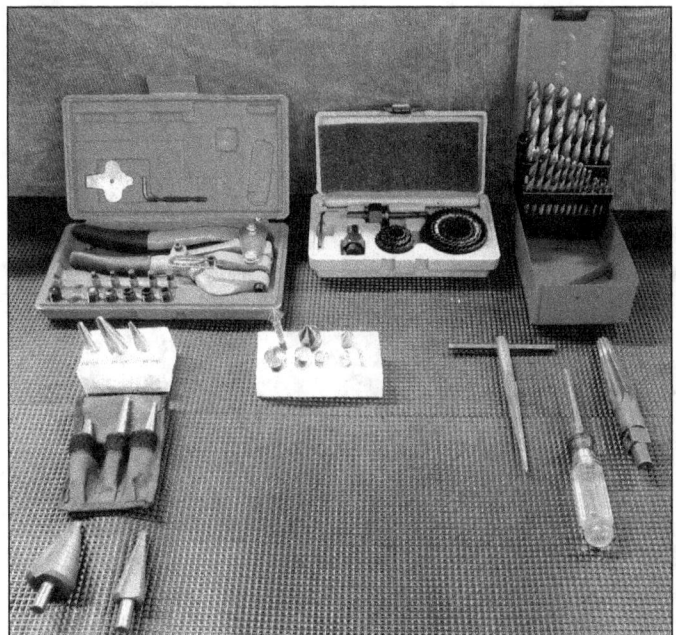

These hole-making, sizing, and deburring tools are used extensively in metal work. On the top row from left to right: a hand punch, hole saws, and a drill index set of drills. On the next rows from left to right: stepless and stepped sizing drills, countersinks, and hand reamers.

sanding are usually best, unless the proposition is to feather edge an area level to its surroundings. Then, circular sanding motions are most useful. Sanding pressure depends on the grit, backing, and lubricant (if any) that you are using.

Edge Deburring

Since many cutting operations leave rough edges on metal, it is usually highly desirable to deburr them before you can call them finished edges or weld them to other metal. While edge deburring can be accomplished in many ways, the slickest ways involve the use of tools specifically designed for this purpose. These are edge deburrers and machinists' knives, which are run along the edge to be deburred. The pressure on the tool must be enough to make it cut, but not gauge, the work piece. This may take a little practice, but it is a skill that pays dividends after you acquire it. Commercially sold deburring wheels from 3M Scotch-Brite, Norton, and Brite Star, among others, can also be used for edge deburring.

Drilling, Piercing and Punching

Making round holes with clean edges is often important in metal work. In the case of sheet metal work, the common, everyday twist drill has been the mainstay of creating holes for centuries. Unfortunately, it is largely ill-suited to the task of making precise holes, and only marginally preferable to gnawing holes through sheet metal with your eye teeth. Holes drilled with twist drills tend to be irregular in shape, and to have massive burrs on their back edges. These holes can be sized, made round, and deburred with reamers and countersinks, or larger drills, or step and stepless drills, but the results are usually far from perfect.

Fortunately, there are better ways to drill holes when their quality matters. It involves the use of step and stepless drills (see below).

Piercing with an oxy-acetylene torch, or plasma arc cutter, are not among those better ways. They are fast and can be tempting for making holes in thick sections, but they produce far more ragged results than drilling with twist drills.

If you have the equipment, punching produces round, burr-free holes that require little, or no, afterwork. Lever punches are good for making small holes in mild steel, up to about 20-gauge. Beyond that, you need more power than a hand punch can deliver, specifically hydraulic or screw-generated pressures.

The new kids on the block for making clean, round holes are step drills and stepless drills. Step drills produce remarkably round and smooth holes in exact dimensions in sheet metal. Stepless drills do this in minute increments. They produce a continuum of sizes and can be used for precise fitting and cleaning up holes, much like reamers, but often with far better results.

Edge Treatments and Bead Rolling

When you look at a car, almost any car, one thing that you are *not*

CHAPTER 6

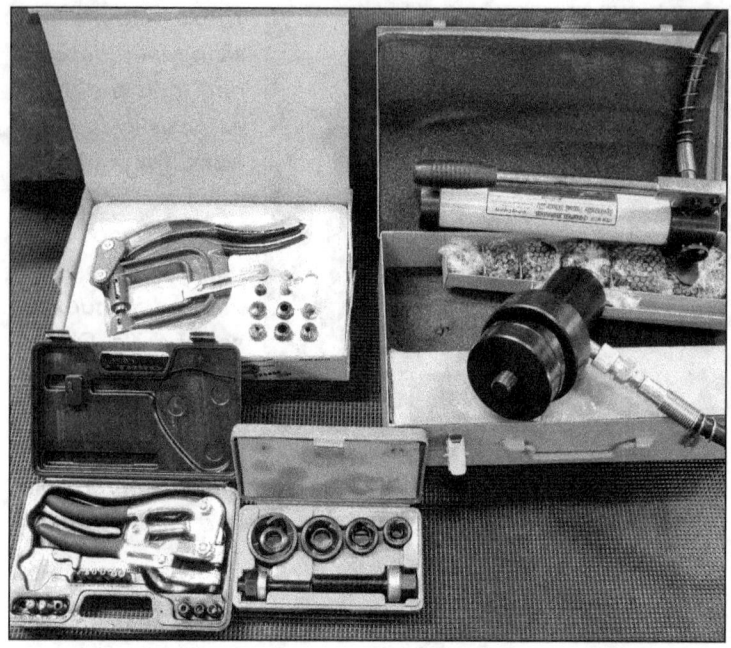

Punches come in many sizes and formats. On the top: a long-reach hand punch for making small holes (left) and a hydraulic punch for making holes of up to 3½ inches in diameter in light sheet metal (right). On the bottom: a short-reach hand punch (left) and a screw-type electrician's punch set (right).

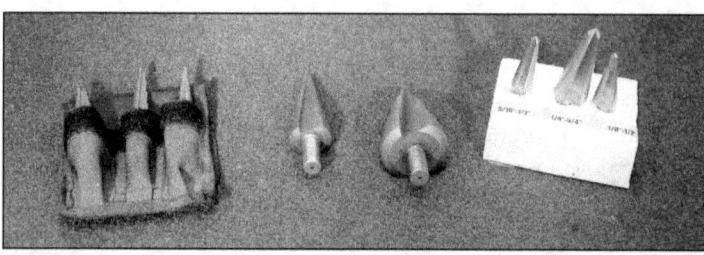

The five-step drills on the left carve out precisely sized relatively flat and burr free holes. They are best used for sizing, not opening holes. The three stepless drills on the right fine-tune hole sizes and remove burrs. Always use low drilling pressure with these devices.

The edges of this reproduction part will be visible in the new part. That is unfortunate, because it will be difficult to protect those edges from corrosion. Unfortunately, there is no choice because the original part had visible edges. Finishing these edges as smoothly as possible will help.

likely to see is raw metal edges. This is because they tend to be sharp enough to cut human flesh and because it is very difficult to apply and keep coatings on them that are thick and durable enough to protect them from rusting. Often, they are covered with trim, which hides these issues. No fabrication should leave visible or touchable raw metal edges. Aside from the hazard that they present, they look awful.

Hiding panel edges under trim is not always practical or useful. Neither is tucking them conveniently out of sight. One obvious way to deal with them is to fold them over on themselves with a small radius bend at the newly formed edges. That works in areas like the edges of hoods and fender wells, particularly if you make the folded edge disappear from view by placing it on the backside of the panel.

Factories used to deal with the metal edges that they couldn't completely hide by wrapping them around wire. Later, they developed production dies that could form edges into rolled round formats without a wire inserted in the fold. This was an improvement on wire edging, because it reduced the likelihood of rusting that the close tolerances of wire edges and inability to reliably coat them internally produces. Unfortunately, wire edges and rolled edges are quite difficult to achieve in custom metal work. However, both can be done with bead rolling as their basis.

Other solutions to the edge problem include sweating U-channel over them, and welding them out to rounded configurations. That last one requires considerable welding and finishing skills.

OTHER PROCESSES AND SKILLS

The "business end" of a Magee wire edger wraps sheet metal panel edges over and around a core wire in one motion. This process is no longer used in production. Today, in production, visible panel edges are usually bent into tight radii.

Finding or making custom louvering dies, like these, is one way to create louvers—the hard way. Obviously, changing louver length involves inserting or removing sections from this type of die.

Decorative rolled beads both strengthen and enhance the appearance of this reproduction panel. It is amazing how much strategically located rolled beads can do to stiffen panels and to add authority to their appearances.

Louvers and Exotic Trim Formations

In the quest for something different, practical, and stunning, fabricators have often created repetitive formats that are easy to describe and very difficult to actually create in metal. Functional louvers are a good example of this kind of custom metal adornment. Louvers can also serve a vital function of allowing cooling air to circulate behind a panel.

While it is possible, with great difficulty, to hand hammer louvers that look professional, it is much easier to do this with a louver press, or with a louvering attachment on a power forming machine, such as a Pullmax. Many exotic trim formats, like louvers, are best done with the specialty equipment that is intended to create them (more on louvers in Chapter 11).

Using Tension

This is an enormously useful technique for shaping, or reshaping, metal into consistent mild contours in two or three dimensions. Put the area that you want to reshape under overall pressure or

This louvering attachment for a Pullmax makes louvers in one format, and of any length, in a simple process. The die cuts and forms the metal in the louver, including its formed ends.

This dent-pulling system illustrates the tensioning concept on a small scale. The welded electrode is levered away from the dent, as its edges are tapped lightly to release it. This pulls out the dent, even with the impact applied in the wrong direction. Tensioning makes all the difference.

Bead rolling has many uses beyond making edges. A bead down a panel strengthens it by work hardening the metal in the bead. Often, this is used to strengthen panels, and to reduce or prevent vibration-induced flutter in them. Bead rolling can also be used to achieve artistic or decorative effect.

tension to force it into the direction(s) that you are seeking to shape it. Then, strike it locally toward the desired contours, or away from them if necessary for reasons of access. The combination of overall tension, or pressure, and local impact tends to work together to move the metal smoothly where you want it to go.

General tension can be applied with tension plates that are spot welded, MIG welded, brazed, or soldered to panel surfaces. After the tension plates are attached, they are pushed or pulled with levers or hydraulic rams and, while this is being done, local impact is applied to the metal where you want to move it. When the results are satisfactory, the tensioning or pulling attachment plates are removed and the surfaces are ground, filed, or sanded back to smoothness. Many other tensioning arrangements are possible and can even be worked into three dimensions with the right setups.

Wire Edging a Panel

One particularly interesting application of bead rolling is to use it as the basis for creating a wire-wrapped edge on a panel. In this sequence, a bead roller is used to create a pocket to contain a wire at the edge of a panel. The rolled bead is then closed partially in a brake and then closed completely around a wire with a hammer and flattening tool. This process can be used to make a straight or curved wire edge. Curved wire edges are more difficult to make than straight ones because reliefs must be cut into the rolled edge as it goes into and out of curves. These cuts must be welded shut and/or filled with body solder.

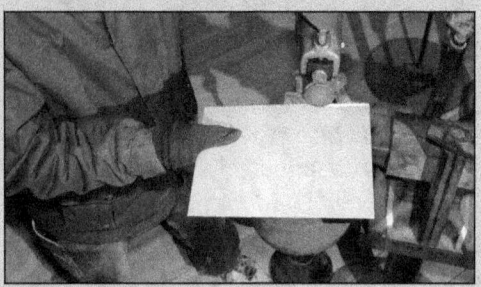

To replicate a wired edge, the first step is to bead roll a deep grove at the edge of your metal. Experiment with the proper depth and distance from the edge to use. These vary with metal thickness and wire size.

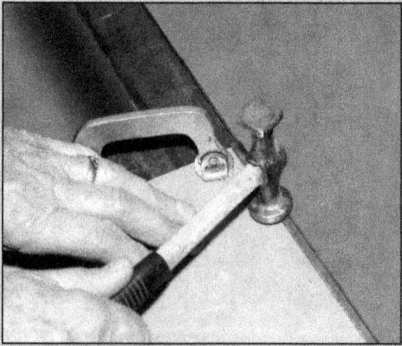

The third step in hand forming a wired edge is to hammer down the edge over the wire with a low-crown hammer. This must be done very carefully to maintain uniformity and to avoid scarring the metal.

The second step in manually forming a wired edge is to take the bead-rolled piece and brake its edge to a more acute angle than the bead roller left. An angle of no less than 90 degrees between the panel and the formed lip is desirable at this point.

The final step in manually making a wire edge is to tighten and slightly offset the hammered edge with a highly unsophisticated tamping tool, like this one. Manually making wire edged parts becomes much more difficult when curves and crowned surfaces are involved.

CHAPTER 7

FINISHING PROCESSES AND TOUCHES

At various stages in any metal fabrication project, as major processes have been applied to metal and completed, there are a few finishing processes and touches that should be performed before the metal is passed on to the next phase of the project.

Checking Final Dimensions, Contours and Attachments

While metal fabrications should always be checked against templates, forms, patterns, and the other standards that you created to guide your work as it progresses, there comes a "moment of truth," when forming operations are completed and final dimensional checks are made. This is usually before final surface finishing and metal treatment operations are undertaken, because it involves basic testing for correct contour, shape, and dimensions. If any attachment holes, slots, ledges, or other mating or docking features exist, they must be checked for proper fit and alignment to their surroundings.

While small surface changes may occur later, when minor amounts of body filler, sprayable filler, primer,

This diagonal-shape checking template for this fabrication confirms a lot of important dimensions and symmetries in one overlay application. It was used to guide the fabrication of the top of this piece, as well as to make final shape and dimension checks.

No jig or common measuring instrument or device could provide the instant indication of crown accuracy that the reflections from the overhead lights do for these fenders. It would take sophisticated laser scanning equipment to validate the fabricated fender (right) as authoritatively as do the reflections off those lights.

AUTOMOTIVE SHEET METAL FORMING & FABRICATION

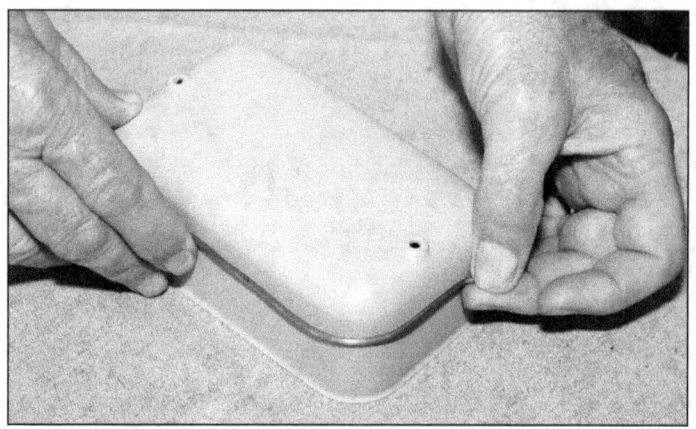

The copper wire used to confirm this fabrication's corner format was bent over the original part of which this is a copy. This is about as simple and useful as templating gets.

and spot putty may be applied, these will not change basic shapes or dimensions. Final shape and dimension checks should be made before, or just after, these finishing steps are completed. The advantage of making them before finishing operations begin is that you avoid the chance of damaging delicate, finished surfaces, particularly if corrections have to be made.

While the original patterning devices that you created for your job are great guides for informing you as to how accurately you have finished it, they are not always the last word. For example, where your fabrication has elements of dimensional consistency or symmetry, these should be checked for conformity with approaches such as making the same measurements at different points to prove consistency. You should also use procedures like diagonal measurements to verify symmetry.

Beyond that, there are aspects of surfaces that may be too subtle for your jigs, patterns, and measuring instruments to pick up. These can range from very mild crown to slight slope, relative to other parts of a fabrication, sometimes measured in only thousandths of an inch, but highly visible, nonetheless. How light hits and reflects off a surface, for example, is usually critical, but may be too fine to measure with patterns, templates, or measuring instruments. Sometimes, spraying primer at a part and looking at it in different lighting conditions and from different angles can reveal these kinds of subtleties.

Templates are often more helpful for comparing old and newly fabricated parts than the old parts are. However, in this case, the original part was more useful for checking the hold-down hole locations than was the elaborate template that we created for this purpose.

Weld Finishing

Weld finishing deserves special mention in completion operations, because so many metal workers fail to do it well enough to completely hide weld dimples and seams. This is not a "close" or "almost" proposition. If you leave spot-weld tags, sinks, or dimples, or MIG or TIG weld lines visible in your metal work, people *will* notice them. That is because they tend to occur in fairly predictable places, and are obvious for what they are if they rise above or fall below the surrounding panel, even under paint.

Spot welds must be finished completely level to, or slightly below, panel surfaces and then raised with filler to panel level in their low areas. How many times have you seen part of a spot weld above a panel and part of it below the panel? It is easy to avoid, and should not be tolerated.

Spot welds are nasty things if they are visible through the paint that covers your sheet metal fabrication. The trick is to finish spot welds to, or below, panel surfaces and then fill and level any pits that they leave.

TIG welds tend to be inherently close to level when they are done correctly, but still need to be ground flat to work, and then filled to raise any low areas to level. After they have been ground flat to panels, MIG welds almost always need filling to level alongside their beads. In both cases, this is part of metal finishing.

Metal Finishing

The term, "metal finishing," covers several different processes that have the common goal of moving metal in small areas by very small increments to, or very near, perfection. This is done only after you have achieved the final, basic shape of your fabrication. It is not an efficient way to move a wide area of metal or to move any amount of metal very far. Those shaping operations should always come before the precise techniques of metal finishing are applied. In the main, metal finishing is a way to locate and to correct minor high and low spots in contours that are basically already final. Think of this group of operations as minor adjustment or fine tuning.

The first step in metal finishing is to identify high and low spots and analyze the reason(s) that they exist. If the areas to be adjusted are larger than a business card, they may still be susceptible to metal finishing techniques, but in these cases it becomes imperative to determine why they are where they are. The answer to that query usually has to do with something holding the metal out-of-place, like a stretched or shrunken area(s). These areas that can cause problems can be in the visibly out-of-position metal, or they can lurk in adjacent metal and generate distortion elsewhere. Keep this in mind as you search your fabrication project for high and low spots, because you will have to deal with these problems if they exist. You cannot work around them.

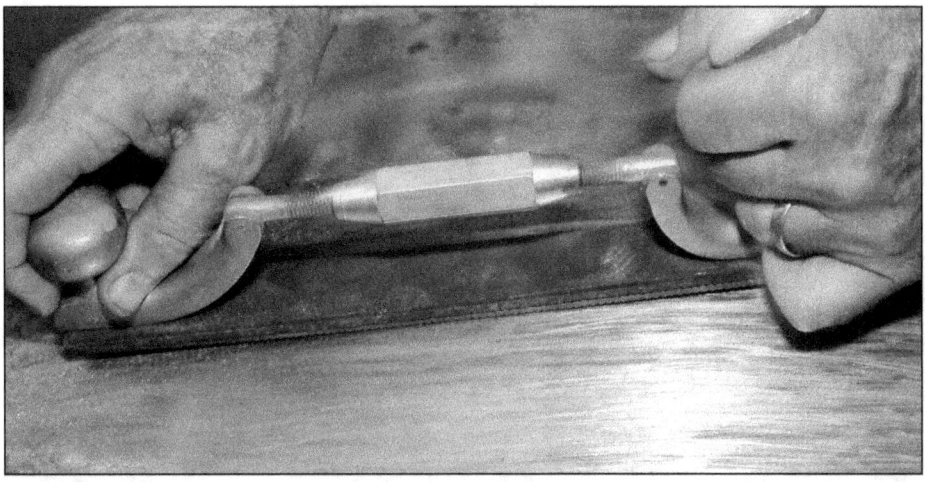

Body filing a surface for indications of high and low spots is one of the best ways to make this critical check. The file can reveal deviations of as little as .002 inch in 25 square inches. That's safely below what the unaided human eye is likely to see.

That search is accomplished with body files, hard-backed sanding pads, disc sanders, and visual inspections. Sometimes, particularly when you are new to this work, dabs of layout dye or Prussian blue (a paste colorant) can aid your search.

Filing to locate panel areas that need to be raised or lowered is the old-time method of finding them. It is precise and very effective. Using a body file correctly (as described in Chapter 6) levels high spots, and reveals low spots. In most cases, if your fabrication was ready for metal finishing, filing completes the removal of high spots. The exception occurs when they are so high that they cannot be filed without going through the metal, or rendering it dangerously thin. In those cases, you need to go back to basic shaping operations, like hammering, off-dolly (See Chapter 5), to lower the specific areas that are too high to file level. When to make that call takes experience. You need to sense when you are filing too far for safety, quit filing, and go back to shaping the metal. In this matter, always err on the side of caution.

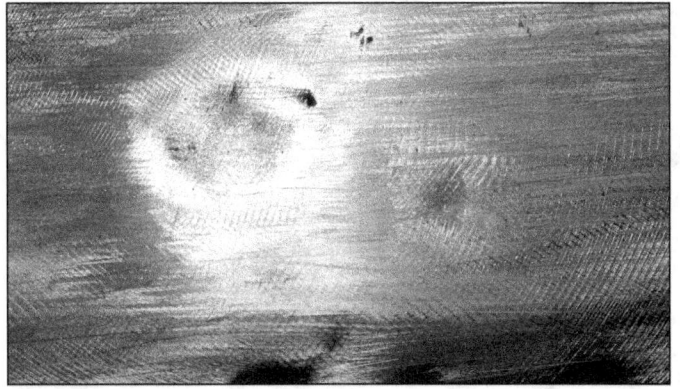

The dark spot in this filed area represents a low region, while the shiny area indicates a high spot that the file has somewhat decapitated. Learning to read filed metal for level is a useful talent.

Moving a disc sander across a panel with the correct motion and row spacing reveals low spots very quickly. Be careful to keep your disc moving across the panel, while maintaining steady, but not excessive, pressure against the metal.

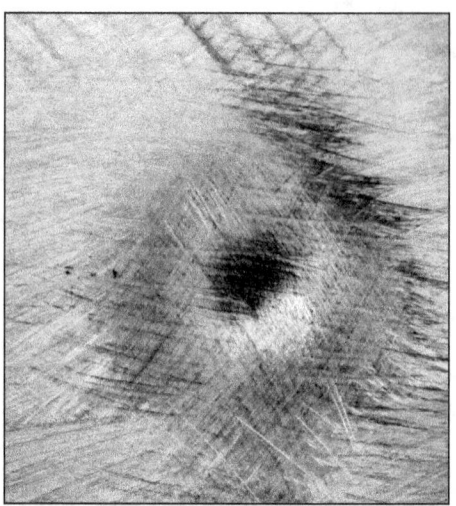

Disc-sanded low spots look like this, except they usually don't have scratches in them. Many of the scratches in this one came from a soft abrasive disc that was used to clean the metal before it was disc sanded.

Used properly, a body file shows high spots as shiny metal and low spots as dull metal. Beyond that, the characteristic score marks of filing are not visible in low areas. Some practice with scrap metal quickly shows what this distinction looks like.

The other major approach to indicating high and low spots for metal finishing is with a 7- or 9-inch disc sander. In most cases, a fine sanding disc, about 50-grit, is best for this job. This can be applied to any panel configuration but is uniquely useful in simple concave areas, where flat body files cannot reach, and in reverse crown areas, where even hard-to-find convex body files cannot reach. Wheels much coarser than 50-grit should not be used for metal finishing, because they tend to remove too much metal, and to score surfaces too deeply for this stage of metal finishing.

The correct tool motion for this operation is to move the disc sander along in the direction that offers the longest access to a flat surface. The disc sanding pad should be held at about 15 degrees to the panel surface, and flexed enough for the outer 1½ to 2 inches of the disc to contact the panel surface. As the disc sander is moved back and forth across an area, its spindle should be tilted alternately in the direction of travel. Thus, the disc should be tilted slightly in the opposite direction at the end of each stroke, when your motion is reversed. This keeps its cutting edge in the direction of the disc's travel. The disc should be moved with enough speed, and mild enough pressure, to remove metal, but also to avoid burning or gauging metal.

At the completion of each stroke, the disc is moved 1 to 1½ inches down the panel for the next sideways stroke, allowing a little overlap on the previous stroke. The result of these motions is a sort of herringbone pattern of sanding swirls in the metal. There are two very useful results from attaining that pattern. The first is that small, local high spots are cut level to the metal by the action of the disc sander. The second is that low spots are indicated as dark areas that usually do not have the disc's characteristic swirl marks across them. This is because the abrasive disc does not reach into areas very far below the panel's surface level. If, as you disc sand, you begin to see areas of blue (burned) metal, you are moving the disc too slowly, pressing it down too hard, or sanding high spots that are too high to be dealt with this way.

Filing and disc sanding are the mainstays of eliminating small high spots and locating low spots in metal. These operations can be performed on a finer level with hand sanding techniques, and even by applying layout dye or Prussian blue to areas that are suspected of being

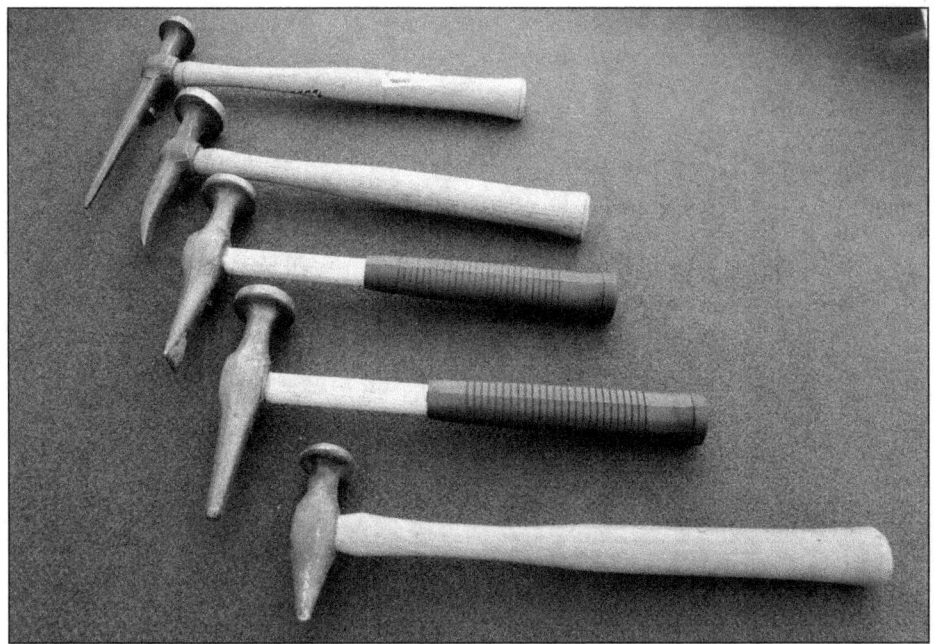

Pick hammers come in many shapes and sizes. Learning to use a pick hammer properly takes a lot of practice. The bottom two hammers are the most useful in this group for general work.

The dry magnetic particle inspection method shown here uses a black light and fluorescing powder to locate cracks. A strong magnetic field is applied to areas where cracks are suspected. This causes the magnetic powder particles to line up, north to south, along the edges of any crack. The black light causes the powder to fluoresce, making the crack lines easy to see. This kind of inspection is worth the effort if you suspect the existence of a crack, but cannot see one with simple magnification. The arrow points to the edge crack in this photo.

high or low. In this approach, you file or sand with abrasive paper wrapped tightly around a file or paint stick, and note where the die or Prussian blue is removed (high spots) and where it is left in place (low areas).

There are few tools in the metal worker's arsenal as inexpensive and effective as the pick hammer. Used with reasonable skill, it is capable of moving small amounts of metal in tiny increments. This can mean taking a visibly lumpy or mottled surface and turning it into one that is perfectly formed for its surroundings. Unfortunately, without the skill that comes from practice, a pick hammer can become a weapon of sheet metal mass destruction.

There are only two major issues that you have to get absolutely right to use a pick hammer effectively. You have to hit the right spot, not someplace near it, and you have to hit it with exactly the right impact. Both potential problems are made worse by the fact that you often do not have very good visual or physical access to the area that you are trying to "pick" or "pick up." That is because you often are forced by the arrangement of things to make blind swings toward yourself from the back of a panel, or work in inconveniently tight quarters, or both.

As you begin this work, you can take very small, non-deforming swings with the pick hammer and see where the blows are landing; in particular, whether they are landing on the metal that you are trying to raise. You eventually develop a sense of where the hammer will hit. Even then, cramped quarters in which to swing your pick hammer can make this difficult.

The problem of hitting with the right intensity to raise the metal, but not to raise it above the surrounding metal, is easier to solve. The solution is called *restraint*. Hit the metal incre-

mentally. Who cares if it takes five incremental swings to do what possibly could have been accomplished with one perfectly calibrated harder swing? The risk of over-lifting the metal is reduced by taking restrained strokes. And if one of your five strokes raises the metal a just a little too high, you can disc sand it back to level without unduly thinning it. This is not a proposition where you have to get it right the first time, but

CHAPTER 7

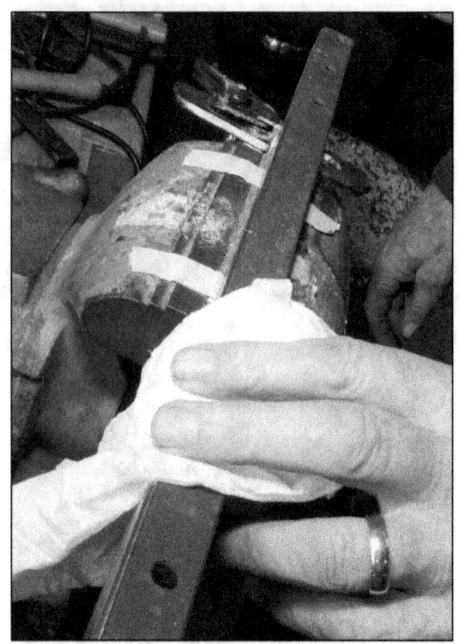

Your fingertips can reveal irregularities in metal as small as .002 to .003 inch. If you place a tissue or rag under your moving fingertips, it reduces the frictional drag caused by the oil and moisture on your skin. That greatly enhances your ability to feel surface variations.

it is one where you quickly regret raising metal above where you want it to end up: level. If you pick hammer metal too high, you can hammer, file, or sand it back, but the less you overdo pick hammering, the better your results will be.

Checking Metal Integrity

While shape, contour, and format can be checked visually and by feel, structural defects that may lurk in formed metal are often more difficult to find. Finishes can hide many surface defects, but have absolutely no capability to strengthen metal, or to make it durable. After work is put into service, the assaults of vibration and flexing can wreck havoc on the most subtle and beautiful fabrications.

The first line of defense is to know where trouble is likely to occur. Areas that have been worked extensively with forming tools and equipment are always vulnerable to fatigue and subsequent failure. Pounding metal thin or pulling it apart in some stretching devices is very likely to make it hard, brittle, and prone to cracking. In fact, in some cases, these processes may initiate small cracks that can grow into bigger ones. After all, in the entire history of metal, no crack ever spontaneously healed or got smaller.

None of this suggests that you should not apply these processes, but it does make it very desirable to keep an eye on their results to look for unintended outcomes.

Cracks are also more likely to occur at the edges of areas where extreme heat (welding) has been applied to metal. The so-called "heat affected zone" next to weld is particularly vulnerable. Again, the first countermeasure is to inspect these areas minutely for evidence of the beginnings of cracks. Using a magnifying glass is a good start. If you see an area that might be starting to crack, using an inexpensive, self-lighted microscope to examine it is well worth the effort. Note that cracking is more likely to occur in areas such as edges and corners, where vibration tends to be focused. Rough cut lines also provide perfect places for cracks to start and to propagate. If such areas also contain heat-affected zones, strongly worked areas of metal, or other red flag factors for cracking, the odds for cracking increase.

If visual inspection does not confirm the existence of a crack and you still suspect that there might be one, magnetic particle inspection is an excellent way to resolve the situation. In the case of non-ferrous metals, such as aluminum alloys, a dye-penetrant approach accomplishes the same purpose. Another approach is sonic testing. No, not the high-tech versions of ultrasound. I'm talking about plinking the metal with your middle finger in suspect areas. The sound that you generate can tell you a lot about the metal's condition, if you know what to listen for. This approach takes practice.

If you find a crack in sheet metal, the best way to deal with it is to determine its exact extent, and then to drill or punch a small hole slightly beyond its end. Then cut the metal away along the crack line for proper welding fit-up and weld it shut—right into the hole that you punched or drilled. The hole acts as a final measure to deflect the crack's forces around a radius, and stop its further progress.

This inexpensive illuminated magnifying device (30X magnification) can often locate cracks and other problems that cannot be seen with the naked eye. This is an easy way to spot and/or confirm problems in metal surfaces.

CHAPTER 8

FILLING WITH LEAD AND PLASTIC

After the metal finishing phase of sheet metal fabrication work has been completed, the work passes on to the next stages of completion—metal preparation, filling, and surface preparation for priming and finishing. This may involve specialists who work exclusively in these areas, or it may involve the same people who did the metal forming and/or metal finishing. In either case, it is important to understand what is involved in the metal preparation, filling, and surface preparation processes, because their success depends largely on what went before them.

What follows is not an extensive discussion of metal filling and preparation for finishing, but rather an overview of these processes as they relate to custom fabricated metal items.

Four Types of Filler

There are four basic types of filler in use today: lead, polyester, sprayable polyester, and spot putty. Each has advantages and drawbacks, and each may excel in some situations and fail in others. In my experience, none of them have magical properties, and none of them should ever be employed to cover up inaccurate or rough metal work. Used within proper limits, they are assets to good metal work and refinishing.

Lead, actually tin/lead alloys with the preferred proportions of those two metals being 30/70 and 20/80, was the original automotive body-filler material. Lead is still used in some shops today, but its use has declined severely over the past 50 years. The advantage of using lead filler is that it is a metal, and more similar to the sheet metal that it fills than any other filler material. It tends to file better than plastic fillers and is more durable. On the downside, lead

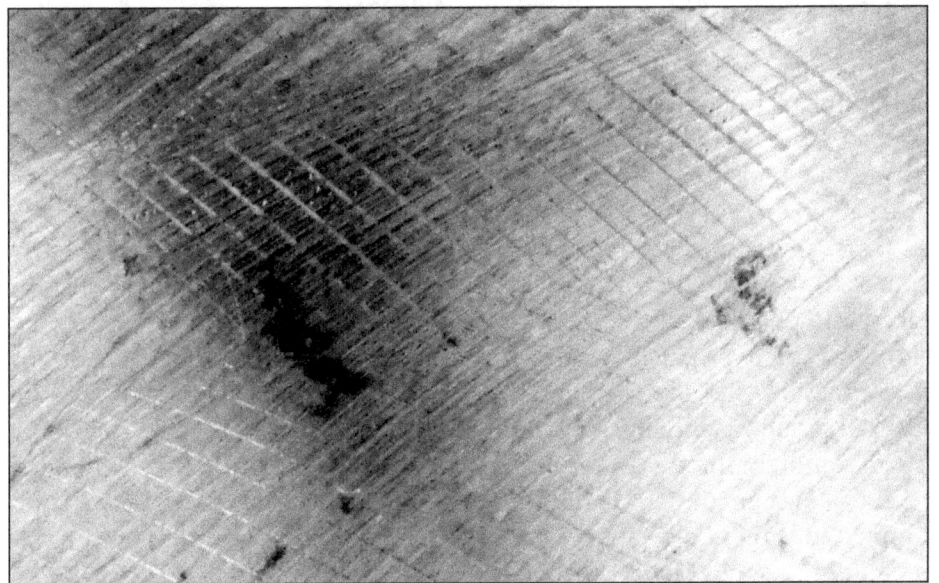

The corrosion residues visible on this metal may not look dangerous, but they are the seeds of corrosion. If you apply a finish over them they fester and expand under it as rusting continues. Eventually, they crack the finish, allowing moisture to attack the metal directly, destroying the finish.

AUTOMOTIVE SHEET METAL FORMING & FABRICATION

CHAPTER 8

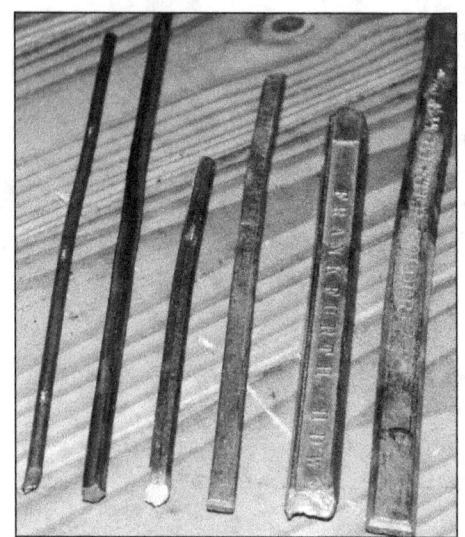
Lead filler starts in the form of lead bars. It is spread over tinned metal to fill and even surfaces. Then, it is shaped to form smooth, even panel contours. Lead is the most permanent filler that there is.

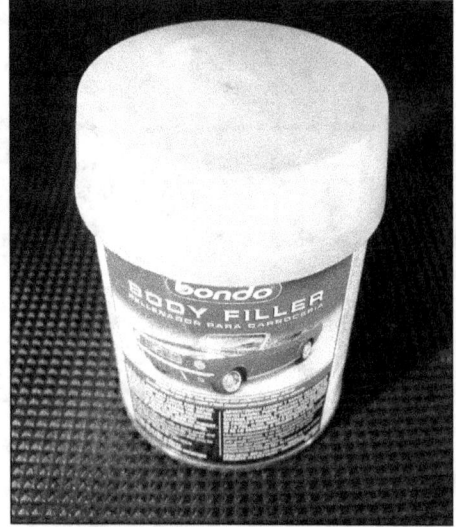
While they lack lead's durability, plastic fillers (like the ever-popular Bondo product) are easier and faster to apply than lead fillers. They are far and away the most popular fillers in use today.

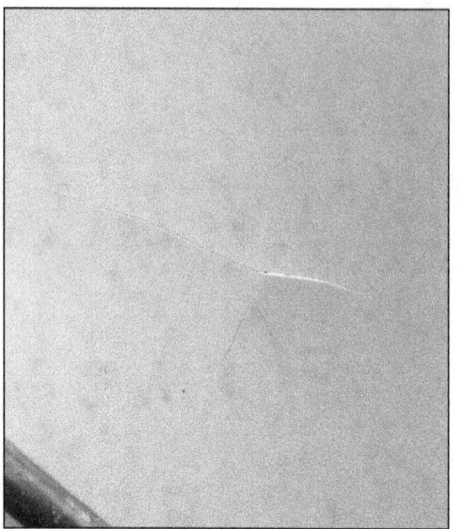
No matter what type of filler you work with, it should be applied in small amounts. This paint failure was probably initiated, in large part, by plastic filler that was applied too thickly. Note that the thickness of paint at the visible fracture indicates that overly thick filler has lifted.

is expensive, relatively difficult to apply, and fraught with environmental hazards. Still, if lead is worked expertly and safely, it is the choice of many custom fabricators and of a few repair specialists.

Polyester fillers burst on the automotive scene in the early 1950s and have grown in popularity ever since. These are two-part paste-type fillers that are mixed prior to application, and then applied with a plastic squeegee, or other suitable tool. They cure quickly, and can be easily and quickly shaped into rough format with a "cheese grater" file before they fully harden. After hardening for 20 to 40 minutes—depending on product, temperature, and mixing proportions—they can be formed with conventional body files and sanding techniques. Polyester fillers are inexpensive, relatively easy to work, and reasonably durable. They are applied to raw metal surfaces, or over adhesion coatings, such as self-etching primers, and adhere mechanically to them.

Early polyester fillers lacked durability because the solids used in them, often talc, tended to absorb and transport moisture. This resulted in rusting under these fillers that caused them to lose adhesion and fall off the panels to which they were applied. The use of better, less water permeable solids solved this problem years ago.

Sprayable polyester fillers have come a long way in the past 30 years. Like paste polyester fillers, early versions of these products tended to lack adhesion, stability, and durability. These are essentially very high build sanding primers that can be used to cover small defects or, inappropriately, to hide relatively large ones. While some people use them for the latter purpose, they tend to leave telltale signs when used that way, like thickened panel edges that look awful and that lack durability. Used in moderation, they preserve most panel detail, and are an acceptable way to achieve final surfaces for painting.

Spot putties are high solids fillers of various compositions that can be used on top of primer coats to fill small surface defects, like scratches and pin holes. They should never be used to create contours, or to adjust shapes, because they are inherently fragile and unstable when applied in any appreciable thickness. Used properly, which is very sparingly, they are a worthwhile tool in the refinisher's tool box. Using them to correct problems in finished metal work is a misguided endeavor that can only end in great difficulty.

Proper Filler Application

In a word, the best application for any type of filler is "thinly."

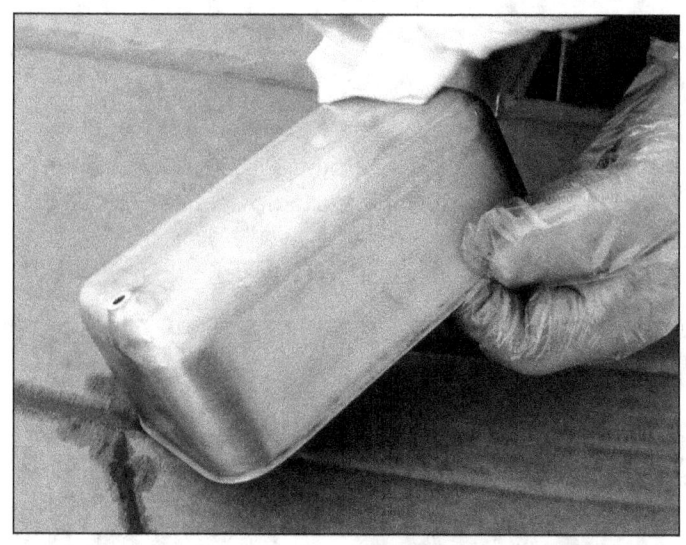

The lead filler applied to this part is visible as areas of lighter gray than the base metal. After the part was filed and sanded, the lead was very thin in these areas. This part has just been treated with metal conditioner.

About 1/8 inch is the *maximum* thickness for lead, polyester, and sprayed polyester fillers, and thinner is always better. Spot putties are usable to less than a quarter of that thickness, and only over primers. All fillers have different coefficients of expansion than the base metals, steel or aluminum, to which they are applied, and offer less resistance to flexing. The result is that they tend to lose adhesion and lift off over time. Add to that the possibility of rust forming and advancing under them, where it exerts enormous pressure to lift them off, and you can understand the problem with overly thick applications of these materials. The thicker a filler's application, the more likely it is to crack, admit moisture that causes corrosion, and lift off.

Beyond *thin*, fillers should be applied only where they are needed, and to very clean metal. Sometimes you apply filler to a broad area of a surface to file or sand it to perfect contours, but in these cases when your shaping and smoothing are completed, very little filler thickness in any place should remain on the surface, and it should be pretty thin where it does remain. At other times, fillers are applied to deal with small, local depressions or spots, which is really their best use.

Aside from avoiding excessive thickness in filler application, there are a few other cautions that apply to all filler types. Fillers should never be used structurally. They lack the strength and stability for that purpose. Their only function is cosmetic. They can only be applied over absolutely clean metal. Yielding to the temptation to use them to bridge over specs of corrosion, or other contamination, always ends in failure, because those defects harbor the seeds of corrosion that eventually release filler piled over them.

Lead fillers must be applied to perfectly tinned metal. This is metal with a thin, continuous, and uniform adhesion coating of 50/50 solder on it. The tinning layer is what bonds the lead filler to the steel panel. Tinning aluminum panels requires the use of special aluminum solders. Any breach in the tinning on base metal leads to poor lead adhesion and filler failure. Unfortunately, it is all too easy to accidentally wipe the tinning layer off of metal when you smooth it with a rag after its application. This tendency must be avoided.

Unlike lead and polyester fillers, spot putty is applied over primer to correct minor breaches in primed surfaces. It is then allowed to dry completely and sanded level to the surrounding primer. If it is used properly to fill very small defects, like scratches, and allowed to cure completely before coats are piled on top of it, it is an effective way to deal with minor surface problems in primer. However, if it is applied much thicker than a few thousandths of an inch, or not allowed to dry properly before recoating, it tends to sink, or absorb top coats, or release paint.

Polyester paste and sprayed fillers have better adhesion if the metal to which they are applied has some "tooth," or roughness. It is important not to polish substrates on which these fillers will be sprayed. Sanding with 150- to 180-grit abrasive paper leaves the right surface for good adhesion.

Proper Shaping and Smoothing Techniques

Any filler, lead, paste-applied polyester, or sprayed polyester is designed for application to surfaces that meet a few basic specifications. They have to be free of all contaminants. In the case of polyester fillers, they have to be allowed to completely cure before they are top coated. Fillers must have and hold the right contours, and blend into surrounding metal. Finally, they must have surfaces with enough tooth for good adhesion of the primer and paint that will be applied over them, but not be so rough as to show deep, visible

Applying Lead Filler

Applying lead filler is neither as difficult nor as arcane as some people think. You start by applying a good flux or tinning butter to the area to be leaded. Of course, the base metal has to be scrupulously clean before you do this. The tinning flux or butter is then heated with an air-acetylene torch until it starts to sizzle and brown. You can apply these fluxes with a scrap of rag or an acid brush.

The first step in applying lead filler is to heat the metal and apply tinning flux to the part. The flux should sizzle on the hot metal and turn slightly brown. Flux serves to clean metal and to prepare it for the next step in leading, which is tinning.

After the area(s) where lead will be applied have been fluxed, 50/50 tin/lead solder is spread on them by heating the metal until the solder melts on it. The solder acts as a bonding coat for the lead that will be applied over it.

Now the surface can be tinned. Using the same torch, 50/50 solder from a coil is melted onto the fluxed area in sufficient quantity to spread it evenly over it with a rag. This coating does not need to be uniform at this point.

Next, the solder is wiped to a uniform coating on the base metal. This is done by heating the solder to a liquid state, and smoothing it over the metal with a rag.

The solder is wiped with a rag over the area that you are tinning. Apply some heat to keep it liquid enough to spread. The first few times that you try this, you are likely to singe your wiping rag, but later you will get the hang of keeping the solder hot, while not immolating your rag.

Still using an air-acetylene torch, take a bar of lead, 30/70 is my favorite composition, and stub it onto the tinned area. This means heating the bar about 3/4 to 1 inch above where it is held against the surface, while occasionally playing your flame over the tinned area around the lead bar to keep it hot. When the end of the lead bar reaches its paste state, it appears to frost slightly on its surface. It can then be twisted off onto the tinned surface.

After you have deposited enough stubs for the shaping and filling that you plan to do, use a mutton-tallow-lubricated maple paddle to direct the lead to where it is needed on the tinned surface. The 30/70 lead has a plastic range of about 130 degrees F (360 to 490 degrees F) in which it is pasty, and can easily be formed.

FILLING WITH LEAD AND PLASTIC

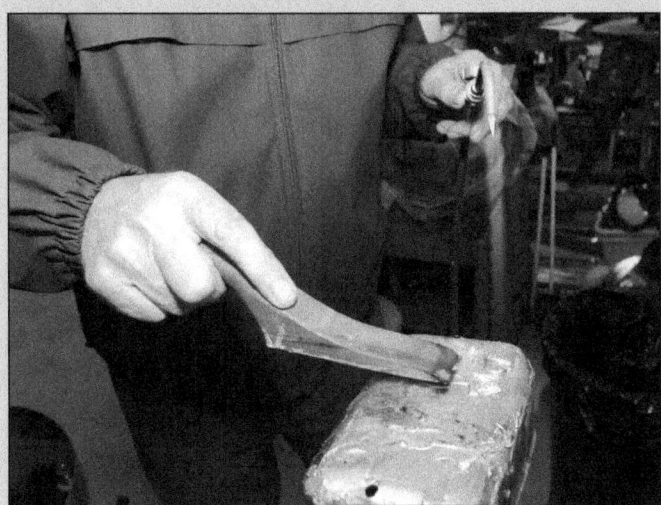

After lead stubs have been deposited on the tinned metal, they are spread uniformly over it with a tallow-lubricated maple paddle. Heat is used to keep the led in a pasty state. The filler must not be overheated, or it will separate into its base metals and become unworkable.

The deposited lead can now be shaped and smoothed with a body file. Smooth, light strokes allow you to have your way with the soft lead, and to file it into desired shapes and contours. At this point, be careful not to gauge it, or to file it too low. Following filing, the lead can be sanded to final format and surface with sandpaper on sticks, pads, or boards, but never with power tools, due to the health hazards of airborne particulate lead.

It is important to "kill" any flux and paddle lubricant residues that may have worked their way up through the lead to the filed surface. This should be done before you file and sand lead, and after your filing and sanding are finished. Scrubbing your leaded surface with a good metal prep solution, vinegar, or ammonia will kill these residues. I prefer to use a metal prep solution for this purpose. (The one shown on page 80 is solvent based and works well for this purpose.)

Using a good metal conditioner to "kill" lead filler is essential, both before and after it is filed and sanded. Killing removes flux and tallow residues that might otherwise interfere with paint adhesion. It also acts to bond paint. Never use an etching primer where you have applied metal conditioner.

Leading takes practice, but it is a skill that is worth learning, because it is useful in performing top-quality sheet metal fabrication in some situations.

Lead filler files like plastic filler, only more easily and smoothly, giving it a definite advantage. If applied properly, lead filler is more durable than plastic filler. A downside of using lead filler is that its filings and dust can become dangerously toxic, if you fail to take reasonable precautions. Therefore you should wear a long-sleeved shirt, trousers, or similar garments as well as a dust mask or a respirator. After working with lead, take a cold rather than a hot shower to remove the metal from your skin. Most overlooked is washing your clothes before wearing them again.

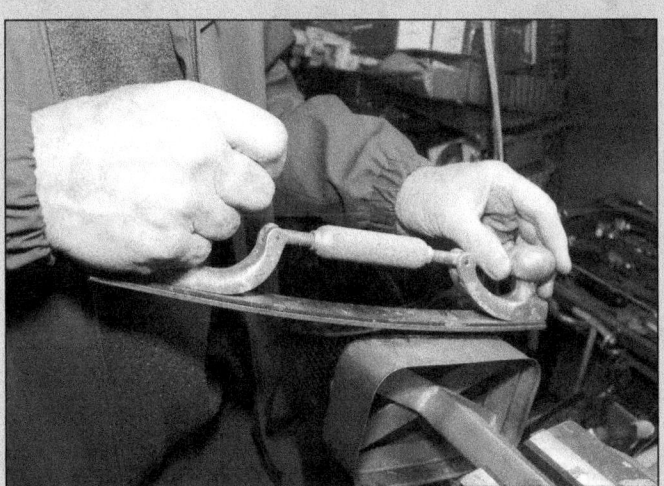

CHAPTER 8

Applying Polyester Filler

Paste-type plastic fillers are far and away the most popular fillers in use today. Most of them are based on polyester resins with added solids. They have the advantage of being inexpensive, easy to work, and durable.

Catalyzed plastic filler is applied to work metal with a plastic squeegee, or similar tool, in thin coats. All fillers are meant to fill depressions. They are not intended to be sculpture mediums. Maximum filler thickness should be held to 1/8 inch.

After you have mixed plastic filler in its can to correct separation of its resins and solids, you combine it with its manufacturer-supplied catalyst. The catalyst must be added in the amount specified by the filler's manufacturer. Filler and catalyst should be mixed thoroughly on a clean, non-absorbent surface.

A few minutes after it is mixed, plastic filler sets up enough for rough shaping. This is done with a cheese grater type of file. You have just a few minutes to do this shaping, because the plastic filler continues to harden very quickly. Be conservative in how much filler you remove with a grater.

The first step in using plastic fillers is to mix the basic filler in its can until it is consistently pasty, combining any liquid resins with the filler's solids. Then mix the filler with its hardener (catalyst) in the proportions recommended by the manufacturer. It is important to mix the filler components completely, and on a clean, neutral surface. For example, cardboard is a terrible surface for mixing filler and hardener, because if it is waxy you can end up with wax contaminating your filler, and if it is not waxy, it can absorb some of the filler's chemical components, unbalancing the filler. Thorough mixing is essential to success.

Plastic filler is applied with a squeegee or plastic spatula in thin, even coats. Keep these coats at minimal thickness. It is better to make subsequent applications than to gob plastic fillers on your work.

After about 20 minutes, depending on product and temperature, plastic fillers can be roughly grated into the shapes that you want. Grating removes material quickly but be careful not to remove too much filler at this point.

primers are epoxy based and most, or all, of them are waterproof.

Chemical adhesion holds two benefits for the metal fabricator. The first is that when these washes or primers are applied properly, they greatly reduce the chance of the metal surface rusting before it is painted. This is because it is difficult for rust to displace or disrupt their chemical bonds to the base metal, and because in the case of the etching primers a level of waterproofing is added.

Unlike top coats, standard sanding primers are *not* waterproof and do not protect raw metal from the attack of moisture. In fact, the aggressive, bi-polar water molecule buzzes through most of them as if they do not exist. Using either a metal prep wash or self-etching primer helps to protect metal for the period between finishing fabrication work on it and priming it. These treatments continue to protect metal with bonds that are difficult for rust to penetrate or break, even if moisture does succeed in getting through primers and top coats after a finish is applied.

The basic rules for using metal preps and self-etching primers are pretty straightforward. In both cases, it is critical that the base metal be completely clean and free of corrosion, oil, and grease. Metal preps should be wiped off after application, as directed, and/or allowed to air dry before priming. They should never be applied more than once, even if they have a somewhat irregularly transparent appearance after they dry. Always be sure to use a metal prep specified for the metal that you are protecting, steel or aluminum.

Self-etching primers should never be used over metal preps. They are inherently incompatible. Use one or the other, never both. Using both types of product leaves all sorts of unreacted chemicals under your finish system. Only trouble can follow in that witch's brew. Older reactive primers, such as zinc chromate, have largely been replaced by easier-to-apply formulations, such as zinc phosphate for many applications. Zinc chromate remains a primer of choice for aluminum alloy materials. Both of these primers should be applied in single thin coats, although zinc phosphate is a bit less fussy than zinc chromate on this issue.

Self-etching primers are not designed for sanding. These primers should be coated with a sanding primer of a different color to avoid sanding into the self-etching primer. In fact, I always coat self-etching primers with a different color of sanding primer, and then build that up with yet another color. That way, if I see the color of the first sanding primer as I sand, I stop before I sand into the self-etching primer under it. If you do sand through self-etching primer, and into its adhesion layer—its reacted underlayer that is in contact with the base metal—you create big corrosion problems at that interface.

I am not recommending aerosol primers. These products illustrate available types of anti-corrosion primers. Zinc chromate and zinc phosphate work well on aluminum. Primers sold as etching primers are excellent for steel surfaces. Never use an etching primer over metal that has been treated previously with metal conditioner.

The reason I go into this detail on metal coating and priming in a book about sheet metal fabrication is that it is all too common to blame the sheet metal worker when things go wrong with the coatings applied over his or her work. Protecting your work with properly applied reactive chemical coatings is good practice. The combination of mechanical and chemical adhesion that results from properly applied metal prep or self-etching primer is always an asset to your fabrication work. It protects it while it awaits finishing and long after that. Both of these approaches also neutralize traces of chemical residues and contamination that may have escaped your cleaning processes.

In the end, a properly prepared metal surface should look smooth and uniform. It should never be shiny and should not have been sanded any finer than with 220 grit. It should be coated with a metal prep wash or a self-etching primer to prevent rusting, and to promote primer adhesion. That is what fabricated metal surfaces should look like when they are sent on to painters to work their own particular brand of magic on them.

TOOLS AND EQUIPMENT

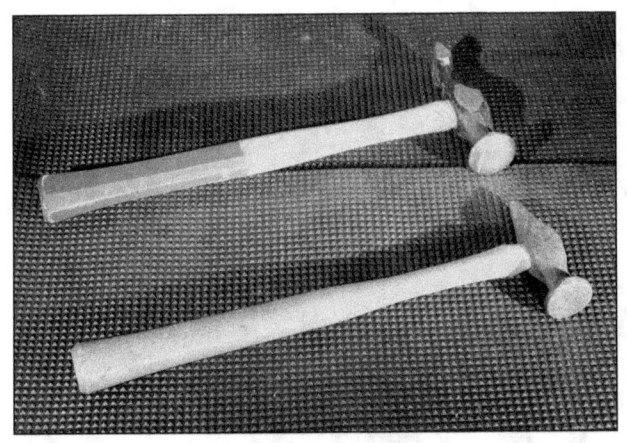

Although I own dozens of sheet metal hammers, these two wonderfully shaped and balanced strikers seem to end up naturally in my right hand most often. The legendary Proto 1427 (top) lives up to its reputation; the New Britain (bottom) is a great but unheralded hammer.

Items covered in other chapters in this book in specific contexts, are mostly omitted from this chapter, or covered in only minor detail.

I realize that my tool selection routine is not very scientific, but I think that my choices suggest to you some very useful tool and equipment categories needed to do this work. I hope that you find it useful.

Hand and Vise Tools

Hammers are the most basic tools in all of metal work. The variety of hammers and mallets is extraordinary. Aside from size, shape, balance, and head and face configuration, hammers can be made from or faced with anything from common iron to varieties of steel, plastic, leather, brass, copper, wood, and numerous other substances. Oddly enough, while I have literally dozens of hammers, there are about half a dozen that I use for 90 percent of my sheet metal work, and just two that I use for close to half of it. They have become like good friends over the years.

Dollies are backups for hammering or are sometimes used as hammers. They can be used for basic bumping operations that move a lot of metal, or to aid metal finishing work in very fine detail. There is a dizzying variety of dollies, from small hand-held tools with numerous surfaces to back up a wide variety of hitting operations, and on to huge dollies that can be the basis for forming large areas of metal over them.

Special-purpose small dollies often support the creation of details in metal forming work. They do this by providing useful backup shapes and surfaces for particular jobs.

Squarely in the "don't stay home without it" category of hand tools are sheet metal flanging pliers. They are endlessly helpful for making those "unofficial" little bends and tweaks, where nothing else quite does the job.

Magnetic vise finger brakes are small, inexpensive, very accurate, and easy to use for making small bends—up to 6 inches in length—in light steel and aluminum sheet, as thick as 18- or 16-gauge (steel). When you are making things like small brackets, vise brakes allow you to work faster and more precisely

This big teardrop dolly offers so many useful shapes and surfaces for sheet metal fabrication that it is hard to imagine a tight radius that cannot be found on it. However, it is plenty hard to find. Very high end fabricator catalogs, auctions, and private sellers may offer one.

A plethora of dollies! On the far left is a long-reach dolly; teardrop and oval dollies are pictured to the right. To the right of those are several general-purpose dollies. The two dollies on the bottom are a shrinking dolly (left) and a plastic-clad dolly (right).

AUTOMOTIVE SHEET METAL FORMING & FABRICATION

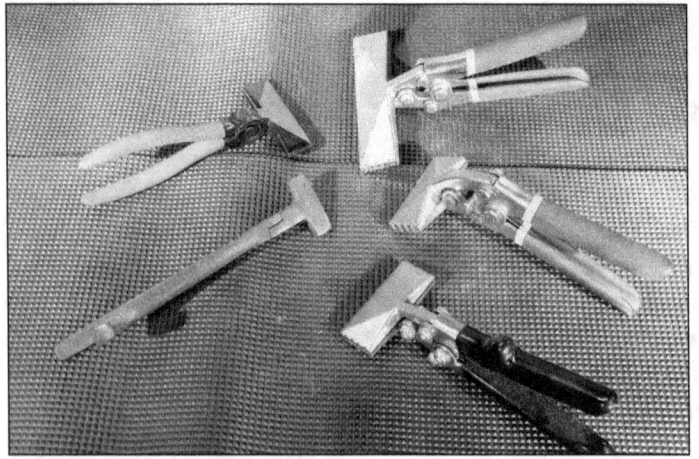

Flanging pliers (a.k.a. seaming pliers) have multiple uses based on manually bending or warping small areas of edge metal. Here, clockwise from top left: 4-inch sheet metal flanging pliers, 6-inch compound sheet metal flanging pliers, angled 4-inch compound sheet metal flanging pliers, straight 4-inch compound sheetmetal flanging pliers, and very old brass 3-inch sheet metal flanging pliers. (The compound pliers have a cam advantage for applying force which the simple pliers lack.)

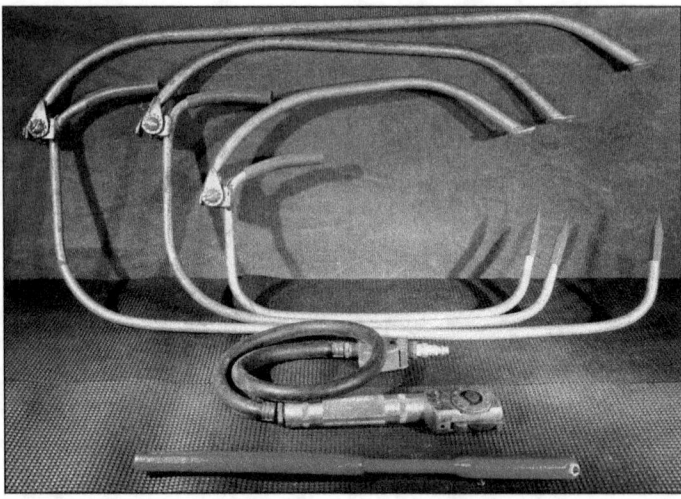

These three tool types address the same problems— limited visibility and access to pick work. The Bull's Eye picks (top) are so cumbersome as to be nearly worthless. The Dial-a-Pick pneumatic pick (middle) works reasonably well. The Steck limited-access pick (bottom) works beautifully and is relatively inexpensive.

These 4- and 6-inch magnetic vise-mount finger brakes are incredibly useful for forming small parts, such as the bend-excluded tab piece in this 6-inch set. Unlike normal brakes, these offer a terrific view around what you are bending. The vise screw drive makes for precision control.

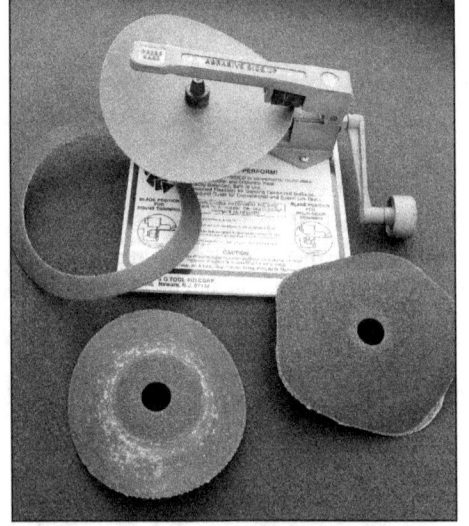

Sanding discs are expensive, and it's a shame to throw them away just because their outer inch, or so, is spent. With a disc trimmer you can trim them back to fresh abrasive areas or into shapes that are great for feathering your sanding.

than using some hulking 16-foot monster brake, and the control that you get with a vise drive is tremendously accurate.

Specialty Tools

The good news is that some commercially available specialty tools work, and work well. Others are a waste of time. There is a terrific difference between something that just addresses a common problem and something that solves it. The Bull's Eye pick set looks like a great idea, but raises more issues than it solves. The Dial-a-Pick is awkward and frustrating to use, but it does work in places that are hard to reach. The Steck close quarters pick hammer is the least expensive of these devices and works the best of any of them. In fact, it is downright handy.

The sanding disc trimmer is not very glamorous, but it more than halves my sanding disc bill every year. The Gas-Saver attachment for

TOOLS AND EQUIPMENT

This Gas-Saver adds greatly to torch convenience, economy, and safety. When I hang my torch on the Gas-Saver's hook, gas flow stops, extinguishing the torch. Once I remove it from the Gas-Saver's hook, gas flows and I can relight it off the Gas-Saver's pilot light.

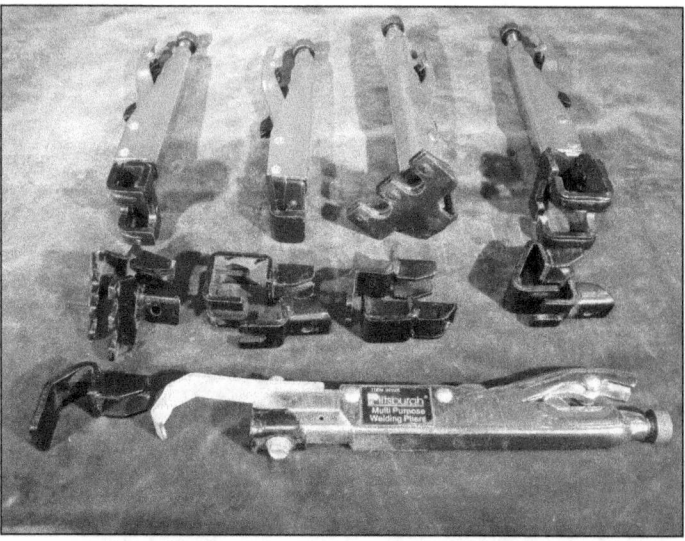

Locking pliers are among the most useful clamping tools. They come in numerous varieties, including long-reach and special-jaw configurations. These are for welding applications. The set at the bottom uses the interchangeable jaws shown above it. Note the special purpose homemade jaw mounted in it.

my oxy-acetylene torch does the same for my flame welding gas bill.

Advice: Don't buy specialty tools or equipment before you have had a chance to use it or to talk to someone whom you trust who has experience with it. Some tools look more useful and competent than they are, and while some tools look hokey, as they say on TV, "it really, really works."

Clamping and Fixturing Tools

Anyone who works much on forming and fabricating projects has probably sometimes wished for a third arm and hand, or, perhaps, for a long, prehensile tail. The need to hold things in place before they are pounded, bent, welded, riveted, etc., can be enormous. When a co-worker is available to help position things for you, that usually solves the problem, but some holding jobs are too long term for that. Numerous devices fill

Holding things together, and in position, is a big issue in welding. Counterclockwise from the top: Cleco holding devices and their installation tool; specialty clips for securing sheet metal edges; a couple of ever-useful spring clamps; and two particularly useful types of welding magnets.

The corners of the intersects in cross-rolled beads never roll out quite right. I made this jig to straighten them. I pound a bolt shank against the metal both ways and into my jig. Abracadabra, I get a perfect bead cross roll corner joint.

AUTOMOTIVE SHEET METAL FORMING & FABRICATION

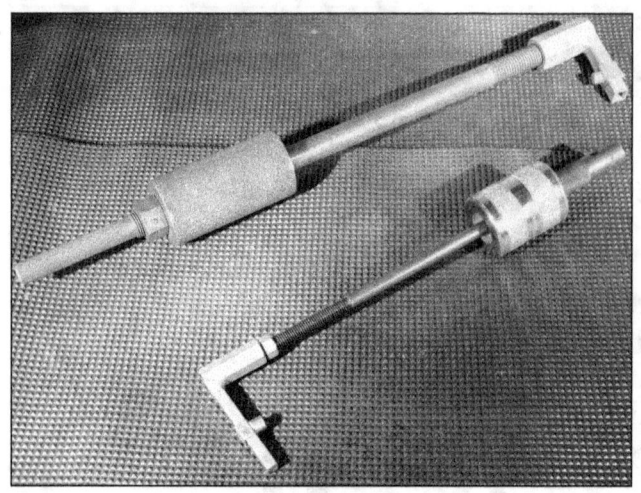

Some of the best tools that you will ever own are made or adapted. These homemade slide-hammer back puller attachments are great for pulling out low metal that you cannot work directly or with prys. The sliding impact points on their cross beams are adjustable for depth.

These dollies were homemade for special-purpose work. They can be mounted in a vise and used as small anvil dollies, or they can be hammered against recesses in metal. They make terrific hammering back-ups, no matter how you use them.

that gap. Locking pliers in various formats are among the most useful hand tools for that and other purposes.

Close behind them are Cleco-type devices that are designed specifically to hold sheet metal parts in alignment prior to welding. Some very ingenious magnet-based tools are also very handy for this purpose, as are various types of clamps and spring clamps.

There are so many terrific and effective holding, clamping, fixturing, and positioning tools out there that it is a shame to resort to crudely balancing parts, while fervently hoping that they will stay in position long enough to do whatever you need to do with them. You will often lose that bet.

Making Special-Purpose Hand Tools

Some of the most useful tools in sheet metal fabrication work are tools that you fashion for yourself. Sometimes these are special-purpose tools that you need just once. Other times they are more general tools that have multiple uses and serve for many years, often in ways that you did not anticipate when you created them. My slide-hammer puller attachments were made for pulling inaccessible dents out of a trunk lid. Making those tools was the fastest way to get that job done. Since then I have used them in several fabrication situations where access to the back of an area was difficult or impossible.

Some tools are made by modifying existing tools, so that they can be used where the originals cannot. Bent T-dollies and special prying tools fit into that category. It is surprising how often tools like that are made for some specific job, but are later quite useful for solving other problems. That is why I never discard special tools that I make. I often find some valid use for them later or can modify them to fit one.

Among the most useful tooling ever created in fabrication work is hammerforms for specific shapes that you need to pound out of sheet

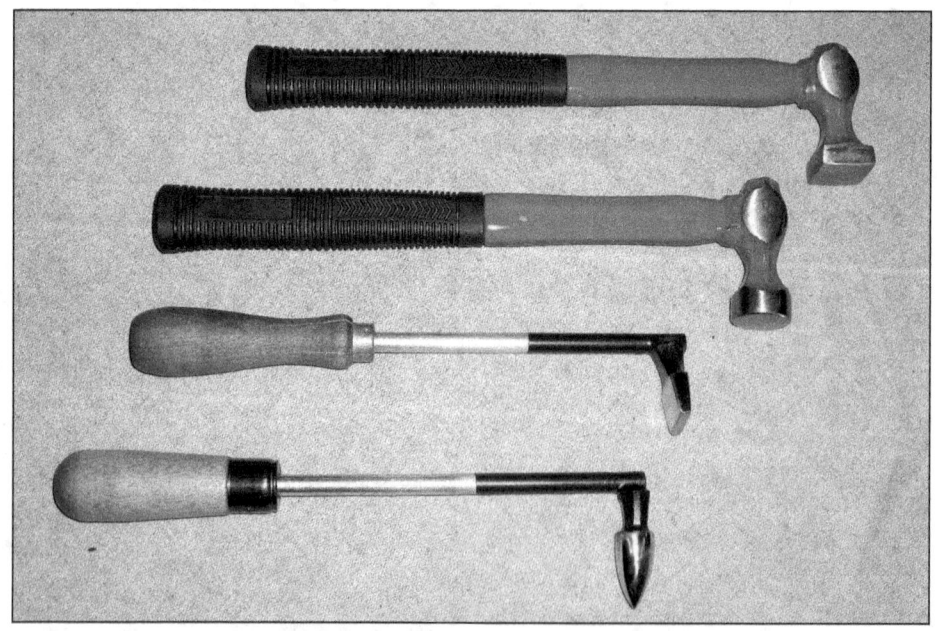

Hammer heads with short overall length are always a great asset where you have limited room to swing a hammer. These were fabricated from an inexpensive set of body hammers. I use them for flattening and picking in close quarters.

metal. These can be indispensable for one-off jobs, particularly where high replicative fidelity is required. They can also greatly improve your quality and efficiency when you have to make the same part, or section, several times.

Then there are those wonderful items that you find, or that find you, and that prove incredibly useful for purposes for which they were never intended. An old tire patch anvil and some shoe lasts are among my favorite adaptations in this class. Both provide surfaces and configurations that can be perfect helpers for some forming and finishing jobs. Keep your eye out for these tooling opportunities when you sort through old junk. You may be surprised at the uses that you can conjure up for things that are completely unrelated to forming sheet metal.

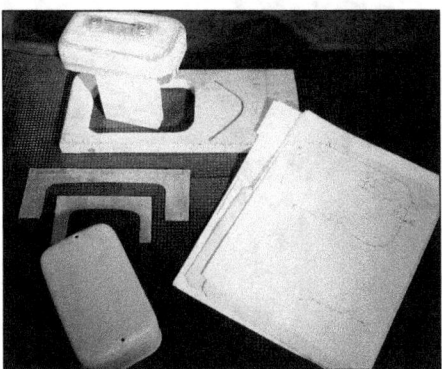

The hammer form, data, and templates used to fabricate the electrical box cover (lower left) were essential to the job, particularly that hammer form. These will be boxed and saved just in case I ever need to make another of these covers or to be modified for some other purpose.

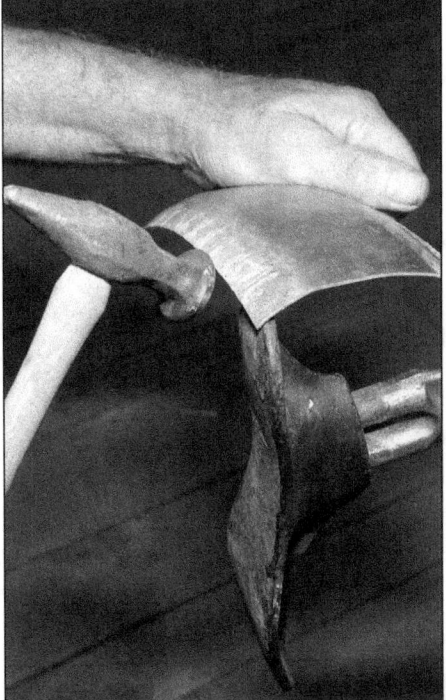

You'll never guess what the thing shown in this photo being used for hammer backup is. Oh, you did! Right, it's a shoemaker's last for nailing shoe soles and heals. It also works wonderfully as a backup for shaping metal, particularly when you have to reach into narrow spaces.

Below: This edge shrinker/stretcher is endlessly useful for forming and curving narrow pieces of metal, which are, themselves, essential parts for many panel fabrications. But my favorite use for them is to flatten warped pieces of flat stock after something that I do distorts them.

Imagination in finding new uses for old tools can be very helpful in fabrication work. No one has much contemporary use for this narrow old tire patch vulcanizing form, but it makes a dandy hammer form for all sorts of shapes.

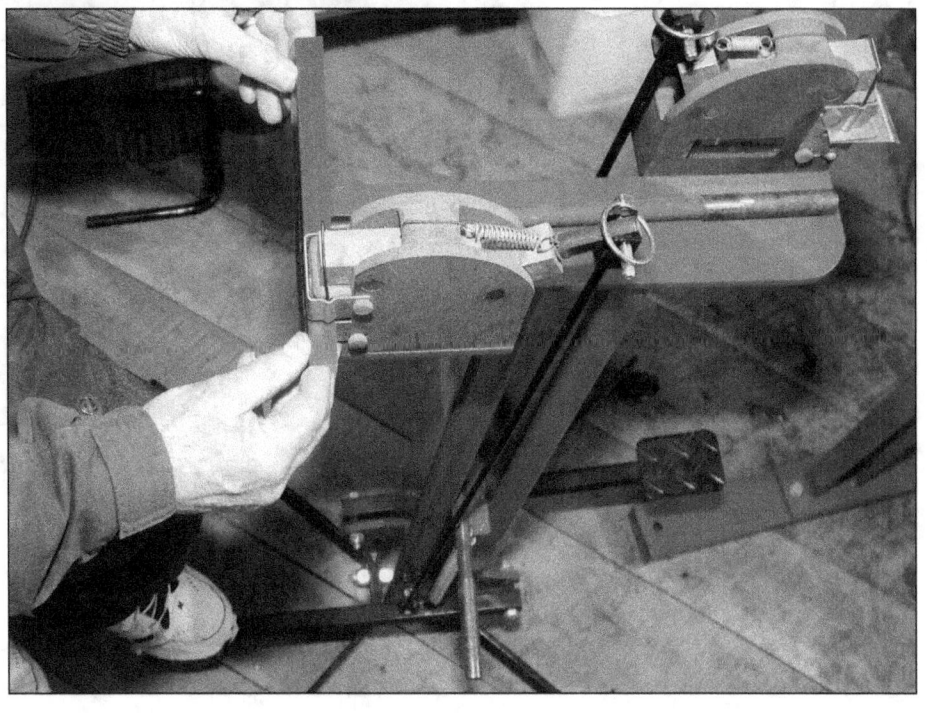

CHAPTER 9

Small Equipment

Often, small hand- and foot-operated equipment is the stuff that allows you to do what simple hand tools cannot do, or can accomplish only with great difficulty. This is handy stuff that ranges in size, quality, and price.

Mechanical shrinkers and stretchers—sometimes combined into one shrinker/stretcher device with interchangeable jaws—are among the most useful of all small sheet metal shop equipment. Used with imagination, they are capable of creating right-angle edge pieces in three dimensions. It is really astounding how many uses these simple devices have in metal fabrication. They are relatively inexpensive for what they can do, and come in both hand and foot air-operated versions.

Recently, somewhat larger versions of mechanical edge shrinker/stretcher tools have become available in units that can reach up to 8 inches beyond panel edges. In addition to edge shrinking and stretching, these units make it possible to mechanically shrink and stretch areas that used to require the use of either high-heat metal shrinking techniques or very expensive, machine-mounted mechanical shrinking/stretching equipment.

Slip rolls bend uniform curves into metal with perfect consistency.

Slip rolling is often a first step in complex forming operations. It can impart final shapes or create the basis for further forming. Slip rolling misses forming the ends of pieces. Plan to trim those ends or to hammer form them against one of the rolls to shape them.

Recently, 8-inch depth shrinker/stretchers in hand-control and pedestal-mount foot-control versions became available at very reasonable prices. They rough up metal surfaces a bit in shrinking and stretching them, but they get the job done. This is a hand-operated shrinker version.

This foot-operated pedestal version of an 8-inch stretcher won't match the speed, versatility, and precision of a power hammer driven device, but if you don't have a power hammer, this kind of tool can take you a long way.

TOOLS AND EQUIPMENT

Bead rolling is as often structural as it is decorative. It frequently serves both purposes. Originally, the beads were die stamped into this part. In this reproduction, they are being rolled. In both cases, they give the panel profile and work harden the bead areas, and that makes it stronger.

They do this by pressing the metal between one moveable roller and two fixed rollers. Adjusting the distance between the moveable and fixed rollers controls the amount of curvature imparted to the metal in its pass through a slip roll. Adjusting one end of the moveable roll in this device differently from the other results in curves of different radii at each end of a piece that is rolled this way. Thus, a conical shape is rolled.

While not essential for many basic fabricating procedures, bead rollers are very useful for creating decorative adornments, and for providing strengthening ribs to help panels counter vibration induced flutter and light mechanical deformation (see also the brief discussion in Chapter 5).

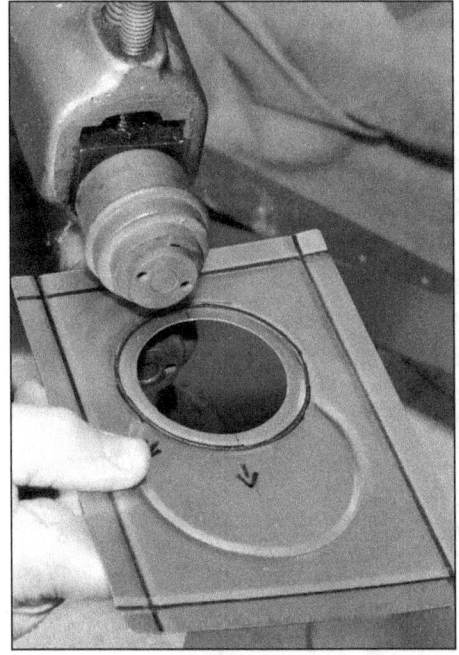

The edge bead was rolled into this piece after the decorative, circular beads. Note that rolling the edge bead is warping the piece. The easiest way to flatten it is to figure out where its edges are stretched or shrunk and to correct that problem with an edge shrinker/stretcher.

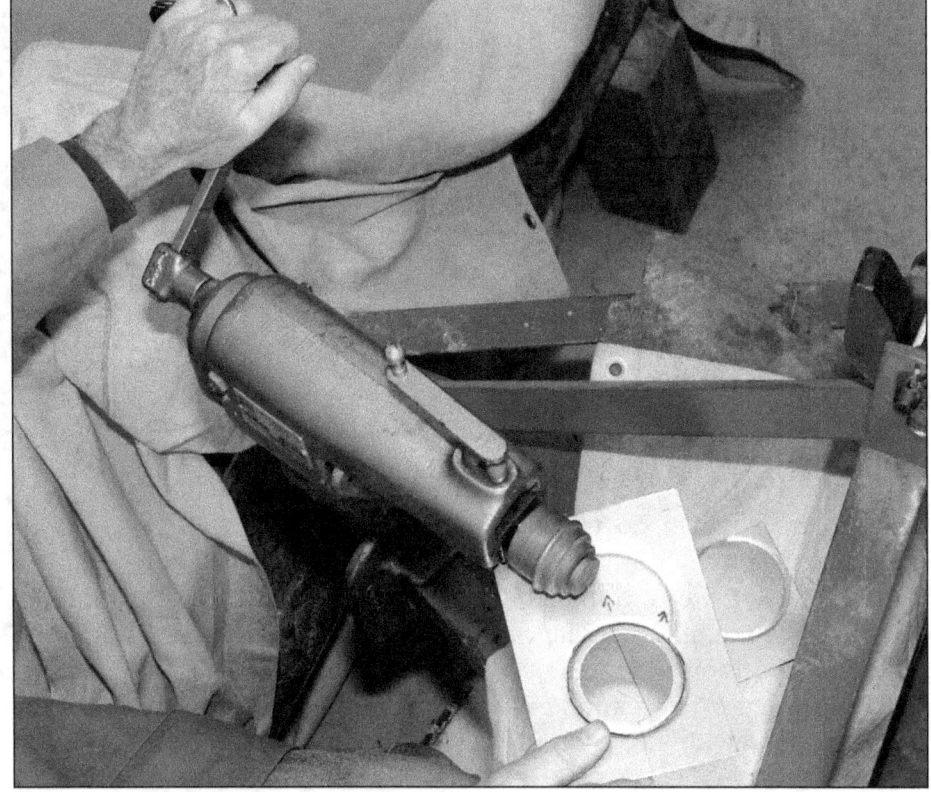

Rolling circular beads like this takes a visible line to follow, a good eye, and some practice. The key to success is to go slowly and to correct small mistakes as you roll along, before they become big ones. Note the practice piece under the part that is being rolled.

AUTOMOTIVE SHEET METAL FORMING & FABRICATION

This big Beverly shear cuts metal more accurately than any other common method that I know. If you want to cut very fine detail, this is the best way to do it. Cheaper versions of the Beverly shear never seem to quite measure up to it.

It was well worth the time spent converting this old spot welder to foot operation. The hand-held unit remains easily removable. Note the piece of insulating fiber that is inserted between the bottom welding arm and the work piece's side to prevent shorting through the welding arm.

Bead rollers are sometimes hand driven, either with a wheel or crank, and sometimes motor driven. They differ in quality and in reach. The deeper they reach, the more expensive they are, and the more useful they become. A good bead roller comes with a dozen, or more, different width and profile bead wheels, and it is always possible to custom-make new tooling to fit your specific purpose.

Stationary hand shears frankly lack sex appeal. They tend to seem expensive for what they do, particularly the higher quality ones. And all that they do is to finely cut metal. That's all. But they do it so much more accurately than do the hand snips and shears described in Chapter 5 that they are worth considering. You can trace the most delicate cuts with great precision with these cutters. Once you use one you will never want to be without a bench-mounted shear.

Spot welders are necessary for many fabrication projects; after all, several thousand spot welds are what hold most modern cars together.

This multifunction machine handles 22-gauge mild steel in widths up to 52 inches. It's a slip roll, a finger brake with up to a 90-degree capability, and a shear. It does all of those things a bit clumsily, and creaking and groaning along the way, but it's inexpensive and compact.

However, unlike the robotically spot-welded "bodies in white" of modern automobiles, sheet metal fabricators have to make these welds one at a time. One thing that can make this work much easier, while enhancing its quality, is to use a foot-operated spot welder, leaving both hands free for aligning and positioning the pieces that you are welding. Frames

TOOLS AND EQUIPMENT

that hold spot welders and convert them to foot operation can be purchased or fabricated. The one that I made for my own use took about half a day to fabricate and works perfectly. It's a real time saver.

Multi-Purpose Devices

The combined 52-inch sliproll/shear/finger brake device is a member of the class of light, very versatile, multi-functional equipment. It represents great economy over buying these capabilities singly in the form of three separate pieces of equipment and it does each of its designated jobs acceptably well. Unfortunately, it lacks the ease of use and precision of the three separate devices that it is supposed to replace. For occasional use, it is fine. If, however, you plan to use any of the functions of this kind of tool regularly, you will be far better served by buying dedicated tools for these purposes. It's a matter of budget, outlook, space, and need.

In fabrication work, it is often necessary to bend and join tubular sections to create substructure and framework pieces and systems. A post-type tubing bender is a very capable machine for forming many kinds of curves in tubular sections, including some with increasing and decreasing radii. With the right dies, it can even handle small, square tube stock.

The rolling-type wheel bender also works well for making circular bends of large radii, and can be induced to do changing radius bends to a lesser extent than the post bender. It is particularly useful if several identical bends must be made in matched pieces.

The hydraulic tube bender can be used to make large, constant radius bends in tubing, but it is a cumbersome way to accomplish this. A more useful application for it is to increase bend radius in existing curves for the purposes of final

This roll bender can handle fairly large diameters of soft, thin-wall metal for making wide-radius bends. Don't expect light equipment like this to bend heavy stock. Think more of electrical conduit and decoration.

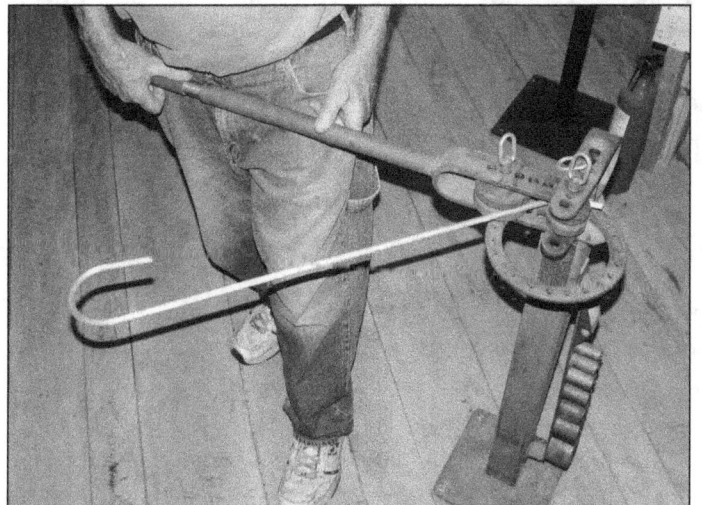

Post benders, like this one, make consistent bends in round and small square stock. Scrolling attachments can take you into the realm of art. Sometimes, when you need a consistent curve for a bracket or support, this is a good way to form it.

If you do want to bend sterner stuff, this hydraulic bender is a good choice. To bend consistently with it, you have to index your pipe in segments as short as 1/2 inch. The rubber taped to the support rolls lessens denting and marring of the pipe.

CHAPTER 9

Notchers use hole saws of various widths to cut consistent circles into tubing, or square sections, to make junctions for other round sections. Either brazed or welded, this construction is compact and strong. It has been used to fabricate air frames for most of aviation history.

Air-driven power tools exist in great variety. Here are some interesting examples (from left to right): A portable belt sander, a scissors metal shear, a small needle scaler, a percussion hammer, and a 4-inch air disc grinder. The needle scaler and percussion hammer are useful for moving small amounts of sheet metal.

adjustment and fitting. Hydraulic benders are also capable of deforming much heavier tubing stock than post benders and rolling benders, should you need to do this for an item like a roll bar.

Up to a point, these three types of tubing bender all make bends without collapsing the tubing on which they are used. One way to further prevent tube collapse when you are bending a tube is to fill it with sand and crimp and weld its ends shut. The sand contained by the crimped and welded ends prevents collapse while you are bending, and can be removed later.

Notchers are used with hole saws in drill presses to cut straight or angled saddle ends on tubes, for the purpose of fitting them to the sides of other tubes, for welding at various angles. While this function can be duplicated crudely by grinding or filing tube ends into the necessary formats for fitting them up, a notcher is really invaluable and unsurpassed for this function.

Power and Hand Tools

There are far too many useful electric and pneumatic hand power tools for sheet metal fabrication work to be able to note even a small fraction of them here. (Some of them were covered in Chapter 5.) For both air and electric hand tools, the tendency over the years has been to develop versions that are lighter, cheaper, and easier to use (sometimes at the cost of durability). In some cases, tools like small electric grinders and air die grinders have become so inexpensive as to virtually become throw-away items.

Some commercially available hand power tools that were never intended for sheet metal work end up being very usable for forming and finishing endeavors. The air belt sander, percussion hammer, and needle scaler are good examples of this. Air belt sanders were originally developed for cabinet work, but are great for sanding and finishing hard-to-access places in sheet metal work. The air needle scaler was intended for cleaning the slag off arc welds, and the small percussion hammer was invented to expand the skirts of collapsed pistons. Both of these tools can be used to move metal in finishing processes. If you think hard about it, you can probably come up with several new sheet metal applications for existing tools intended for other purposes.

Blacksmith Tools

Blacksmith gear would seem to be an odd category of tools to have application in sheet metal fabrication, because we usually think of blacksmiths as working with heavier sections of metal, such as horseshoes and farm equipment. Yet, blacksmith paraphernalia often has great application to this work. The basic blacksmith's anvil is so ingeniously designed and evolved that it offers a

TOOLS AND EQUIPMENT

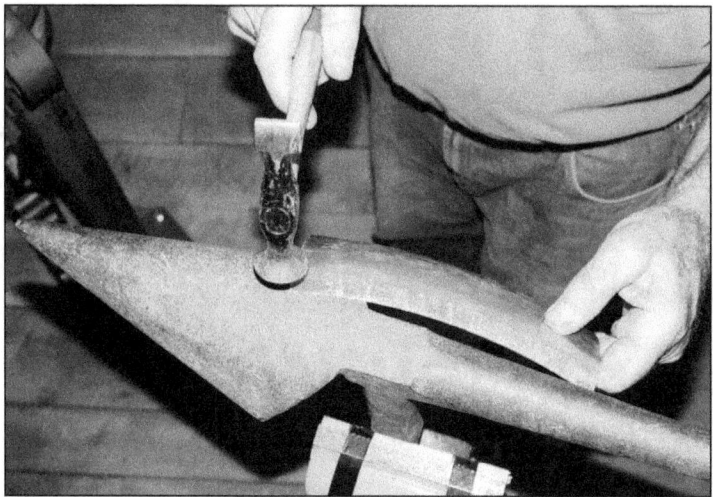

This horn anvil is really an attachment for a blacksmith's stake tool set. It ordinarily mounts in a plate, along with a dozen other strange and wonderfully useful attachments that perform various functions. Here, it is mounted in a vise.

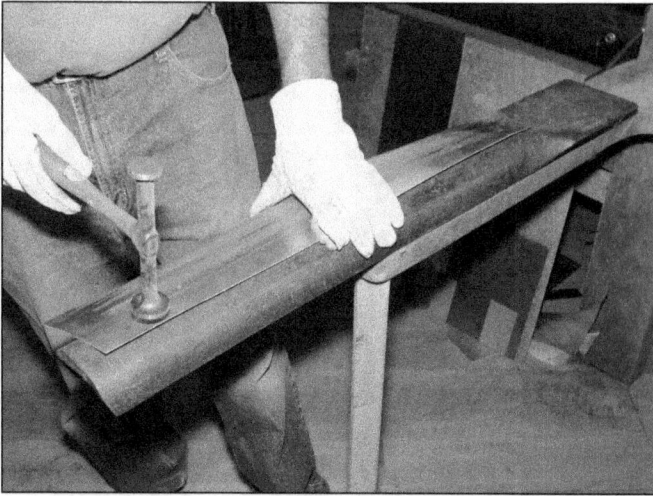

This stove-pipe anvil is terrific for forming and adjusting long pieces into fairly consistent curves. It was originally intended for hand fabricating stove pipe. I find it particularly useful for work on rocker panels.

myriad of useful surfaces for forming sheet metal. Its horn has variable curves, its sides are great for making angles, and the basic flat, and its edges, are perfect for lightly hammering metal evenly level.

When you get into specialized blacksmithing tools, such as the long horn anvil attachments and stakes in a blacksmith's bench tool set, you have working surfaces for almost any conceivable hammer forming job.

Long before there were rocker panels, blacksmiths hand-made stove pipe from flat stock. A good stove pipe anvil on a good mount is nearly ideal for fine tuning almost any rocker panel or other long, mildly curved structure that you may have to form or fix.

In days of yore, blacksmith's vises bolted to work benches, with one long leg that reached and mounted to the floor. That was so that blacksmiths could pound down on something in the vise without having the thing move or damage the bench to which the vise was attached. The floor took the impact and helped to position the vise laterally. These tend to be very good vises that load up all kinds of torque in their jaws, holding the things placed in them with great tenacity. Mounted to a plow disc stand, or other base that acts as the anchor for a stand, they become holding devices that you can walk around to access your work from any angle.

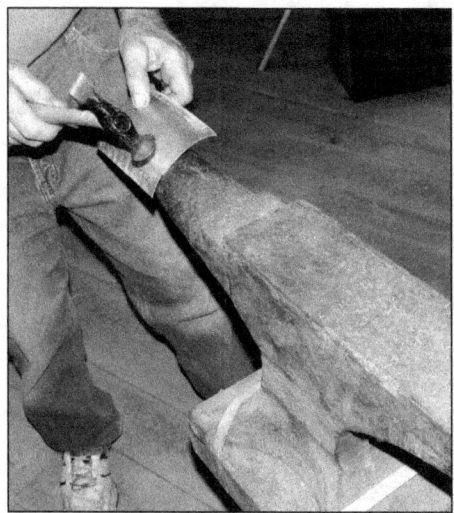

This 175-pound anvil is the king of blacksmith tools. It offers a huge array of surfaces and features for shaping sheet metal. This one is mounted free standing. You can walk around it as you work on it.

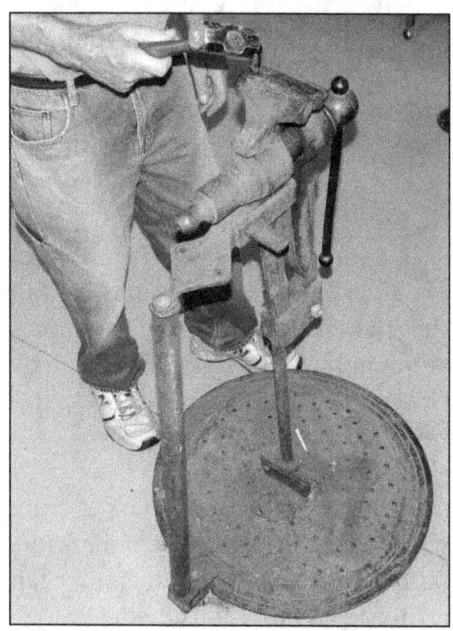

This blacksmith's vise is seriously tough and can take a lot of punishment. Here it is being used to form a small bracket piece. It is mounted on a person-hole-cover, allowing easy access around it. Its main support goes to the floor, making it very stable under hard pounding.

AUTOMOTIVE SHEET METAL FORMING & FABRICATION

CHAPTER 10

THE ART OF THE ENGLISH WHEEL

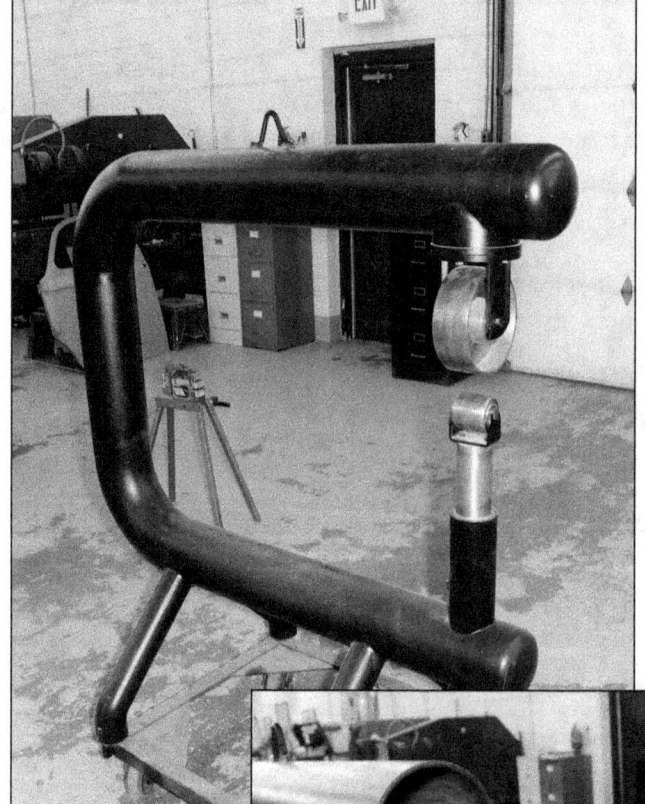

This modern formed and welded tubular English wheel is a thing of great beauty. It has stability, accuracy, and ingenuity. Note that the wheels can be rotated for different angles of approach.

As an added convenience, the designer of this wheel included anvil wheel storage in the top of its tubular frame. You guessed it—I want one. Who wouldn't?

There is something wonderfully elegant about the English wheel. This device is often shrouded in myth and bathed with romance, but what it does is really quite simple, which is stretching and/or smoothing metal. How it does those things is also simple: It exerts pressure on a narrow band of metal as it is passed between the two tensioned rollers of the English wheel, making it ever so slightly thinner, longer, and wider. Roll enough strokes with the right pressure and overlap settings, and in the right directions and locations, and you have the basis for forming a crowned surface, made to specification. Not much myth or romance is available in any of that.

The myth and romance enter when you consider the remarkable results that a good operator can achieve with an English wheel. However, that successful outcome depends on the skill and judgment that an English wheel operator rolls into his work: his choice of anvil (lower) wheel with regard to configuration (radius), the tensioning of the wheels, and every aspect of manually pushing and pulling a piece of sheet metal

THE ART OF THE ENGLISH WHEEL

This custom, hand-formed Inskip Rolls-Royce body represents the heights to which the sheet metal forming and fabrication arts can take you. It combines originality, imagination, and superb craftsmanship.

Even an inexpensive English wheel has considerable utility. I wouldn't try to form a car body on it, but it serves well for smoothing and forming small panels. Beyond that kind of service, its accuracy and consistency begins to pose problems.

puzzler. Suddenly, what seemed simple in concept has numerous variables, and a mind boggling number of combinations become available with those variables.

English wheels may vary in construction, but all contain the same basic parts. Most important among these is the C-clamp-shaped frame. Originally, these frames were cast, but have since been fabricated from round, square, and rectangular tubing and from welded, bolted, or riveted flat plates. In any construction, it is the purpose of the frame to hold the rolling wheels in alignment under pressure and to load varying amounts of torque between them when they are tensioned at various settings.

Other important parts of an English wheel are the actual rolling wheels and a method of tensioning them against sheet metal. The wheels are usually made from hard steel and run on ball-bearing axles. The top wheel is the "rolling" wheel, and is roughly three to four times larger in diameter than the bottom, or "anvil" wheel. The top wheel is most often flat, while the bottom wheel is supplied in multiple radii for different jobs, or different phases of the same job. Finally, an English wheel has some type of adjustable tensioning device that the operator can manipulate with his hand, leg, knee, or foot.

Using an English Wheel

No amount of written instruction will allow you to just step up to the wheel and make things happen as you would like them to. You have to learn how to do that from considerable practice. To get the most out of that practice, be very sensitive to the feel and sound of the metal going through an English wheel. Observe closely the

through them. That last item includes his speed, angle, repetition, overlap, length, and dwell of strokes. There is also the question of the hardness of the surface of the upper wheel. And, most of all, the question of where to place and how to configure those strokes; that one is a real

The cross wheeling pattern is usable for some forming and a lot of smoothing at the same time. When you get the hang of it, it's amazing what you can do with an English wheel.

small changes that occur in it with every pass that you make. Learn what maneuvers, and combinations of maneuvers, result in which outcomes.

One straight pass through the wheel has little visible effect, even with the most radiused anvil wheel available. The likely outcome of that maneuver is a very slight crease in the metal. That is a valid outcome if that is what you are seeking, but it probably isn't. You could get the same result more easily and certainly with a bead roller.

English wheels can do much more than make straight creases: they can create compound curves in metal, a.k.a. crown. This format is created with straight overlapping strokes, the majority of which are in the longest direction of the crown, and then shorter strokes between right angles and diagonally to the initial, long strokes. Your approach in creating a specific crown is largely a personal strategy choice. Many different approaches work. Still, you should have a plan and be prepared to modify it as necessary.

Here is an ingenious arrangement. This fender top patch is getting a slight crease along its center line to duplicate the factory design. Note the use of a creasing anvil wheel and a large, relatively soft castor wheel for the rolling wheel. It looks hokey, but it worked perfectly.

This maneuver demonstrates the English wheel's potential for forming and adjusting crown. It is being used here to add necessary crown to a very specific area of this fender. It is difficult to imagine any simpler way of accomplishing this.

In general, you start with the flattest anvil wheel that you have and with mild pressure, using straight, overlapping strokes. As you begin to see indications of the compound curve that you want to achieve, increase your wheel tension. When you reach a point where the anvil wheel's radius is close to not clearing the metal beyond its contact patch in the crown that you are rolling, go to the next, more radiused wheel, and apply increasing pressure with it. As you progress, you use different wheels to stroke at various angles to your original path, as the situation dictates. You need to balance stretching with forming the crown that you are seeking.

The bad news is that nothing happens very quickly in this work, and the good news is also that nothing happens very quickly in this work. Due to that basic fact, wheeling is a slow but reasonably forgiving process. If you pay attention, it warns you of pending errors. If you concentrate on accurately placed, overlapped strokes, and escalate your wheel pressure and anvil radius as you go, amazing things happen, slowly, right before your eyes. As you get the hang of this craft, you learn to vary your wheel stroke lengths, and to concentrate them more on the areas where you want more crown. This involves a lot of averaging and overlapping. Hint: It is easier to wheel a severe crown, like a bulging hood air scoop, than it is to wheel a large panel with a mild crown, like a slab-sided door. The latter job requires far greater accuracy.

Keep in mind that an English wheel stretches metal in every direction, but more along the sides of its line of travel than fore and aft.

Effective versus Harmful Techniques

What is the most important thing to consider in using an English wheel? Well, I once knew a fellow who, in a fit of inattentive exuberance, ran several fingers into a wheel. As I remember, we called him "Lefty" after that.

The wheel is a subtle tool of often surprising potentials and possibilities. You can keep finding new things to do with it, particularly if you have the capability of making or adapting your own special tooling (wheels) for it. The best wheel artists have developed their own styles of using this tool. You can recognize them in their work.

One thing that a good wheel does almost eerily well is to smooth metal. Get an anvil wheel with the right radius for your job, incrementally

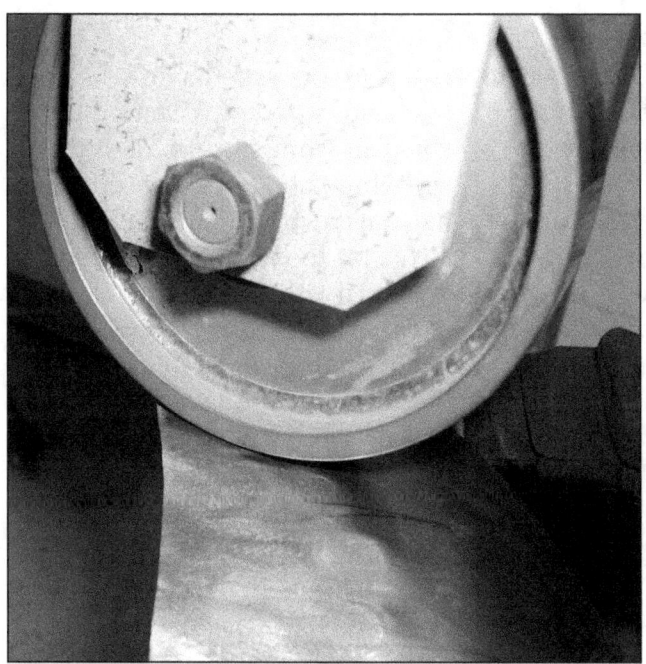
This cross-wheeling approach is being used primarily to smooth the metal in this fender fabrication. Once this is accomplished, the operator can see what the crown and profile look like and make any necessary further adjustments to the metal's shape.

There is a simple way to correct weld distortion in, and near, a panel seam. Start with a sound weld, finish both of its sides perfectly, and then you can wheel over it. If done right, the result is perfect metal flow into uniform crown.

increase wheel pressure from light to mild, and you can watch unwanted minor deformations melt out of metal as you pass it through the wheel. That describes removing even fairly major roughness from a panel or area of a panel. However, it is not a substitute for hammer-and-dolly bumping work.

Even more impressive is the near-perfect surface that can be imparted to metal when light wheeling is employed as a finishing process, after crown forming, and even section welding and weld finishing. Tightly overlapped, low-tension diagonal strokes are the format for this maneuver. If you do it right, you end up with incredibly smooth metal with a faint hint of a herringbone pattern in the panel surface, a pattern that can be seen but is not felt.

And now, the inevitable "don'ts" for novice wheelers. Don't try to make things happen fast with an English wheel. Like teaching a pig to sing, you will not succeed. You will only annoy the hell out of the metal! Keep anvil wheel radii and wheel tension low and safe for each situation. Remember that you are thinning, stretching, and hardening metal with every pass of a wheel, and there are limits to how far you can go. The classic error is to start with a highly radiused anvil wheel and too much wheel pressure. You won't get anything useful out of that, just an irregular and brittle

The overall crown in this patch panel is being adjusted by slightly stretching its edges. You can't make big changes in crown this way, but sometimes a little modification is enough.

mess that will fracture easily where it is thinnest and hardest. This can be a particular problem in very highly crowned areas.

Here is one last wheel caution and trick. The caution is to avoid wheeling over the edge of your metal as much as possible as you work it. Keep an inch away from all edges, and plan on trimming them back to the crown that you want later. The reason for this is that running on and off an edge repeatedly tends to over-stretch it. The trick that results from this caution is that you can adjust crown a little by wheeling along its edges. If you have over-wheeled a panel and created a bit too much crown, you can correct this by wheeling the edges of the panel and slightly stretching it. Of course, you can also shrink the metal in the crown where the crown is excessive by other means. But wheeling around the edges is a bit easier and tidier.

CHAPTER 11

POWER-OPERATED MACHINES

If you haven't actually seen them, you likely have heard of them, and many of you may dream of someday owning one, or more, of them. I'm talking about the big power metal forming machines that are used in places like aircraft factories, prototype shops, and advanced custom and restoration shops. These are power hammers that greatly speed sheet metal work. In some cases they make it possible to do in hours what would otherwise take days, or what could barely be done at all. They are often expensive, and always skill intensive to operate. What they may lack in the elegant, unpowered simplicity of English wheels, they make up for in usefulness and capability. They require fairly extensive tooling to attain their full versatility, and often require pretty steep learning curves to operate them successfully.

In practice, what the big machines do is to mechanize and hasten the key metal forming operations that have already been discussed: shrinking, stretching, and creating crown. They can also support tooling for such specialized operations as uniforming curves and pressing louvers.

This old power hammer is typical of early members of the species. While it could move a lot of metal, it was finicky, noisy, and complicated. Modern power hammers have come a long way since this one was built. However, power hammers of this vintage remain very usable.

AUTOMOTIVE SHEET METAL FORMING & FABRICATION

CHAPTER 11

This Pullmax looks like it has been used heavily. That's okay, if it was well maintained. Shiny paint is the last thing that you should be seeking when you purchase this kind of equipment. You can add that later.

Power Hammers

The first well-known power hammers were the Pettingell and the Yoder. The Pettingell was probably the earliest successful device of this type, and was manufactured for many years, starting in the middle of the first decade of the twentieth century. Carl Yoder invented the power hammer that bears his name a few years later. Both devices have benefited from considerable improvement over the years. Some metal formers still use Yoder and Pettingell hammers today, and swear by them. These early hammers were large, bulky, and noisy machines that could be equipped with a wide variety of tooling, and could radically form metal far faster than could be accomplished with simple hand tools. Of course, there were other power hammers in the twentieth century, like the Helve, but the Pettingell and Yoder remain the best known of the breed.

Several newer power hammers, such as those by Pullmax, Eckold Kraftformer, and Piccolo, have thoroughly modernized these devices. These are much quieter and less cumbersome and finicky than their predecessors. With the right tooling, they can move metal in ways that seem almost miraculous. However, like their predecessors, they tend to be expensive and very skill intensive to use. I have known more than one metal man who thought that acquiring a power hammer would be the solution to most of his problems, only to see it become the center of an entirely new set of vexations.

Big Machine Basics

The big metal forming machines basically consist of a C-configured frame, a fixed-bottom anvil attachment point, and a powered upper ram hammer. Turned on, the hammer approaches the anvil with a

The Pullmax has been around for decades and is probably the most versatile and generally useful of all power forming machines. While it has some limitations that other machines may fill, it is probably the best single forming machine out there.

Newer Pullmax machines are expensive and serious repairs to them can be costly. Pullmaxes sometimes turn up as industrial surplus. If you consider buying one, be sure to take an expert along to evaluate it before you purchase it.

AUTOMOTIVE SHEET METAL FORMING & FABRICATION

POWER-OPERATED MACHINES

The Eckold shrinking heads shown here are performing two operations simultaneously, shrinking and smoothing a panel. The Eckold shrinking device can move plenty of metal, but does it so gently that it does not damage the metal's surface.

The outer edge of this panel is beginning to show the mild dimpling left behind by Eckold shrinking and stretching heads. It becomes more pronounced as metal gets smoother. Note that these heads are installed in a Pullmax power hammer.

This close-up of a pair of Cook shrinking dies shows their configuration. The secret of their operation is to create a V-groove as metal is inserted through them, and then to flatten it, as it is pulled back out. The net effect is an upset or shrink.

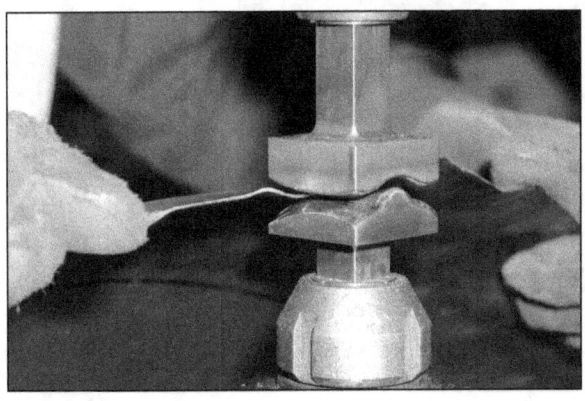

Cook shrinking dies perform radical shrinking that would be difficult to achieve as quickly or certainly by any other method. As they pound, the metal is moved forward through them, impressing a V-groove into it. Then it's flattened by the die's heals as it's withdrawn through them.

force, frequency, and pressure (adjusted distance) that can be set by the operator. There is nothing particularly magical in that action. The real magic is in the tooling that you affix to a power hammer.

For example, the basic and essential task of shrinking metal can be done with the likes of Eckold shrinking heads mounted on a power hammer, such as a Pullmax. These heads mechanically gather metal and shrink it predictably, smoothly, and incrementally, up to and including relatively large amounts. Unlike edge shrinkers and other inexpensive mechanical shrinkers and stretchers, Eckold heads do not damage the metal that they shrink by serrating or fracturing it. Instead, they leave a smooth, slightly pebbled surface that is easily finished to a perfectly smooth, paintable panel. In fact, these shrinking heads smooth rough metal in the process of shrinking it. Eckold stretching heads work the same way, but mechanically spread metal, rather than gather it.

If you are thinking, "Oh, I can manage to shrink and stretch metal without that fancy stuff," you are right. The issues are the quantity of your metal's surface after you work it and the speed and predictability with which you can move it. Power hammers with the correct tooling greatly speed metal work and add certainty.

A friend of mine, an expert metal worker who is not prone to exaggeration, once told me, "Cook shrinking heads mounted on a Pullmax represent the most important advance in metal working in decades." I agree. The Cook heads that he referred to are actually beautifully manufactured versions of a fairly old idea that has been kicking

Using Cook shrinking heads effectively is not a matter of luck or guesswork. You have to develop a plan to move the metal where you want it to go. The marks on this panel indicate the depths of various strokes. Some insertions were made multiple times, between smoothing operations.

This panel edge has been shrunk with Cook tooling, and is now being fine tuned and smoothed with Eckold shrinking heads. It is often necessary to go back and forth between these processes to move metal where you want it to go.

around metal fabrication shops for a long time. In many cases, shops saw the idea in practice and made their own versions of shrinking heads in the same configuration. Cook's modern versions are perfectly dimensioned and wonderfully rugged sets of shrinking dies.

The Cook heads, mounted on one of several power hammer devices, are designed for radical shrinking. This is not the outfit to use if you are just looking for a little local shrinking. It is designed for massive shrinking, the kind of job that turns a flat piece of stock into a fender or swoopy hood. It works, as do all hot and cold shrinking processes, by upsetting metal.

The area to be shrunk in a panel is fed into the Cook dies from their flat intake side. Then, the V-groove dies, just beyond the flats, do their work on the panel, impressing a set of fairly deep V-grooves into it. Then, the operator pulls the metal back through the Cook heads' flat areas. This flattens the V-grooves, upsetting the metal in them by compacting it into itself, thereby performing the exchange of lateral dimension for thickness that is the essence of shrinking.

Using the Cook tooling in conjunction with a good plan, you can rough out almost any crowned shape in surprisingly little time. That plan involves how deep you go into the panel in various places with the Cook heads, and how often you decide to go there. Remember, I said that there was a considerable learning curve for using this kind of equipment effectively.

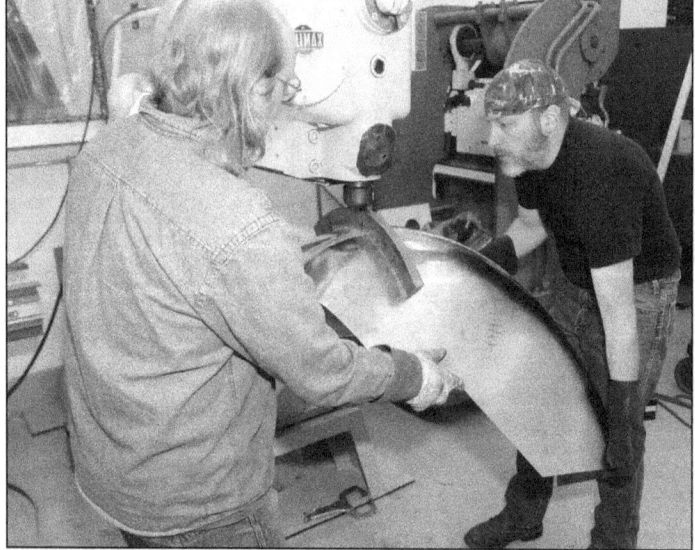
This fender was originally cut out of a large metal spinning, making it a section of a circle, with a uniform radial format. That means that it can be uniformed with the special dies (shown) mounted on a Pullmax. Nice trick, eh?

POWER-OPERATED MACHINES

Soft tooling, such as these nylon dies, is often useful for forming metal where uniformity is important. It is easy to construct soft dies. They are particularly useful for imparting accurate detail to soft metals, like aluminum. The dies shown here are mounted in a Pullmax.

The die set shown here is home-made. This setup is designed to perform radical, local doming, and/or stretching. The lower die forces its domed shape into the metal and backed by the relatively soft upper die, which is actually a hockey puck. This setup works wonderfully to produce local stretches.

The Cook heads leave a somewhat rough surface, but that is easily smoothed out in an English wheel, or in a set of Eckold shrinking dies, or both. Your strategy depends on how far the panel that you are forming has progressed toward its final shape. The Eckold shrinking heads shrink the metal as they remove the Cook roughness, while an English wheel stretches it as it flattens it. Making that kind of call on which way to go takes mainly one thing, experience.

There are many other highly specialized, commercially available tooling sets for power hammers. Most of them are useful for either general forming work and/or for specific jobs. The ones covered above represent the most generally useful types of tooling.

Special Power Hammer Tooling

One of the great opportunities that you get with a power hammer is the chance to create your own tooling for special situations and purposes. This can range from elaborate

This set of traditional louvering dies mounts in a power hammer and stamps louvers into metal. Since panels often contain louvers of different lengths, some louvering dies adjust for length with removable center sections.

This louvering attachment for a Pullmax cuts and forms each louver as metal is pulled along its horizontal axis. You can see the cutter and forming sections of the die in this photo.

To begin and terminate each louver, the handle on the louvering attachment is pulled in the correct direction to impress each end of the louver into the panel. Making louvers of different lengths is a snap with this setup.

dies and shapes to soft dies, and combinations of soft and hard dies. The photos in this chapter that illustrate this opportunity just scratch the surface of what is possible. While standard tooling sets contain many useful configurations, there is always the urge to modify them and/or create new ones.

Jobs like louvering can be done with purpose-built louvering dies mounted in a power hammer. Some of these dies provide an incremental method of adjusting their lengths, so that panels with different-length louvers can be accommodated by one set of adjustable louvering dies.

Another method of accomplishing louvering involves the use of a power hammer attachment. The louver site is moved along a fence under the die. The top louvering die cuts and forms the body of the louver. At either end of the louver, a lever on the attachment is swung in the correct direction to form the louver's finished end. Imagine how difficult and time consuming it would be to try to do this work by hand, without tooling. There are situations where big machine forming is the only reasonable way to go.

Finally, there is specialized metal forming equipment for highly specific purposes. I mention the wonderful Magee Wire Edger, and rest my case. This once-common production tool was used by factories for wire edging everything from wheel barrows to automobile fenders. World War II and progress claimed most of these machines for scrap. The Magee is the larger of two models that were originally available, and one of the few that are left. It is owned and expertly operated by L'Cars of Cameron, Wisconsin. The Magee follows a straight line, or any reasonable curve, in three dimensions. L'Cars has, or can make, the tooling for their Magee machine to wire edge in any usable panel or wire thickness.

The Magee wire edging operation is remarkably slick. In one coordinated move, a wire-and-panel edge is fed into the Magee's forming rolls. This results in a wire-wrapped edge. Over the years, hundreds of special-purpose sheet metal forming devices, like the Magee, were manufactured.

CHAPTER 12

METHODS OF ATTACHMENT

Not long after humankind made its first part, it made a second part. And, shortly after it got that routine down pat, it probably tried to attach a first part to a second part. The art/craft/technology of "jointure" was born. The first acts of joining things were probably mechanical and crude, something slid or was forced into something else and partially, or completely, locked there (think of the attachment of a modern hammer head to its hickory handle). That method is still in use with things like bend tabs and crimp-type joints.

A deluge of permanent and removable fastening methods followed: threaded fasteners, glues and cements, rivets, pop rivets, spring fasteners, soldering, brazing, welding of so many types that it would take a good-size pamphlet just to list them, and many more. Fortunately, sheet metal fabricators need be concerned with only a few of the fastening methods that are available.

Joining metal falls into two pretty distinct categories: welding and non-welding. That demarcation line isn't perfect. For example, brazing is a form of welding, but not really fusion welding, while soldering isn't welding, but it's closer to brazing and welding than to, say, pop riveting. Choosing the right joining process for your job and situation depends on several factors. One is the advantages of working with the skills, tools, and equipment that you already have. Sure, we would all like to own the latest digitally controlled TIG welder and possess the skills to do most of our work in steel and aluminum jointure with perfect

This panel seam is being TIG welded over the tack welds that are visible to the left of the arc. While TIG is the premier choice for quality thin-section fabrication welding, some other methods also work well.

TIG welds. However, the simple truth is that we often lack one, or both, of those prerequisites: the equipment and/or the requisite skills. Besides, you can do credible work using other methods than TIG to join parts and surfaces.

Some fabricators have an affinity for physical attachments like nuts, bolts, and rivets. Others prefer MIG or TIG welding. It is a matter of preference. Below are some of the major jointure techniques and processes, and some of the advantages and disadvantages of each.

Non-Welding Jointure Techniques

Sheet metal screws, bolts, captive nuts, fastnuts, trim clips, welded and threaded studs, etc., are the quick and dirty methods employed by many automakers on their new vehicles to fasten some sheet metal parts to other parts and to substructures. The methods that use these items tend to be fast and non-skill intensive to perform. That's why factories use them. Unless they are being used to duplicate authentic factory methods, they should have little place in custom or restoration sheet metal fabrication.

Many of these factory methods are "blind" fastening techniques, meaning that they can be performed completely from one side, the outside, of a surface, without access to the related inside surface. This saves time and expense. In some situations, this makes it possible to secure parts that could not be fastened easily if access to their inside surfaces was required.

Rivets

As far as I know, pop rivets are fine for making household repairs to items like lawn chairs and refrigerator shelves. However, in the interest of protecting the public decency, Congress and the state legislatures should outlaw their use on custom cars and restored vehicles. These fasteners are both ugly and prone to generating corrosion in their immediate vicinities. This is particularly true if you insist on using pop rivets made of different metal than what you are joining, say, aluminum alloy rivets through steel, or steel rivets through alloy panels. Did I mention that I hate pop rivets?

By way of atonement for that outburst, I wish to state, categorically and emphatically, that I like, admire, and revere good "plain rivets." These have a formed head on one end, while the other end of their solid shaft is left blank for you to form, or as riveters call it, to "head." Installed correctly, rivets present attractive heads and good strength.

For more than 100 years, rivets were the mainstay for holding together ships, bridges, boilers,

There are dozens of devices to attach panels to substructure and to each other. From left to right on top are: a captive nut, a captive fastnut, a weldable captive nut, a self-positioning fastnut, and two simple fastnuts. Bottom: sheet metal screws with various head configurations. The screws and three left top row items are blind attachments.

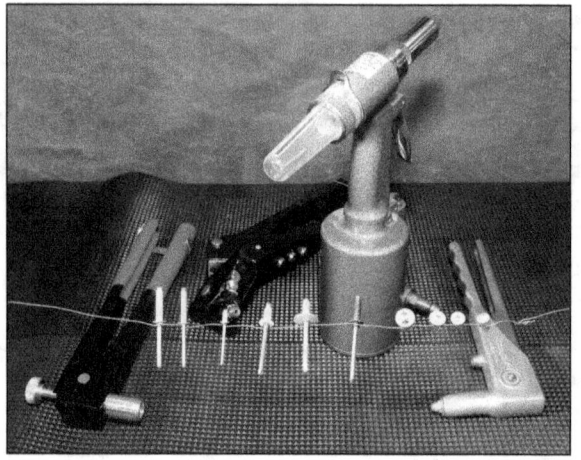

Behold deservedly despised and thoroughly despicable pop rivets (front), and their dastardly installation tools, in all of their ugly, rust provoking glory. If you leave them where they're visible, they're an embarrassment, and if you try to hide them, they come back through primer and paint to haunt and curse you.

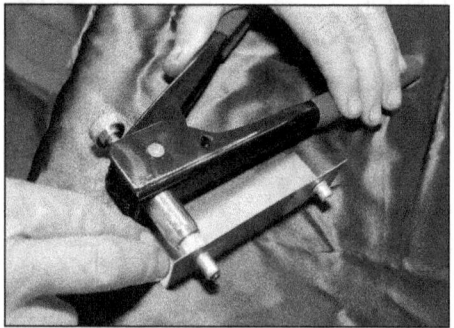

This nut riveting setup attaches threaded receptacles into sheet metal holes with a pop-rivet-type bond. The attachment on the right is completed. The one on the left is uncrimped. The aluminum nut rivet in a steel panel will be replaced with the correct steel nut rivet.

METHODS OF ATTACHMENT

An air rivet set is used to head a plain rivet. A finished rivet is shown on the right. A bucking bar in a vise is being used to back up the rivet that is being headed. You can also perform this operation manually with a hammer and rivet set.

locomotives, automobile frames, aircraft skins, and many other assemblies that were deemed too critical to fail. Of course, the rivets used in automotive fabrication are considerably smaller than those in most of those applications. I was just soliciting some respect for these old-fashioned fasteners. There are few sights lovelier than a series of perfectly positioned and formed rivet heads. Rosie the Riveter may not have been a pin-up girl, but her work was definitely pin-up quality.

Rivets are coming back in automotive custom fabrication work, maybe because they are pretty. Unfortunately, unlike their disreputable and distant cousins, pop rivets, their installation requires access to both sides of an assembly, but that can be pretty limited access, and is not always a critical consideration. Like pop rivets, conventional rivets are made from many different materials, including brass, copper, aluminum, and steel. Always use rivets of the same material that you are joining or you will have massive corrosion problems at the rivet sites.

Small rivets are installed cold, using a rivet set and bucking bar. Their heads can be crudely formed with a ball peen hammer, but a good rivet set is a much better way to head them. While welding and other attachment methods are often, but not always, covered up with filler and paint, rivets can be left to stand proud and look beautiful. Like really good welding, their visibility can potentially enhance the beauty of a sheet metal fabrication.

Installed correctly, rivets not only present attractive heads, they also offer good strength. However, unlike threaded fasteners, it is difficult to determine how tight installed rivets are, so it's best not to use them in torque-critical applications.

Adhesives

In recent years, body adhesives have come into increasing use in car manufacturing and auto body repair. Some of these adhesives yield strong and durable results, and can be used to advantage for some fabrication purposes. Many of them are designed to be used in tandem with resistance ("spot") welding or crimping, and provide added strength, along with sealing, sound deadening, squeak reduction, and corrosion resistance. These materials are available from local body shop supply locations and mail order houses. If you are not familiar with them, it may be worth your while to find out about them.

Crimping

Crimping, on the other hand, is a venerable and proven method of forming seams. Most door skins are crimped over their cores on three sides, as are hood skins, and some other assemblies. Crimping can be used in sheet metal fabrication to great advantage, as long as provision is made to protect the metal under the crimped seam from corrosion. Clean metal and a good seam sealer are the best defenses.

Soldering

Soldering has many valid uses, but little place in joining automotive parts or panels. Joints made with it are simply too weak for serious fabrication attachment purposes. Soldering should never be used for this function.

Brazing

Brazing is a process between soldering and welding. While soldering

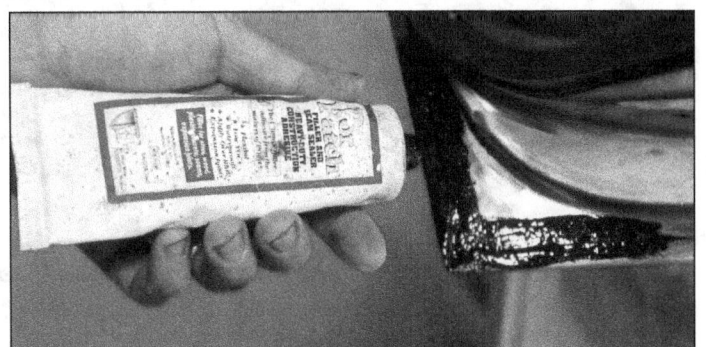

One secret to making successful crimp joints, such as door edge seams, is to get the metal at the joint interface as clean as possible and to apply a good seam sealer under and over the joint before it is completely closed.

is based only on the capillary attraction of melted solder to metal surfaces, and provides mostly mechanical adhesion, brazing uses higher temperatures and involves some molecular commingling of the braze and the brazed material's surface molecules. However, unlike true welding, brazing does not involve extensive molecular fusion bonds between surfaces and the grazing media. Brazing is done with brass rod or granules, or with silver based rod or wire (often called "silver soldering" in that case, but really a slightly lower temperature version of brazing).

Oxy-acetylene heat is used to braze joints. The brazing rod is coated with a flux (often borax based) either by its manufacturer, or by dipping slightly heated brazing rod in powered flux to adhere it to the rod, just before using it. Braze flows into areas between parts by capillary action, forming a thin and strong bond between them in these narrow spaces. It can also be formed into a raised bead over a joint, much like a conventional, rippled weld bead.

For fabrication work, brazing has two drawbacks, which may or may not be decisive in a given situation. Because it lacks the penetration of true welding, brazing cannot rival welding in strength. Also, brazing can promote a phenomenon known as "hydrogen embrittlement" at and near areas where it is used. This is a tendency to embed hydrogen atoms in metal. Hydrogen atoms are often found at the roots of cracks and tend to promote cracking. The flux used in brazing causes hydrogen embrittlement and can be a serious problem if sheet metal joints are subjected to strong and repeated mechanical forces or vibrations.

Although factories sometimes used brazing to make certain panel joints, it is not generally considered an appropriate procedure to use for this purpose today. While brazing's relatively low application temperatures are attractive for controlling distortion in sheet metal, there are too many problems with brazing to use it for all but a few non-critical fabrication joints. If you decide to employ brazing for panel jointure, it is best used for making lap and/or offset lap joints, never butt joints. (See Chapter 5 for a discussion of lap and offset lap welding configurations.) Besides, there are simply too many better ways available to join thin sections of metal.

Welding

A number of welding technologies are currently available. Each has certain benefits and drawbacks for joining sheet metal. While arc welding is still commonly used for structural welding, MIG and TIG welding are the preferred method for joining sheet metal. MIG welding is performed at lower amperages and therefore transfers less heat than arc welding. TIG welding is much slower and more difficult than MIG welding, but it does not produce as much heat and the results can be exceptional. Oxy-acetylene welding was commonly used for sheet metal joining, but MIG and TIG deliver far better results, so it has fallen out of favor.

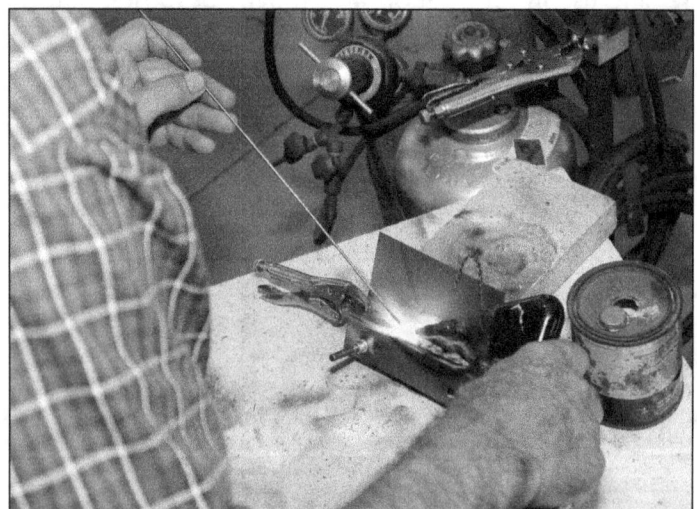

Brazing is not a good choice for making panel seams. As you can see, compared to electric welding, it produces excessive heat that distorts metal. Its flux can promote hydrogen embrittlement that later can cause cracking.

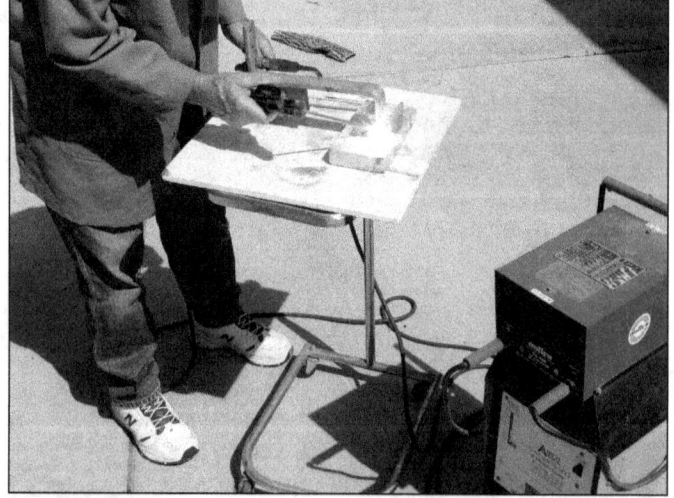

Stick welding has a place in automotive fabrication. Welding heavy structural supports, like this one, is an example of that place. However, there are far better ways to weld thin-section sheet metal.

Stick Welding

Stick welding was the first electric welding technology. It uses a flux-coated stick electrode to arc low-voltage, high-amperage current to a work piece joint. In this process, the arc melts and fuses metal transferred off the electrode into material on either side of a joint, forming a strong, fused bond. The flux that coats stick welding electrodes vaporizes into a gas and then coagulates into a slag. In both forms, it covers and protects the joint area from the rapid oxidation that would otherwise occur at welding and cooling temperatures. Other additives in the flux promote desirable characteristics, such as weld puddle formation, flow, and wetting.

Although stick welding was once used for sheet metal seams by both factories and body shops, it is rarely used to join sheet metal edges today. Again, there are just better ways to make sheet metal joints. For structural welding, stick welding is still very much in use.

MIG Welding

Welding using metal inert gas (more properly GMAW, for gas metal arc welding) was invented to reduce the waste of stick welding stubs. Early MIG welding was done with flux-cored wire, some of it still is. Modern thin-section MIG welders use a shielding gas to protect hot welds from excessive, high-temperature corrosion. These welders have become inexpensive, easy to operate, portable, and very effective. MIG is used extensively in the industry and is the welding mainstay in most body shops.

MIG welders operate on the "short arc" principle. An energized wire electrode and an inert gas (often C25, which is 25 percent CO_2 and 75 percent argon) are continuously fed out of the welding "gun's" tip, toward the grounded weld target. When the wire contacts the target, it creates an intense short circuit that melts the metal, and melts the welding wire's tip off, and onto the target metal. This melts a puddle in the welding target seam, as well, while producing a short-lived gap between the welding wire and the target, as the wire's tip melts off. Thus, the short circuit is broken, until more wire extrudes from the MIG gun and reestablishes contact with the target metal. Then, another short is established, repeating the cycle, typically about 200 times per second. This repeated cycle produces the molten puddle of commingled base and electrode metals that is the basis of fusion welding with consumable electrodes. It also gives off a characteristic "frying egg" sound that is often used to verify that wire speed (akin to amperage in stick welding) and voltage settings (somewhat like the rod-to-target distance in stick welding) are correct for the proper short arc cycle.

MIG welding can be used directly on steel materials. It can also be used on aluminum panels with a spool gun, which is an auxiliary gun that feeds aluminum wire a very short distance into a weld.

TIG Welding

Welding using tungsten inert gas (more properly GTAW for gas tungsten arc welding) is the premier shop welding process. It's a slow way to weld and requires considerable skill to perform, but the results are worth it. TIG welding utilizes very expensive equipment. Its most desirable characteristic is its very intense but highly concentrated local arc. That results in very little heat spread and distortion in metal near the weld area. This is often a terrific advantage. TIG welding's slowness makes it possible to better control what is happening. It just doesn't rush you. Also, TIG heat is so local that it is not necessary to leave much fit-up gap between parts to account for expansion during welding. TIG welding is usable on steel, stainless, and aluminum alloy materials. It is the method of choice for aluminum and stainless welding.

This modern MIG welder is fast, efficient, and reliable. Units like this one, from various manufacturers, are relatively inexpensive and nowhere near as skill-intensive as TIG and gas welding formats. That's why MIG welding is a favored approach to sheet metal fabrication welding.

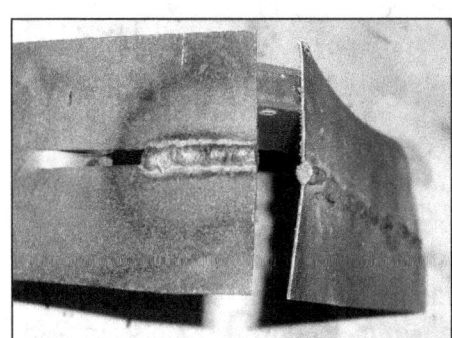

MIG welding is versatile and strong, but uses much more local heat than gas welding. This is a MIG seam weld closing a 3/16-inch gap! I don't recommend fit-up gaps this large, but I wanted to demonstrate what you can do with MIG welding when you have to.

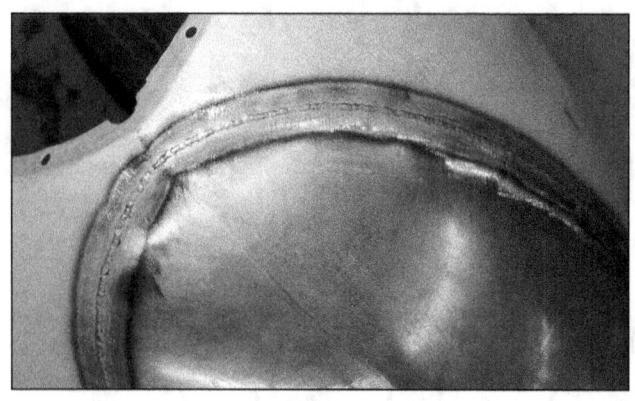

This TIG-welded fender top patch is strong, well penetrated, and tidy. It will be easy to grind and finish it. Almost no fit-up gap was used, but because TIG heat is very local, there is little welding-caused distortion to deal with.

Some TIG outfits use air-cooled torches, while others are liquid cooled. TIG is performed with a shaped tungsten electrode immersed in a shielding gas. The "tungsten" arcs to the target weld area, melting the metal there. A consumable rod may be fed into the weld puddle, as necessary, to provide extra metal for the puddle and resulting weld bead. TIG welding is probably the most difficult common welding process to master and certainly the most precise and controllable.

Oxy-Acetylene Gas Welding

Oxy-acetylene gas welding is at the other extreme from TIG in many respects. This method was once common in metal fabrication, but is now rarely used, simply because both MIG and TIG results far surpass what is commonly possible with torch welding (unless the torch welder possesses extraordinary skills).

In oxy-acetylene welding, a flame is used to move a molten puddle of metal down a weld seam, with filler rod added as necessary. Unfortunately, this process produces vastly more local heat than MIG and TIG electric welding approaches, causing all kinds of distortion issues. The arcane art of hammer welding makes it possible to control and reduce the effects of oxy-acetylene distortion, but it requires extreme skill and coordination, and still does not equal the results of electric welding. Aluminum torch welding is also relatively difficult, and is really closer to brazing than welding.

Spot Welding

Spot welding, a.k.a. "resistance welding," is the most common joining process in manufacturing automobile bodies today. It is commonly employed on steel panels, but there are special spot welders that perform welds on aluminum and stainless as well. Spot welding produces a superficial fusion weld of no great strength by simultaneously pressing together a spot in the metals to be joined, while running a very high-amperage current through the contact points (electrodes) that are doing the pressing. This creates an intense short circuit at the site of the pressure and fuses a spot in the surfaces of the two metals together. The copper welding electrodes used in spot welding are not consumed in the weld, but tend to pit, erode, and oxidize rapidly as the process is repeated. It is often necessary to dress or change them after you weld several spots.

The secret of great spot welding is to set the duration time for the weld long enough to produce a good bond, but not so long that the electrodes burn through, or too far into, the metals in the weld. Beyond that, it is important that the welding electrodes are clean, flat, and correctly configured. This means dressing and/or changing them fairly often, as they are used to maintain the correct tip area and surface quality. It is also critical that the layers of metal that you are spot welding are clean and physically in good contact with the welding tips, and with each other, at the site of the weld.

While spot welds lack the strength of welds made with other processes, they work well as a gang, that is, if they are used in sufficient

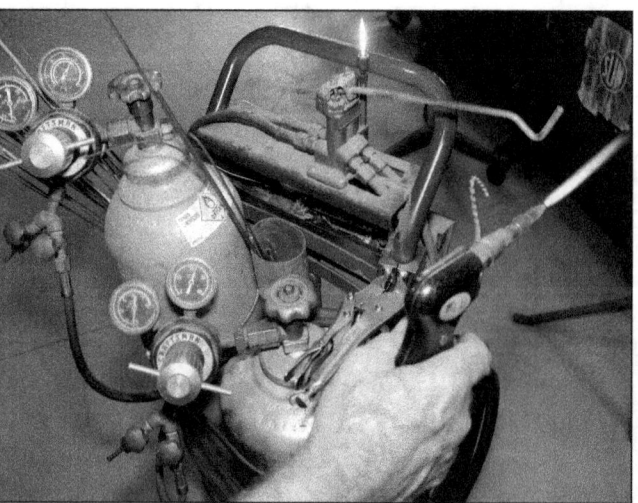

This oxy-acetylene welding outfit is fitted with a GasSaver. When the torch is hung on the Gas-Saver's hook, it shuts down the gas flow and extinguishes the flame. When the torch is removed from the hook, gas flows again and the torch can be lit off the GasSaver's pilot light.

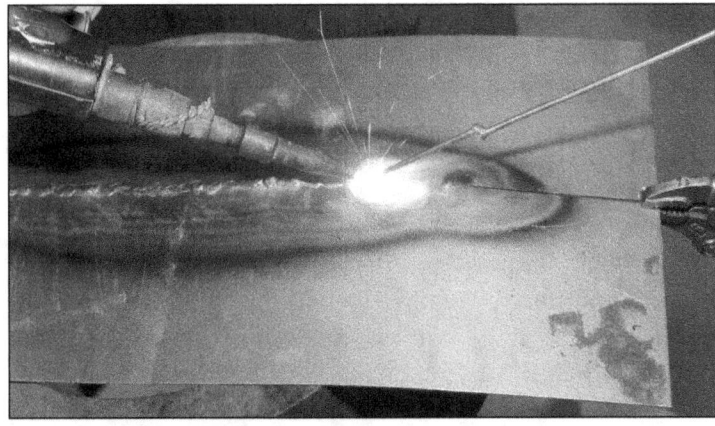
Gas welding sheet metal seams is an obsolete approach. It takes a lot of skill, and the results have more distortion than electrically welded seams. Getting a neat ripple pattern is very difficult and takes a lot of practice.

Our homemade conversion for a hand-held spot welder to a foot-operated unit saves a lot of time and produces improved results. It's great to have two hands free to position and hold what you are spot welding when you operate the welder with your foot.

numbers to attain good overall bond strength. Modern auto bodies are held together by upwards of 3,000 spot welds. It is that duplication that gives this technique adequate strength to hold vehicles together. Spot welds that are strong enough to do their job always leave surface dimpling in the welded metals. It is good practice to clean and level these areas after this process is completed.

There are spot welders available that produce blind spot welds; that is, welds performed entirely from one side of a part or panel. These can be very handy when you are dealing with limited access, or no access, to the back of the panel that you are welding.

Tips for Fabrication Welds

No matter your welding approach or what your skill level and experience are, there are several considerations that are critical to successful panel welding.

Tip #1

Use welding techniques and equipment appropriate to the job. While a stick welder fitted with sheet metal rod can be used to make sheet metal welds in fairly thick sections, this is not a particularly usable approach to 22-gauge mild steel materials. Spot welding works for some kinds of non-critical joints, but continuous welds are required for others. Always consider the needs of a situation when selecting a specific welding or other joining technique.

Tip #2

Always use good-quality supplies and equipment. Buying welding equipment and consumables from Skip's Welding Supply, Delicatessen, and Off-Track Betting Facility is probably not a great idea. Some supplies, such as welding consumables, are of vastly better quality than others. For example, there is welding wire out there that is consummate junk, and that should not be used for anything but tying off trash bags. Brand-name welding wire from a reputable supplier outperforms unbranded wire just about every time, usually by a large margin.

Tip #3

Metal welds better when it is clean than when it is contaminated. If you try to weld over rust, grease, or paint, you end up with inclusions of these things in your finished welds. This compromises their strength and paintability, and can cause major

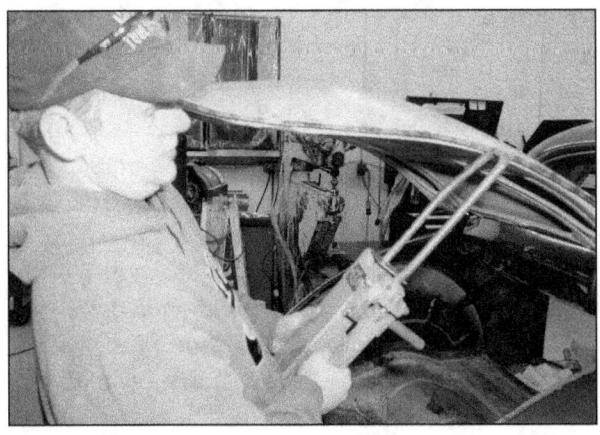
The secrets of making good spot welds are clean metal in good contact, well-maintained electrodes, and correct timer settings. Spot welders are heavy, making them somewhat hard to handle without a counter-balance reel. Good overall strength requires multiple spot welds.

CHAPTER 12

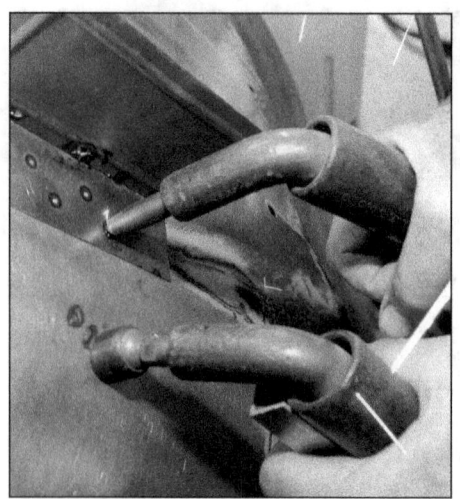

This blind spot-welding system can make welds completely from one side of a job. That can come in very handy when you lack decent access to the back of what you are spot welding.

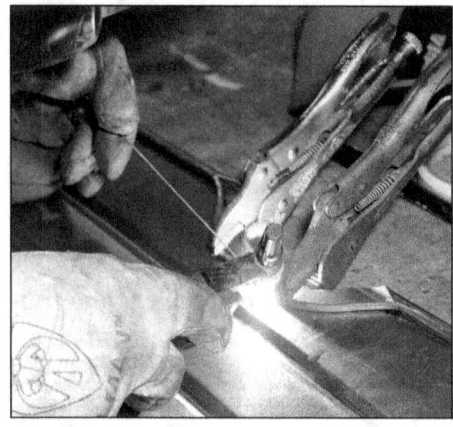

Joining the wrapped wire in this panel requires keeping everything perfectly in place while you weld. Two sets of locking pliers work flawlessly to accomplish this. After it is joined, the wire will be wrapped with the metal that extends beyond it.

ple, while it is possible to MIG weld 22-gauge metal with .030- or even .035-inch wire, it is much easier and better to use .023– to .025-inch wire. Settings are the same way. Many different amp and voltage settings produce welds in the same material, but some combinations are far more effective than others. It is your job to discover and remember which ones work best for you, and in which situations they excel.

Tip #5

Whether you are using gas, MIG, TIG, or resistance welding panels, fit-up is always a critical issue. In the case of MIG welds, the fit-up of parts should separate them by between the thickness of a dime and a nickel. That may seem like a lot of gap to fill, but it really isn't. Fitting them closer than that causes distortion, as the part's edges expand against each other when they are heated. Larger gaps than that are hard to fill and compromise the strength of the welds. On the other hand, TIG welding uses such local heat that it requires almost no fit-up gaps, because there is very little expansion. It pays to know the best fit-up for what you are doing and to provide it continuously for your welds.

Tip #6

Along with gapping welds properly, it is important to fixture the pieces that you are welding securely, to prevent them from moving while you are welding them. Welding a moving target adds an unnecessary degree of challenge to the job, but gains nothing in return. This is particularly true when parts move in relation to each other as you try to weld them. It is worth taking the time to use fixturing methods like locking pliers, magnets, Clecos, etc., to hold what you are welding securely. Then, it is best to make tack welds where they can take over the holding job.

Tip #7

The biggest enemy to great fabrication welding is the distortion that comes with welding heat. TIG welding largely avoids this problem. MIG and torch welding can be accomplished in ways that reduce it.

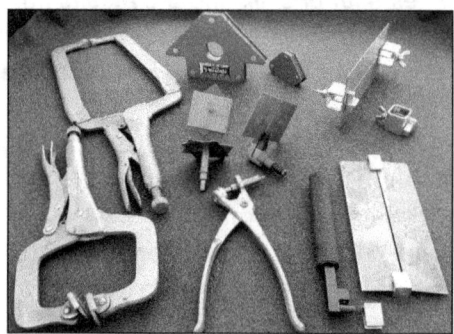

Locking pliers (left) are great for holding sheet metal parts in place for welding. Welding magnets and Cleco holders (center) work wonderfully for setting up welds. Edge holding devices (right) can be great aids to welding sheet metal.

Specialty locking pliers can make holding things in place easy. The ones at the top have several different jaw configurations. The one at the bottom has interchangeable jaws (just above it). It is shown here with one custom jaw, with the jaw that it replaces (left).

appearance problems down the road. It is always worth the time to clean metal before you weld it.

Tip #4

It is important to use the right settings and specification materials for your welding purposes. For exam-

METHODS OF ATTACHMENT

The copper welding spoon (left) is a fairly new innovation in thin-section welding. It works well, but almost requires a second person to move it along behind the seam as you weld. The welding tape (right) protects the backs of welds from oxidation during welding.

Weld-through primer is offered by several suppliers and works well to protect welds from rust. It can be used with MIG, TIG, or spot welding. Its best application is in lap and offset lap welds, particularly when they are spot welded.

The first line of defense against heat-induced distortion is to keep welding heats down. The best way to do this is to avoid running long, continuous weld beads. There are two easy ways to do this. The first is to weld tacks or short runs between tacks or short runs, filling in until a weld covers your seam. This greatly reduces heat buildup by allowing cooling in each tack or short bead before the next is applied to it.

A variant of this is to build short bead sections on the ends of cooling bead sections. You can do this with any form of bead welding technique, gas torch, MIG, or TIG. You weld a short bead, say 1/2 to 3/4 inch, and stop. After the fresh end of the bead has cooled considerably, but not completely, you add another similar bead to it. This greatly reduces heat buildup.

There was an old trick used in stainless welding that employed backup tape on the backside of the weld. When you wanted to protect that area from oxidation, you applied a backup tape bandage to it. It worked. The back of the weld would be as clean, or cleaner, than the shielded front. The tape used a

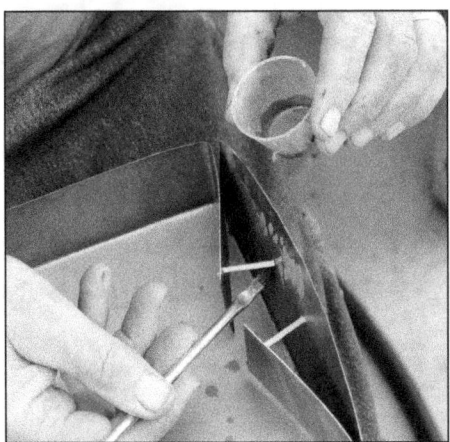

Weld-through primer is basically a heat-resistant, zinc-rich paint. If you can't spray it conveniently behind a weld area, you can brush it into the places that you need to protect. Note how this battery box's overlaps are held open to allow brush application access for weld-through primer.

high-temperature tolerant adhesive and a fiberglass bandage that gave off a neutral gas at elevated temperatures. This sealed the area and kept it bathed in an inert gas. Unfortunately, backup tape was expensive and finicky to use.

A modern tool performs many of the same functions, and is both inexpensive and reusable. It is called a welding spoon, a curved, portable copper backup plate with a handle. The spoon is held directly behind an area being electrically welded. It doesn't create an inert gas environment, but it does prevent welding drop-out, i.e., melting through the material that you are welding. It also removes heat from the backs of welds, reducing distortion.

Welding spoons aren't needed for TIG welding but can save a lot of grief when you are welding very thin sections with MIG. Since I use both hands to guide a MIG torch, I usually have someone else move the spoon under the area that I am welding.

Tip #8

Use weld-through primer where two pieces of material are lap or offset lap welded together. These types of joints are very vulnerable to rust, because the small spaces between the metal sheets tend to attract and move moisture and contaminants by capillary action, creating the perfect environment for rust to start and propagate. After welding is completed, it is difficult to get paint into these spaces to protect them.

Weld-through primer is a zinc-rich (typically 95-percent zinc powder) paint that tolerates high heat. The zinc in it is conductive, so you can spot weld through it. Painted between metal that is welded, particularly spot welded, the paint offers some barrier protection to moisture, and, to some extent, fuses into the weld. The zinc in the paint protects steel in the same way that galvanizing, which is also a zinc coating, protects a bucket. Zinc ions have a tendency to migrate into scratches and other breaches, making zinc a sacrificial ion coating. Aren't those ions nice? If you use weld-through primer where metal sheets join, it greatly retards the formation of rust. If you don't use it in those locations, expect to see rust before too long.

CHAPTER 13

SMALL DEMONSTRATION PROJECT: THE LITTLE BLACK BOX

Even if you've been skipping around a lot in this book, you probably noticed that the examples involve two jobs, fabricating two specific parts: a small electrical junction box cover and a large tractor fender. These projects were chosen for demonstration consistency and because they were both very challenging jobs in their own right, and also because they were very different from each other in scale. Both jobs required basic procedures and skills, like planning, measuring, patterning, forming, and finishing, among many others. Both were complex and challenging projects, because those who did them had never tried to do anything exactly like them before. I am happy to report that both jobs came out successfully, at, or beyond, the fabricators' expectations.

This chapter details the crafting of the small electrical junction box cover. Its fabrication will be described from start to finish, so that you can follow it exactly as it progressed. That includes mistakes as well as minor triumphs and successes. (Chapter 14 details the fabrication of several John Deere 1020 orchard tractor fenders.)

On the left is our replica of TLBB (The Little Black Box) in primer and on the right is the original LBB. This was a fairly difficult project, because it presented some problems that were hard to solve. It also illustrated many of the common issues in metal fabrication.

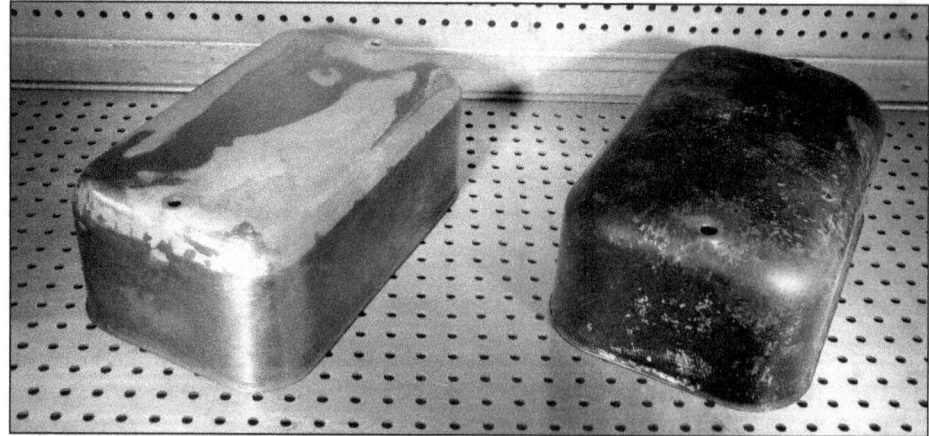

Our reproduced box, before it was primed (left), next to the original LBB (right). This job required extreme dimensional accuracy in some very small spaces. Figuring out how to create the bottom flange was among the most difficult issues in this fabrication.

SMALL DEMONSTRATION PROJECT: THE LITTLE BLACK BOX

We made no attempt to reproduce the inside of the original box, but if we were to do this job again, we would butt weld the top and bottom pieces of our fabrication, producing an accurate replica of both the inside and outside of TLBB.

Meet the Little Black Box

This is an electrical junction box cover from a 1936 KB Lincoln. Like most of the parts in an automobile, it is a mundane, innocuous little part that probably cost the Ford Motor Company far less than a buck when it was new. It was made in one or two draws by deep draw dies mounted in a stamping press. It is quite possible that the inner die was an expanding-type device.

This is a part that probably never gave offense to anyone, unless it got lost or mislaid. The truth is: This kind of small part is very easy to lose or leave off a car in the heat of resolving some great electrical issue. The result of that sequence of events is that there is enough of a shortage of these covers to make them hard to find.

A friend of mine, who owns a 1936 KB Lincoln, was able to borrow an original cover, and asked me to make a replica of it in my shop. I suspected that I could do it, but wanted no part of this job. It looked like it would take a lot of work to recreate such an insignificant part, with little glory available for doing it successfully. My friend pointed out that it was actually very significant to him, because its absence made for negative comment every time he raised his Lincoln's hood on the side where the little black box was missing.

I gave in, and my friend and sheet metal sidekick, Herb Statz, and I set about figuring out how to make this innocuous, little item. Along the way, we made our share of mistakes, learned a few things, and finished the job with acceptable results, and without having to restart it at any point. We proved for certain one thing that I had only suspected, that it would take a lot more work and time to fabricate this part than seemed reasonable.

On the good side, if I ever have to make another similar electrical box cover, or anything like it, I have some ideas for improving our approach to fabricating it. In another try, I'm sure that I could advance the speed and quality of our results. That's one of the great things about sheet metal fabrication work; you have the opportunity to constantly improve your ideas for and approaches to it.

There were three basic problems in fabricating this part. It required high dimensional accuracy, because it has to fit to a closely toleranced, existing base, and its hold-down studs have to align perfectly with the two holes in its top. Even the 1/2-degree inward slope of its sides, from its base to its top, must be preserved for it to look right. The slight concave curve of its long sides should also be maintained for purposes of authenticity.

The second problem in constructing this item is to recreate the small flange on its bottom edge. This is a small detail, but a nettlesome one. It is hard to form this flange around the box's corner radii, after the box shape is achieved, and it is difficult to pre form it accurately enough in the box's four sides to fold them down, shape them, and still have it come out in the same place at all four corner junctions. It is also hard to hold metal in a brake for such a short flange lip, or to trim a larger lip accurately to such a short length. The problem of the flange is not one of those issues that we could solve when we got there. It would have been too late by then. We needed to have a plan for forming that flange from the beginning of the project. As it turned out, this seemingly simple problem had a simple solution. It's great when things work out that way, but I never count on it.

The third problem was location. This box mounts on the firewall of a car and is exposed to terrible conditions: moisture, heat, chemicals, minor impacts and abrasions, and occasional bursts and streams of foul language. More important, it is visually prominent in what will often be terrific lighting. Any defect in it will rival the visibility of a star crack in your windshield, about level with your nose. Of course, the solution to this problem is to form the piece as close to perfection as possible.

The Basic Plan

The first, most basic, and most important step in fabricating the little black box (hereafter referred to as TLBB and LBB) was to formulate a workable plan for constructing it. I would love to show you photographs of our process for doing this, but I

CHAPTER 13

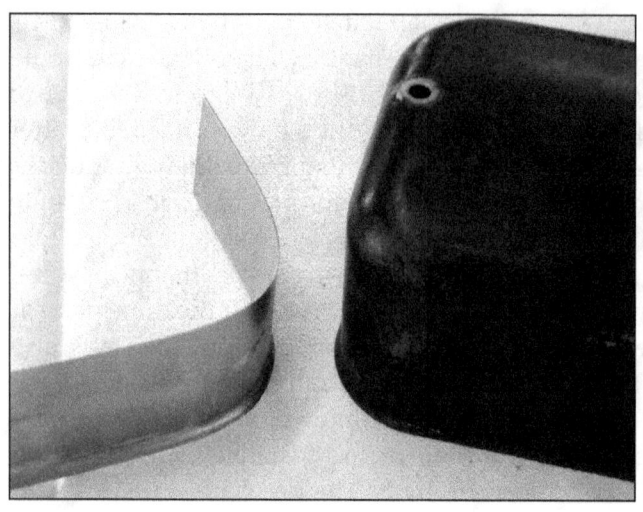

The most difficult issue in planning this fabrication was reproducing TLBB's bottom flange. We succeeded in replicating this feature experimentally in the test piece (left) and used that technique in the final fabrication. Thorny issues in any fabrication are best solved before you start it.

would need a series of CT-scans or MRIs of Herb's and my brains to graphically illustrate it, because the plan was formed in our heads. We discussed all of the obvious, and many of the not-so-obvious ways in which we might construct TLBB. We considered the advantages and drawbacks of each possibility.

In the end, we adopted a plan that maximized both the probability that it would work and the promise that our result would be of excellent quality. Inevitably, we may have missed something, and there may be a better way, or ways, to do this job. I already have my suspicions that there is. However, at the very least, our plan worked, and worked well.

We decided to construct TLBB in two pieces, and then to join them. Breaking TLBB's fabrication into two separate constructions allowed us to deal separately with the problems of each piece. A curved top piece included the metal in TLBB's top and down its sides to where they became flat. The bottom surround piece (hereafter referred to as "the skirt") included those flat sides, the lower corners, and the bottom flange. This division of the job into two pieces isolated the problem of the bottom flange, making it part of a piece that was otherwise simple to form. We knew how to form the top piece, and how to fabricate everything in the skirt, except its bottom flange. That was a big "except," and we had to solve that last remaining issue before we could start patterning and forming metal.

We knew that we would not be able to form the skirt's flange in our sheet metal brakes, but we tried anyway. We were right; we couldn't brake it to hold the radius that we wanted, without braking a lot more metal than we needed in the flange, and then facing a very finicky trimming job. Our next idea was to hammer the flange over a form. We ground a form into some scrap strap iron and hammered a piece of 22-gauge 1018 steel (the material selected for this job) over it. To our considerable surprise, not to mention delight, this worked perfectly. At that point, I noticed that the experimental hammer form that we had ground into the piece of scrap strap stock looked remarkably like the radius on the back edge of some angle iron that we had in our stock rack. So, we used the angle iron for our flange hammer form. The flange that we hammered on the angle iron was an accurate rendition of TLBB's flange radius and width. It was uniform, straight, and of consistent width, just what we needed. That solved half of the problem of creating the skirt's flange, leaving only the issue of how to bend the flanged metal into the format of TLBB's corners.

In the great tradition of imagining problems that don't exist, we had assumed that bending our flange around TLBB's corner radii would either flatten or fracture it. However, when we couldn't think of any clever way to avoid this, we decided to simply try bending it to see what would

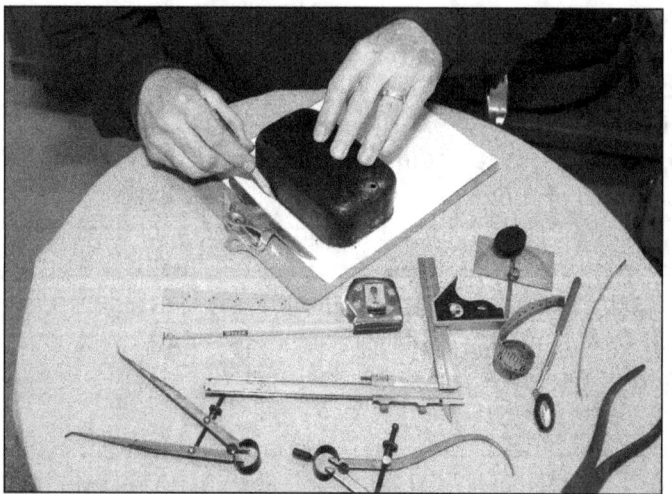

The first steps in any good fabrication involve measuring and modeling the part or panel that you intend to make. Even if you are creating a new piece or panel from scratch, you need data for it. These measuring tools are basic to this phase of fabrication.

116   **AUTOMOTIVE SHEET METAL FORMING & FABRICATION**

actually happen. Imagine our surprise and glee when we discovered that bending a piece of our flanged material around a socket with a radius similar to that in TLBB's side bends resulted in no flattening or fracturing. Our flanged test bend sample made the bend easily and gracefully, while remaining undamaged and flat. And the moral of that story is: *Always try simple, straightforward approaches first, even when they appear to have little likelihood of success.* Hey, they may work and save a lot of time and effort in the bargain.

Our planning was now complete, having solved our major fabrication issue by discovering that it wasn't much of an issue after all. We could now proceed to fabricate TLBB.

Preliminaries

After planning, the next step in fabrication is to record the exact dimensional reality of what you are going to make. There are many ways to take and to record the measurements that are necessary to support good sheet metal fabrication work. What you do, and how you do it, depends on the job, on your preferences, and on your available instruments. Since we were duplicating a part and not creating a new one from scratch, we were in possession of the original, so capturing all relevant dimensions might not seem to be very important. In fact, it was, because the original piece did not lend itself to checking several critical dimensions of the new piece that we were going to fabricate.

For example, the bend radii at the top edges and side corners of TLBB could not be gauged and transferred usefully, directly from the original box to the new box. Templates were

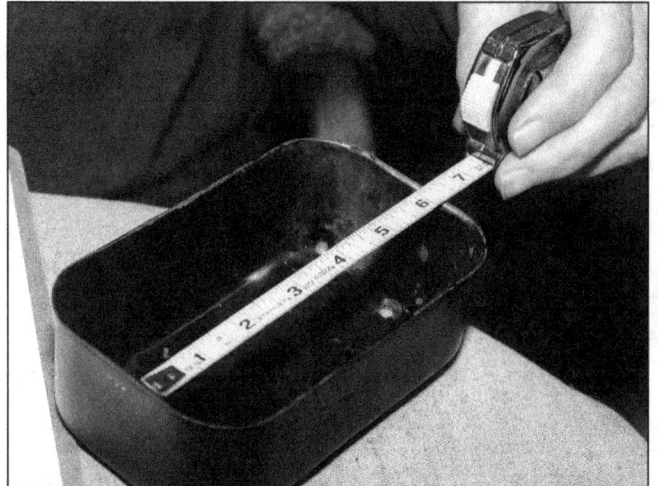

Some measurements are pretty basic and employ standard measuring tools, such as tape measures. In this fabrication, tape measuring is not accurate enough for final measurements, but it does produce rough data to confirm fine data that will be gathered later.

This depth measurement is accurate enough to be useful for the area that is being measured. I like to gather all kinds of data, sometimes by different methods, and then sort through it for what will be most useful and accurate for later use.

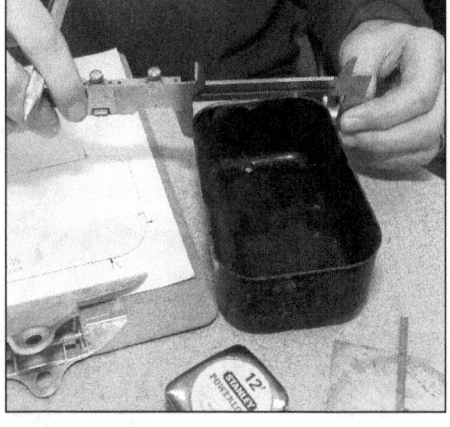

The critical flange area in this fabrication required precise measurement. The technique that is shown here fits that bill. It is important to record all of the data that you gather as you gather it.

needed to capture that data in ways that would allow meaningful comparisons of the original to the new piece. To do the essential validation of our work, we needed relevant data and patterns that accurately and usefully interpreted the original part.

For me, the best way to accumulate information on a part like TLBB is to measure it in every way that I can think of, collect the data, and sort out how to use it later, as I need it. If I don't do that, I often find that

I missed measuring some useful, or even critical, dimension, or that the measurements that I took might have been more useful with different measuring and patterning approaches, or with different measuring devices. My obsessive approach to measuring, modeling, and patterning may serve you well, or it may drive you nuts. The important thing is to take enough measurements, in different enough ways, to reach a good comfort level with the data that you collect.

CHAPTER 13

 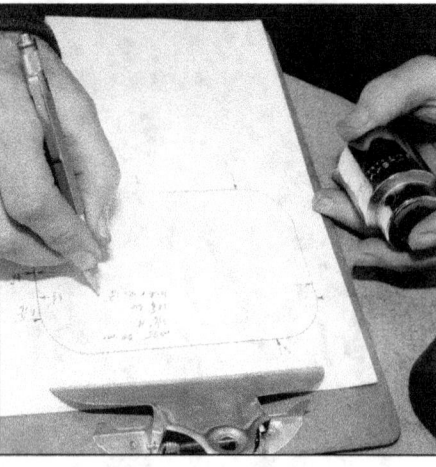

This step involved modeling the original part. We selected a 1/2-inch socket that was very close to the radius of the inside of the corner contour of TLBB, noting which socket it was. This gave us a model of the contour that we could later use for light forming purposes.

This pin-type profile taker is very handy for capturing fine details and contours. These instruments are relatively inexpensive and come in various types and sizes. A larger plastic version of this tool is shown at the top of page 119.

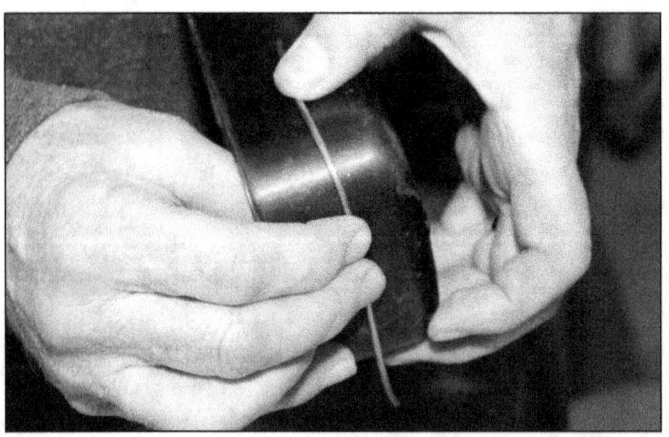

Using a piece of #12 copper wire to capture TLBB's outside corner curve gave us a simple way of validating it in our fabrication. It is much more useful for that purpose than the original part would have been.

My feelings about this are conditioned by too many encounters with situations where I wished that I had taken some measurement or created a jig that would later have been useful, but that I had not thought of or bothered to take or to create. It is also a good idea to take redundant measurements in different ways. Some may turn out to be more useful, accurate, or permanent than others.

In taking and transferring the measurements for TLBB, we tried to consider what would be useful and accurate information, erring on the side of too much rather than too little data. We tried to use all of the traditional methods and models employed in measuring and modeling, such as calipers, pin-type profile takers, and tape measures. We also tried to be innovative, taking a critical circumference measurement with measuring tape borrowed from my wife's sewing box, marking the small and critical hold-down stud holes onto a paper pattern with a tiny lead pencil that was left over from some long-ago forgotten magazine subscription promotion, and preserving a physical facsimile of TLBB's skirt corner radius by noting and recording its similarity to a socket wrench in my tool chest. That last one was just in case our skirt fabrication's corners required a pattern form that was substantial enough to take a little light hammering.

And for all of that, our first concrete move in transferring TLBB dimensions to our work was to trace the original cover's skirt flange directly onto a piece of wood. We didn't use our data or patterns for that, because we had the original piece, and it was more accurate to trace TLBB's footprint directly from it.

SMALL DEMONSTRATION PROJECT: THE LITTLE BLACK BOX

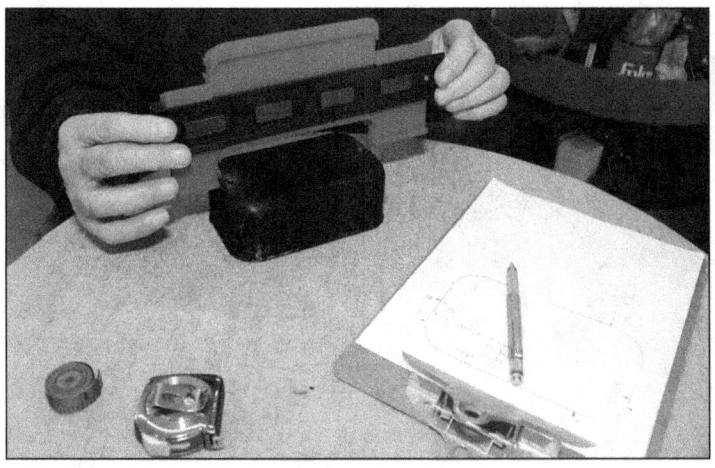

This large, plastic tab-type profile pattern taker is very useful for capturing contours in long and/or deep pieces. Its magnetic base can be used to hold it in a position. It can also be ganged to a second similar unit for use on very long items.

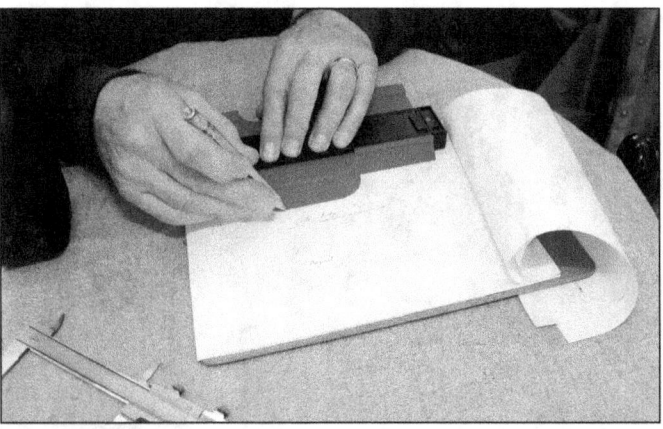

All data should be labeled and recorded as quickly and accurately as possible in a permanent format for later reference. It also should be clearly labeled. What a profile represents seems obvious when you take it, but years later it may become a mystery.

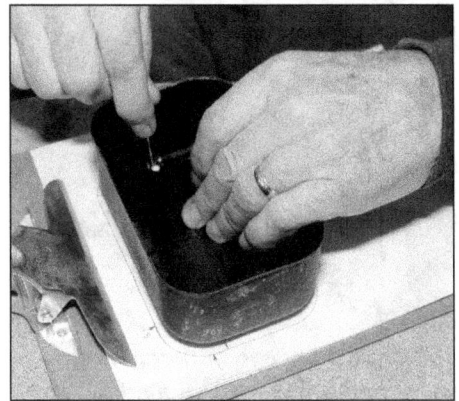

It was critical to accurately locate the hold-down stud holes in TLBB's top for later reference. A tiny Time Magazine *promotional pencil from thirty years ago was perfect for scribing through these holes. If you didn't save one, a mechanical pencil lead in a brass capillary tube will do.*

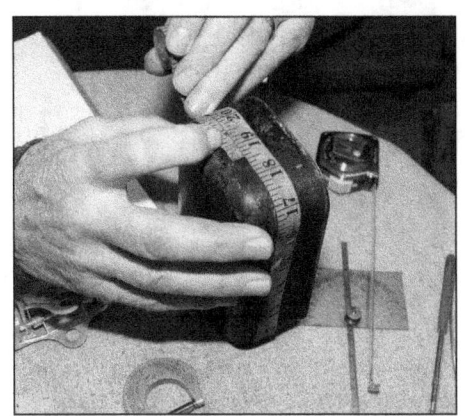

A cloth sewing tape might not seem very appropriate for measuring sheet metal, but it can yield summary measurements of irregular shapes that can be difficult to take any other way. I often use a cloth tape to confirm the total of measurements taken by more accurate and conventional means.

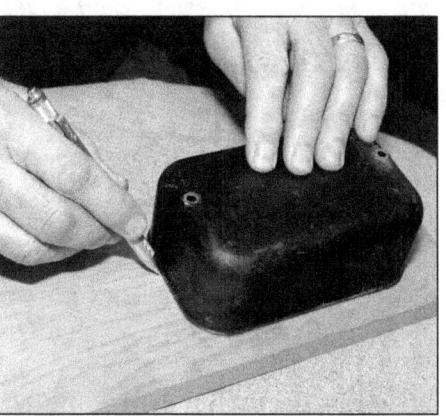

If you have an original part that can be used to model shapes or patterns, you will find it better to use it directly, instead of using some representation of it. Patterns are used where you don't have or can't use an original part for modeling or dimensions.

Forming the Top Piece

I did use our dimensional data to calculate the width of TLBB's skirt flange, from its outer edge to TLBB's inner bottom dimension. Subtracting that width using a compass gave us the actual inside bottom dimensions to which we would form both TLBB's top section and skirt.

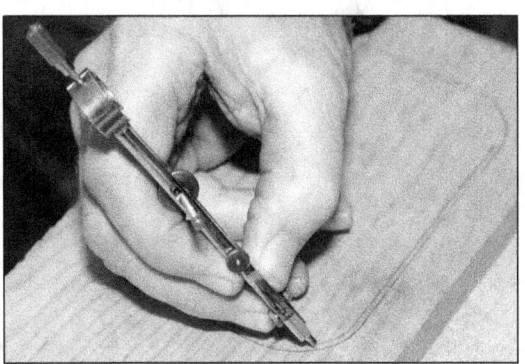

A compass is used to subtract TLBB's flange width and material thickness from its outside dimensions to represent its inside footprint. The tracing of the original part has been aided by data from measurement and modeling to produce a dimensional representation that could not be traced directly.

We cut a piece of 1-inch-thick pine board to shape as a hammer form for TLBB's top piece. The wood from which we cut it was very useful for fine tuning the top piece's bent edges and for forming TLBB's skirt section.

Initial three-dimensional shaping of the top hammer form wood was done on a table disc sander, with its table set at 45 degree to the disc, an average of the hammer form's rounded angles.

Sawing our pattern out of wood, along the line for TLBB's inner bottom diameter gave us two useful models, one for forming the top of the box over the cutout piece, and the other for patterning its skirt from the piece from which the top cutout was taken. The thickness of the saw blade roughly accounted for the 1/2 degree of outward slope in TLBB's skirt, from its top to its bottom.

The cutout piece was now shaped into a hammer form for TLBB's top section. The piece from which it was cut (hereafter referred to as the "outline piece") was laid carefully aside for later use.

The top pattern piece was mechanically sanded to our estimated contour of TLBB's top's side contours, and then hand filed to further refine its shape. At this point, we discovered that our hammer form was too shallow to indicate where TLBB's sides stopped curving, so we glued and screwed additional wood to its bottom. Later, we added thin sections of wood to its top to give us

The sanded 45-degree flats on the hammer form's top edges were further sanded on an inflatable pneumatic drum sander to average that edge into the curves of the original piece. At this point, we were only seeking the rough shape. Note that our hammer form has acquired a base.

The top curves and corners on the hammer form were now filed for consistency and straightness. This is still a rough approximation of TLBB's actual shape. The base that we screwed to our hammer form is already proving to be useful.

We added wood to both the top and bottom sides of our hammer form to give it more depth. A sheet metal lateral template, made from the original part, was now applied to our hammer form. It fit very well.

SMALL DEMONSTRATION PROJECT: THE LITTLE BLACK BOX

High spots were marked with blue die on the hammer form and sanded with an electric detail sander. Note that a metal shield is being used to protect an area that we wanted to avoid sanding.

Final shaping of the hammer form was accomplished with a file wrapped in 180-grit abrasive paper and with the same paper backed by various softer materials. The hammer form was constantly rechecked against our metal template.

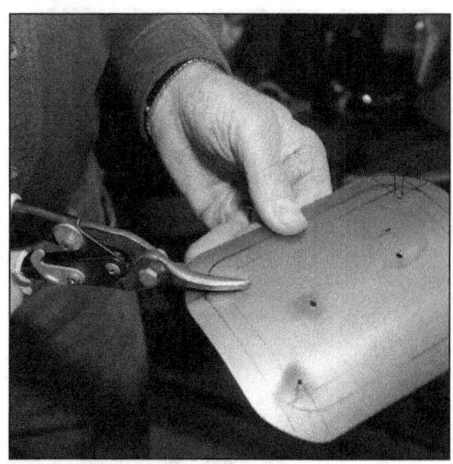

Herb cut corner reliefs into our top piece stock. Some of our patterning transferred to the piece. The holes at the cutout apexes will prevent cracking. The two center holes are for securing the piece. Note the mild lateral curvature that we slip rolled into the metal.

We annealed the corner areas before we even started to form our top piece because we knew that they would work harden quickly. You can see the curve that we had slip rolled into the piece to capture the original's lateral curvature.

A large plastic mallet was the first tool that we used to bend the top piece's sides in and corners around. Even annealed, there was some springback in the metal after it was hammered. Note the top hold-down piece that secures the work piece to the hammer form.

enough material to more accurately indicate TLBB's top contours. Using a metal pattern template of TLBB's top lateral contour that we had made from the original part, we refined the shape of our pattern with some mechanical fine sanding. Sanding the top pattern piece with a file wrapped in 180-grit paper advanced its dimensional accuracy. Checks against our templates indicated that our accuracy was, at worst, a few thousandths of an inch off in a few places.

This may seem like a lot of work just to make an accurate hammer form, but it is nothing compared to the amount of work that would have been required if we had tried to form our piece over an inaccurate pattern and had to correct those inaccuracies.

Our next move was to transfer the paper pattern for the top piece to the metal. Then, the following step was to slip roll the top piece into

CHAPTER 13

After the rough shape of the top piece was hammered out with the large plastic mallet, it was refined with a traditional hammer and dolly approach. The dolly was used to keep the top of the piece from springing up, while glancing downward blows were struck with the hammer.

The outline pattern was used to confine the top piece as it was hammered into correct edge curves with door skinning and ball-peen hammers. Note the top piece's upside-down mounting on its hammer form. Also note the adjustment screw in the outline pattern's entry cut for minor sizing adjustments.

roughly the mild lateral curvature of TLBB's top. Herb then cut out what we estimated would be the correct amount to close the top's corners around our form. Our gap estimate ended up being too large, but not so large that we could not weld the top pieces' corners shut.

Because we knew that to match the original part we would have to massively deform the metal in the areas of the top piece's corners, Herb annealed the metal in the corners to make it as soft as possible for that part of the job.

The metal top piece was now screwed to the top of our top hammer form, and its sides were persuaded into desired rough contours with a plastic mallet. This was followed with some sterner hammer and dolly work to bring the top's corners and sides into closer approximations of their correct shapes.

The top piece was now circumferentially bound with a hose clamp, pulled into proper shape, and measured. The amount that it had to be pulled in was noted, as a guide to how far the metal still needed to be moved.

Next, the outline pattern piece was used to refine the side bends in TLBB's top piece. A door-skinning hammer and a ball-peen hammer were used for this work. The top piece was beginning to come into its correct shape.

The top piece was now circumferentially bound with a large hose

We did more work with several different hammers to bring in the top piece's sides, and make them straight. Our hammer form certainly came in very handy as a mount to hold the top piece while we worked on it.

clamp to bring its sides pretty close to their final contour dimensions, and the top's inside lateral dimensions were measured to check their accuracy. The measurements indicated that we needed a smaller radius bend on the top's long sides, as well as laterally straighter side bends. At this point, our long side bends were

AUTOMOTIVE SHEET METAL FORMING & FABRICATION

SMALL DEMONSTRATION PROJECT: THE LITTLE BLACK BOX

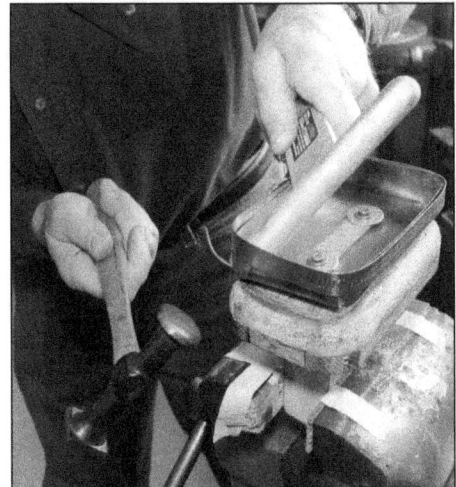

With the surrounding hose clamp still in place, a bar dolly and a mildly crowned hammer were used to bring the top piece's corners into place. Note that the hose clamp is raised slightly in the area of the corner that is being shaped.

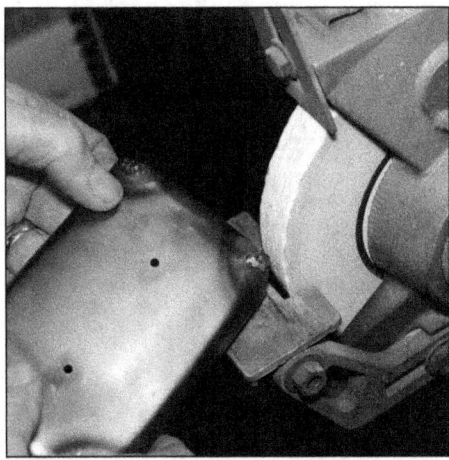

Since welding the corners shut required closing 1/8-inch gaps in some places, far more than is ideal for this kind of situation, there was a plenty of weld area and lots of extra weld metal to finish. Our first step to remove it was to roughly shape the outside corners on a bench grinder.

The second step in finishing the corners was with a right-angle pneumatic die grinder and a slightly flexible disc. An 80-grit paper was used, because it cut slowly and gave us lots of time to work carefully.

The insides of the top piece's corners were ground with a grinding burr in an air die grinder to remove excess weld and to shape them. This method rapidly removed metal from the concave areas.

An electric grinder with a tapered conical stone was used to smooth the inside corner areas that had been ground with the grinding burr. This brought them to a smoother finish.

slightly bowed. These deviations were now corrected with more hammer forming.

Our attention now turned to forming TLBB's corners as accurately and smoothly as possible. At this point, we realized that we had cut corner gaps that were a bit too wide (about 1/8 inch) but not so wide that they could not be welded shut. After welding the corners, we finished the outsides of the welds on a bench grinder and with various grinding discs. The insides of the corners were ground smooth with an air die grinder and with conical grinding stones in an electric grinder.

We had left plenty of extra metal when we cut out the piece for TLBB's top. We now measured exactly how far back to cut the top piece's sides to mesh at the correct depth for the skirt depth dimensions that we had selected. Applying tape to indicate the top's depth cut line, we marked its edge with a felt-tip pen against the tape, and sawed the top piece to dimension with a hacksaw. Final height dimensioning and flatness for the top piece were achieved on a belt sander. The top piece was now finished.

CHAPTER 13

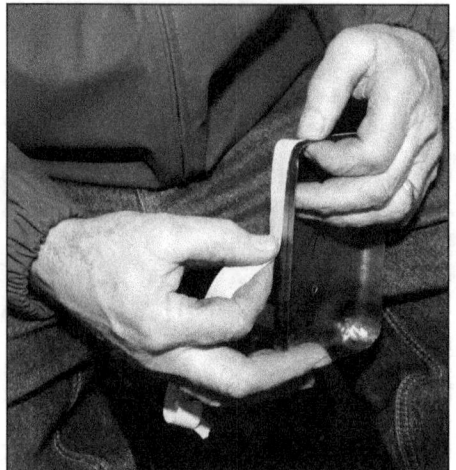

We knew the exact depth at which to cut the top piece for dimensionally correct assembly to the skirt. The line visible in the photo was a reference for flatness. Tape was applied at exactly the correct cut depth, and its position was marked against the tape's bottom edge.

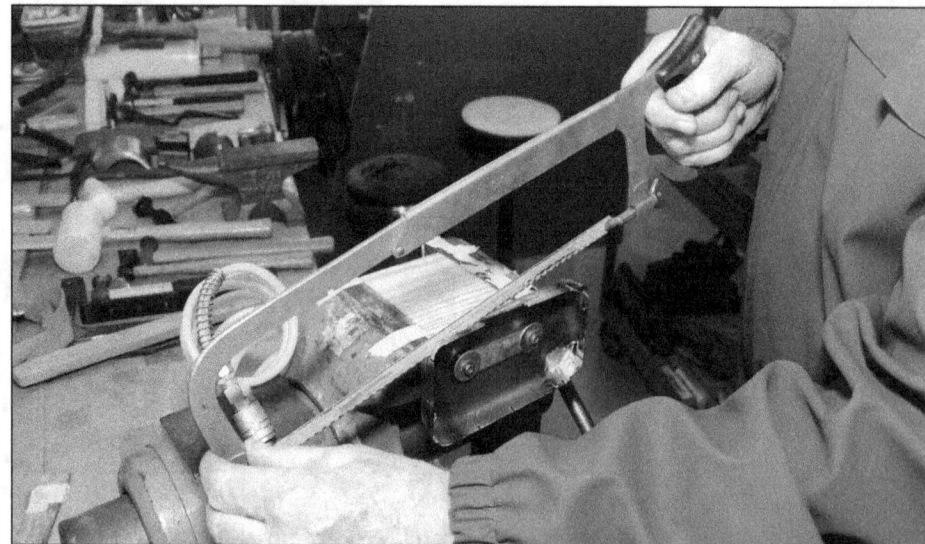

We went real high tech in our choice of cutting tool to trim the top at the marked line—a good, old hacksaw. There are fancier ways to do this job, but none that are much better.

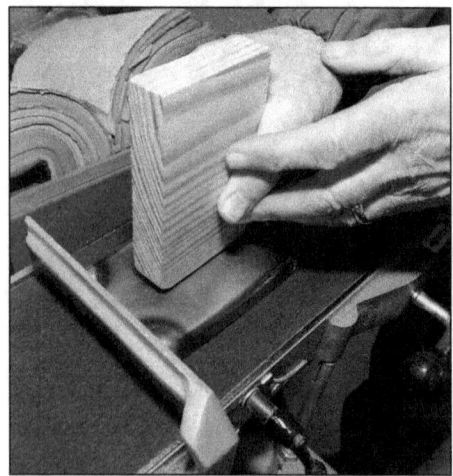

Of course, our hacksaw cut left rough edges, and deviated slightly in places, from our marked cut line. Those deficiencies were corrected by sanding the top piece's lower edge on a belt sander.

Making the Skirt

Our early experiment had informed us that we could hammer out the skirt's flange over a piece of angle iron, and that we could bend the flanged material into TLBB's skirt corner curves without damage or distortion to its flanged area.

The first step was to create a sufficient length of flanged metal to fabricate the skirt. By clamping the skirt metal against the angle iron at both ends for position, we were able to move the setup through a vise, and hammer the flange accurately in the vise clamped area as we went along. The whole process took less than 20 minutes. Worrying about how to do it had taken hours.

The flanged skirt metal was now bent around the outside of the top piece form, with the form upside down. The initial bending was done by hand, with the skirt material clamped into place as bending the corner areas progressed. At this point, we were aiming for a rough shape, not a finished one.

The skirt's corner areas were now lightly persuaded into the wooden outline piece with a plastic mallet to give them the correct contours. It was important not to dent the corner areas in this process.

When all dimensions were correct, particularly the sewing tape measured circumference of the skirt, its seam was cut to the correct length and welding gap, and butt welded together at its ends. The skirt's height had been calculated and cut

Using our proven technique for flanging the skirt's edge metal, we hammered the top of the strip over a piece of angle iron. The clamping pliers kept the skirt and angle iron in position. This rig was moved through a vise and hammered in the area gripped by the vise.

SMALL DEMONSTRATION PROJECT: THE LITTLE BLACK BOX

The skirt metal was now bent by hand around the base of the top piece hammer form, and clamped to it as each bend was completed. Note that we used wood strips to protect the skirt metal from the clamping pliers' jaws that held it to the form.

The skirt's corner radii were improved with a plastic mallet, which had to be used carefully to avoid denting the metal. We also rolled our radius socket inside the bends to shape them. Note the overlapping metal in the top side of the skirt. It was trimmed later.

After trimming and welding, the skirt's butt-welded seam was ground inside, and outside, with a grinding burr mounted in a right-angle die grinder. Diagonal measurements of the skirt's flange area indicated that it was perfectly symmetrical and dimensionally correct to the original.

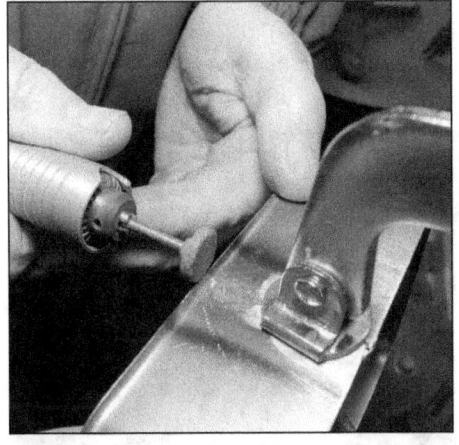

A small grinding stone in a Fordham Tool was used to shape and refine the metal in the flange where the piece had been butt welded. It was amazing how little work was required to shape the flange area.

Here are the two parts of TLBB, ready for assembly, and the original piece in the foreground. If you look carefully, you can see some bulging in the side of the new skirt, near the flange. This was corrected after assembly.

to reach the bottom of the top piece's horizontal curves. The top was cut to exactly the same point, and fitted to the skirt.

The skirt's butt-weld seam was now finished with a die grinder and with small abrasive wheels. Particular attention was paid to the flange's butt-weld seam area. The completed skirt was checked for dimensional accuracy and symmetry. It passed, requiring no further adjustments. In fact, when the flanged area of the new skirt was held face-to-face with the original piece's flange, its accuracy and flatness were amazingly close. Some surface defects in skirt's side metal were noted for later correction.

Assembling the Two Pieces

The two pieces of TLBB were now ready to assemble . . . deep breath! They were fitted, fixtured, and welded. The weld was made in spaced

AUTOMOTIVE SHEET METAL FORMING & FABRICATION

MIG tacks, to avoid unnecessary heat distortion, and because it was unnecessary to run a continuous weld bead. Since solder filler would be used at the weld seam, and since there was no need for great strength at that seam, a continuous weld would have been superfluous. Also, a lap weld configuration was used rather than a butt weld. This was to allow for additional body solder depth in the critical seam area, where the side and corner bend radii would meet and have to be finished. It was easier to shape and file body solder than sheet metal and welds, and fill solder gave us more lead filler thickness to finish to accurate contours. However, we maintained that depth at a maximum of about 3/32 inch.

After grinding the welds close to flush to the metal, it remained to perform several filling and finishing operations on the assembled piece. These included tinning, leading, filing, sanding, etc.

Trying to get a firm grip on this small part with the likes of clamping pliers would have damaged it, while fumbling with it on a bench would have been awkward, uncertain, and uncomfortable. The original wooden form on which the top piece was hammered would not take the heat of tinning, and it really didn't hold the piece very well, anyway. All of that justified cutting and brazing some scrap steel into a tight-fitting work stand for our new LBB. I strongly recommend making work stands in these situations. It takes little extra time and material to do this, but the benefits are more than worth that effort and material. In this case, our LBB work stand was returned to our scrap box to be recycled into something else, or used as a hat rack by someone with a very small head.

Our LBB replica was now tinned and leaded, with particular attention to low spots, such as a few that we found around the skirt's welded vertical seam. (See Chapter 8 for an extended description of the tinning and leading processes.) Since considerable shaping was still required on the filler in the side and corner areas of the seam that joined the top to the skirt, lead filler was the best choice, due to its superior shaping and anti-corrosion properties.

After tinning, the cover was marked and drilled for the two stud holes that would secure it to its base. Although these holes had been carefully modeled during the measurement and patterning phase of this project, it was more certain to line up the original box with the newly fabricated box for the purpose of positioning the drill points for holes than it would have been to use our paper pattern. You can use an original piece for templating purposes if you have one, but at other times this is not possible or practical.

The two parts of TLBB were joined with MIG tack welds, and the welds were ground flush to the metal. Using tack welds provided adequate strength and prevented the distortion that a continuous MIG weld would have produced.

I'm a big believer in making work stands for most jobs. This one took less than half an hour to construct, but saved a lot of time and frustration. It was made out of brazed pieces of scrap metal, a short piece of 1½-inch square tube for the base and some 2-inch strap steel for the cross-supports and surround.

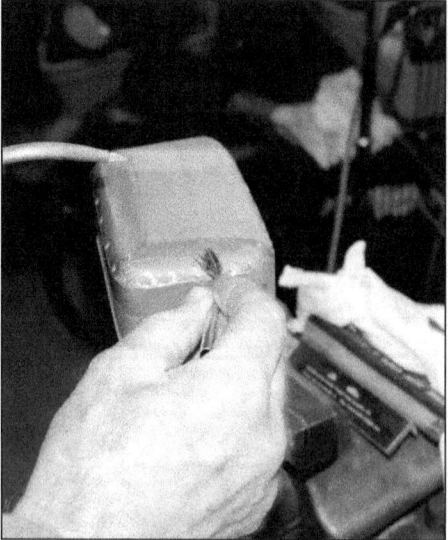

The assembled, welded LBB was fluxed in preparation for applying tinning and body solder. Note that it had been gently bead blasted to remove all contamination before it was fluxed.

SMALL DEMONSTRATION PROJECT: THE LITTLE BLACK BOX

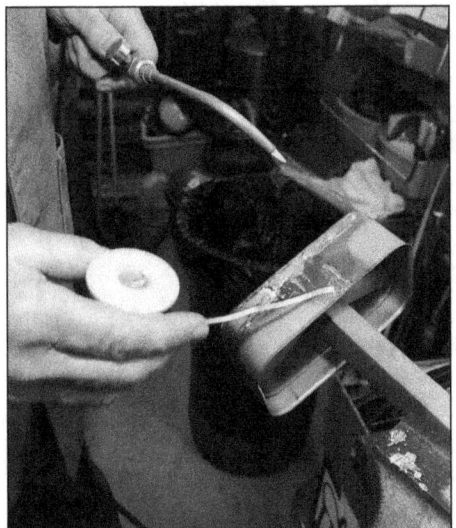

The fluxed areas were now tinned with 50/50 solder to provide adhesion for lead filler. Note how handy the work stand is for holding TLBB in a variety of positions. The tinning shown here is being applied in the skirt seam area.

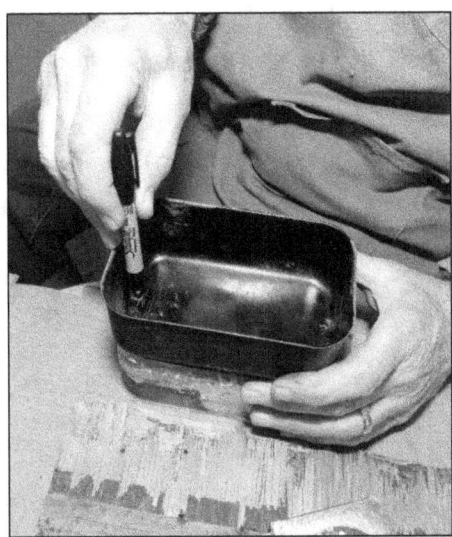

We tried to transfer the hole positions for the hold-down studs from one of our paper patterns, but found that holding the original LBB upside down over our fabricated piece made for a more accurate marking job.

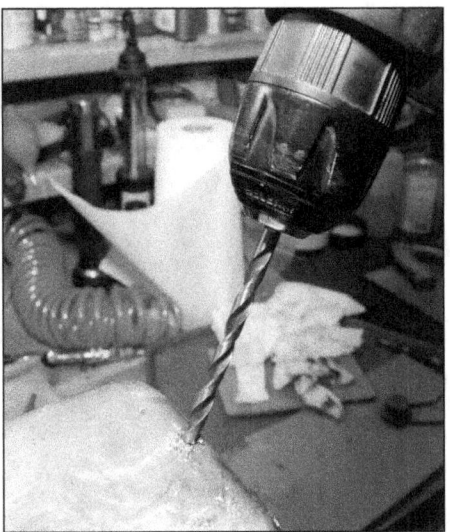

With the exact positions of the holes determined, we drilled them into the fabrication with a twist drill. Note that the drill is angled to the top of the piece because the holes are in the end curves of TLBB. Also, note the tinning solder on TLBB's top.

We stubbed a generous amount of lead filler material onto the top of the box because some of the final shaping depended on having enough lead to file.

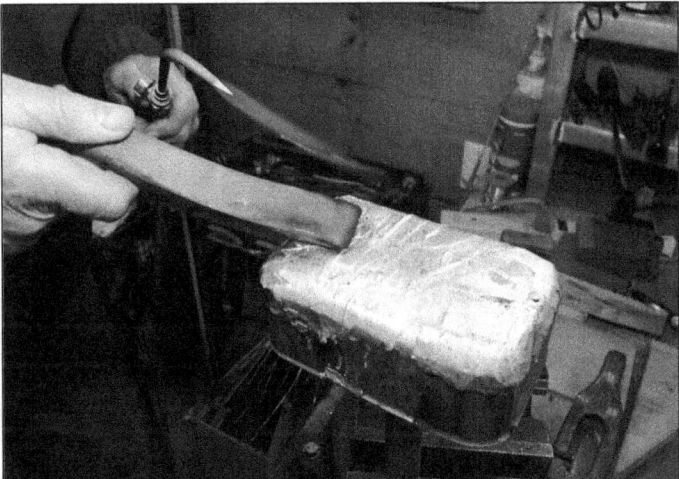

The lead filler was now moved into the areas where it would be needed for filing. While plastic filler could have been used more easily for this job, I find lead much easier to shape accurately than plastic filler.

With the mounting hold-down holes drilled, lead was stubbed onto the tinned areas of the box and spread with a lubricated maple paddle to where it was needed to raise low spots and form contours. This is all pretty standard stuff, but we were doing it in an unusually small scale. It felt a bit more like jewelry making than sheet metal fabrication. In fact, it was the complexity and scale of this job that made it so challenging.

With the lead application completed, TLBB was filed to correct contours and to a pretty smooth surface, pending final sanding. At this point, it looked smooth and symmetrical. When looked at side-by-side with the original box, it looked very accurate. However, there were two problem areas: the areas of what was supposed to be raised material around the hold-down stud holes. These were little raised metal bosses designed to take the pressure from the threaded,

CHAPTER 13

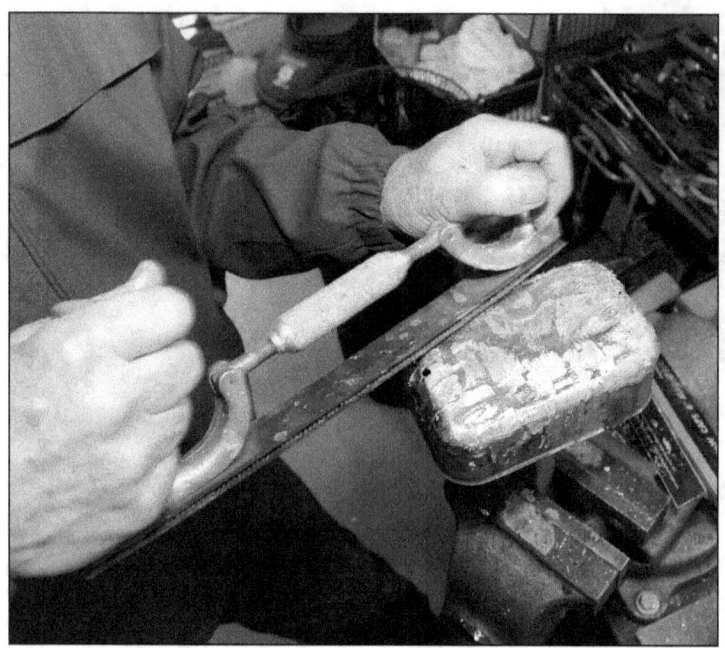

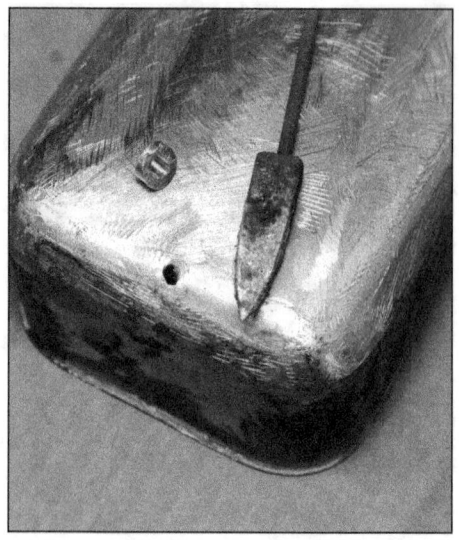

The lead filler filed easily, and allowed us to correct a few contour problems as we filed it. In particular, there was still some bowing in one of TLBB's long sides. We were now able to correct this by filing our lead filler carefully to eliminate it.

We had been unsuccessful in working out the area of the hold-down-hole bosses in TLBB's metal top piece, so we made little brass bosses and soldered them over the hold-down holes. We used a soldering iron to pile a little body solder up against them for later filing.

single winged hold-down nuts. In the original piece, these areas were visibly raised, but we were unable to hammer them out sufficiently in our fabrication's sheet steel to get the right elevation in the new piece. We considered building them up in body lead and filing their detail into the piece, but lead would provide an insufficiently hard and durable surface for repeated tightening of the hold-down nuts. To correct this deficiency, we fabricated brass extensions for the hold-down holes, and soldered them into place. Later, we filed and finished the brass pieces and the solder around them. That completed the leading work on TLBB.

TLBB was now inspected minutely with a magnifying glass for dimensional deviations, and marked where they were found. Metal was

After adding the hold-down-hole bosses and filing our box, it looked very close to the original box. What shaping remained was completed mostly with abrasive paper, backed by various hard, soft, and softer backings.

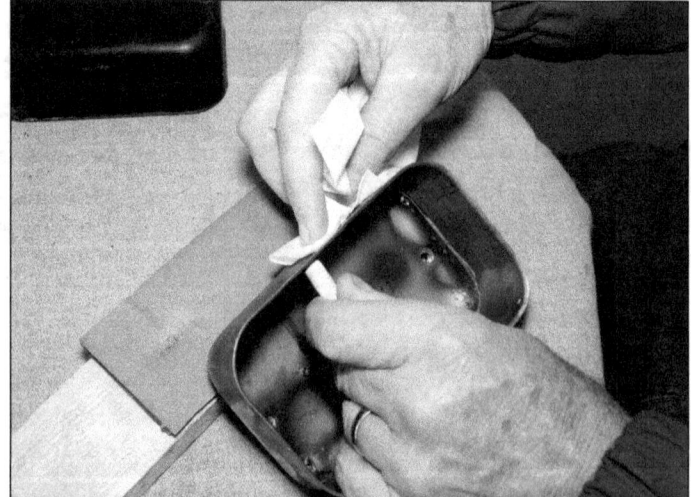

At this point we looked at and felt the unleaded side surfaces of TLBB very carefully, and marked them for high and low spots. There was no point in attempting this fine tuning before leading and filing the top of TLBB was completed.

SMALL DEMONSTRATION PROJECT: THE LITTLE BLACK BOX

Using our marks for guides, we employed some short-reach hammers to push out any low spots. By the way, we fabricated our short-reach hammers out of common body hammers. These are very handy items.

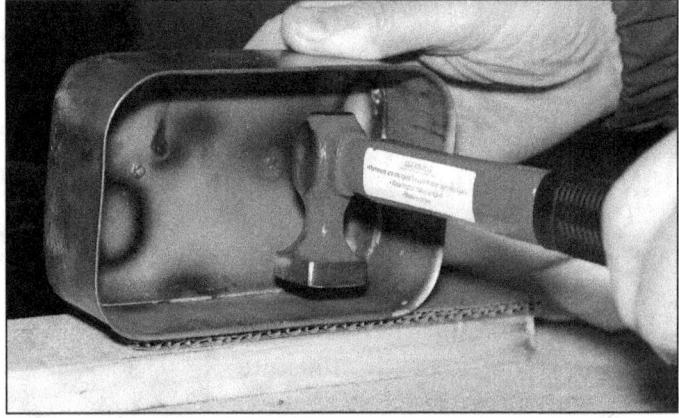

This is the other end of the hammer in the photo to the left. Some areas were picked out, while others were moved more generally with larger hammers. The corrugated cardboard backing provided an almost perfect basis for moving metal of varying areas in small increments.

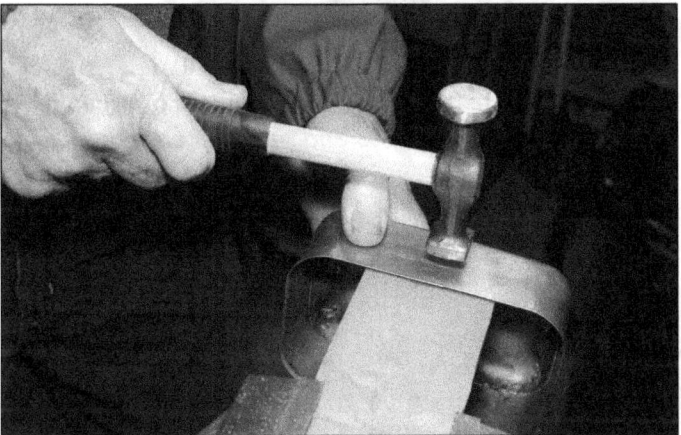

Placing this cardboard-backed piece of pine in a vise allowed us to extend it inside TLBB for some area hammering of high spots. Note that the use of square-faced hammers in these areas allowed us to work close to the side's top bend and its bottom flange.

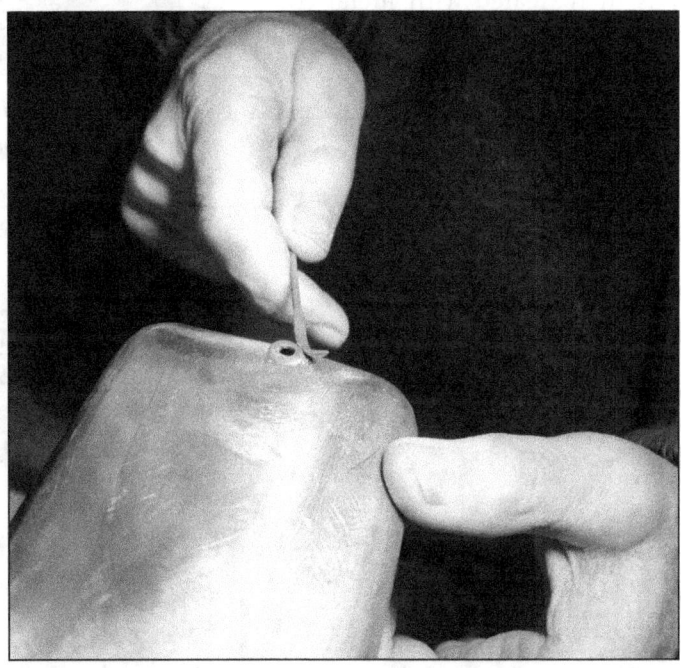

Final shaping of the brass bosses in the hold-down-hole areas was accomplished with several rifling files. These areas were then sanded smooth with 180-grit paper, backed with the edge of a piece of 1/4-inch-thick medium-hard rubber, with its edges shaped for specific parts of the job.

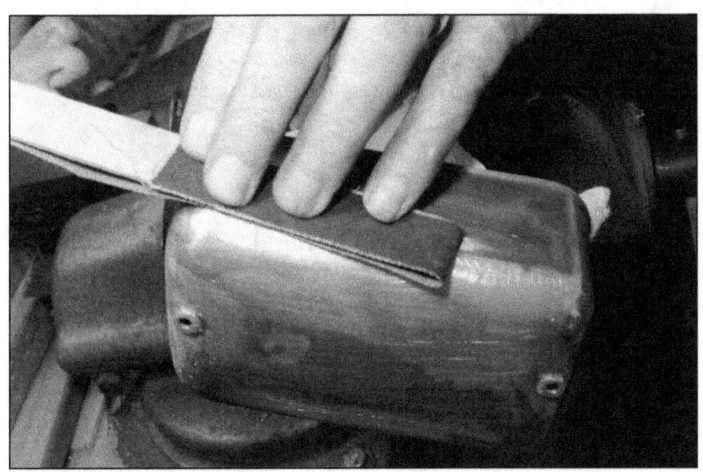

Most of the final sanding of the box's curved sides and corners was done with 180-grit emery cloth wrapped around a paint stick. This method of sanding produces very accurate results.

moved out, where necessary, with special short-reach hammers that we have fabricated from parts of regular body hammers. Where outside areas were high, they were gently moved in with conventional body hammers. With a little bit of filing with a body file, our LBB had nearly perfect dimensions and very true surfaces.

Final shaping of the hold-down areas was completed with miniature rifling files. They were then sanded smooth. The whole box was then sanded with various emery cloth grits, mounted on both hard and soft backings. This produced a final surface finish for painting. The piece was then treated with metal conditioner to kill flux and leading residues, and dried and primed.

Pulling a strip of emery cloth along the top's curves and corners provided a little final smoothing. This averaged their shapes and removed any remaining small, local irregularities.

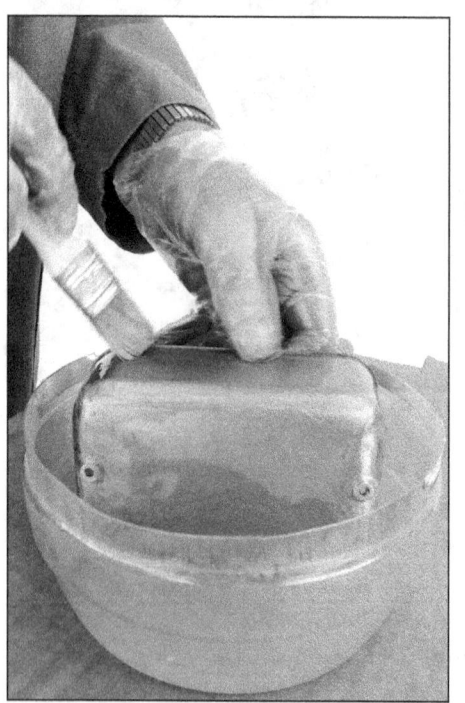

An important final step in this fabrication (before priming it) was to treat the entire box with metal conditioner. We immersed the whole piece in a solution of conditioner and brushed it into every surface. We then let it react and wiped it off.

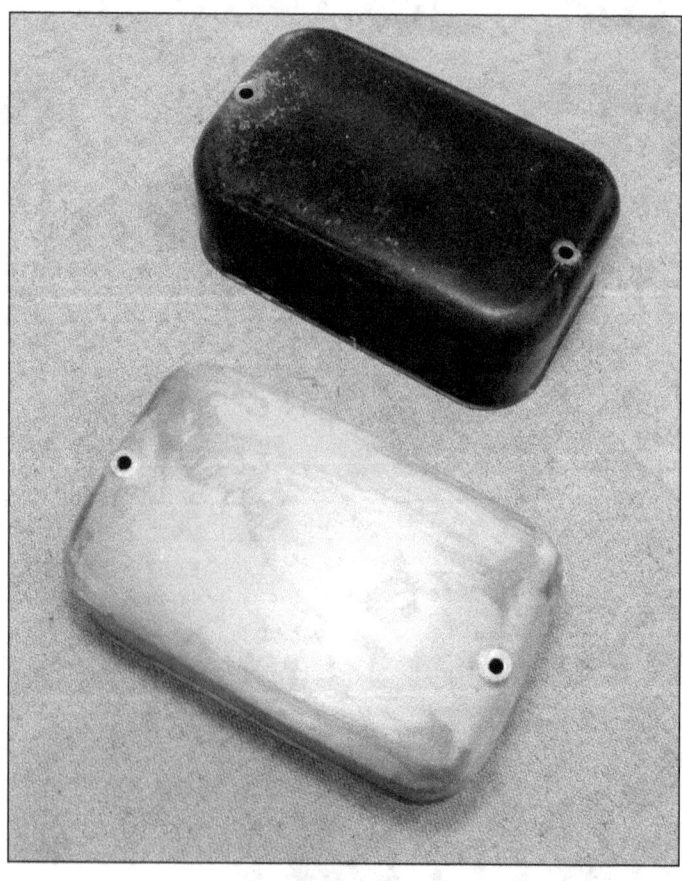

This is what our finished LBB looked like before we primed it. We used a sanding primer, and then sanded it for final smoothness and adhesion. You can compare our fabrication (bottom) with the original part (top).

CHAPTER 14

LARGE DEMONSTRATION PROJECT: FENDER FABRICATION

You have already seen parts of this project in various stages and contexts in previous chapters. You may have wondered what it was. Now I describe how this ambitious sheet metal fabrication was pursued to success in beginning-to-end sequence. This project was mostly the work of Wayne Ayers, a master sheet metal fabricator and technician at L'Cars in Cameron, Wisconsin. He was assisted by L'Cars' extremely knowledgeable shop metal foreman, Blaine, and by highly talented co-craftsman, Matt.

The job was to fabricate three pairs of John Deere orchard tractor fenders. This was a difficult fabrication for several reasons. Each fender is a large piece that is formed into a perfectly symmetrical segment of a circular cross section, and then refined at its leading and trailing edges for left and right applications. Its symmetry means that any inaccuracy will be highly visible. These fenders are seen from both sides, so every inch of every surface must be true on both sides.

Originally, these parts were formed in some kind of giant spinning operation, and then edge trimmed and wire edged. The original material was 16-gauge mild steel, a thickness necessary to take the impact and stress of orchard work. The two inner fender braces were originally stamped in single pieces of 12-gauge steel. Since the new fenders were to be used only on tractors in museum settings, it was not necessary to duplicate the exact thickness of the original materials, so the fender bodies were formed from 18-gauge, and the

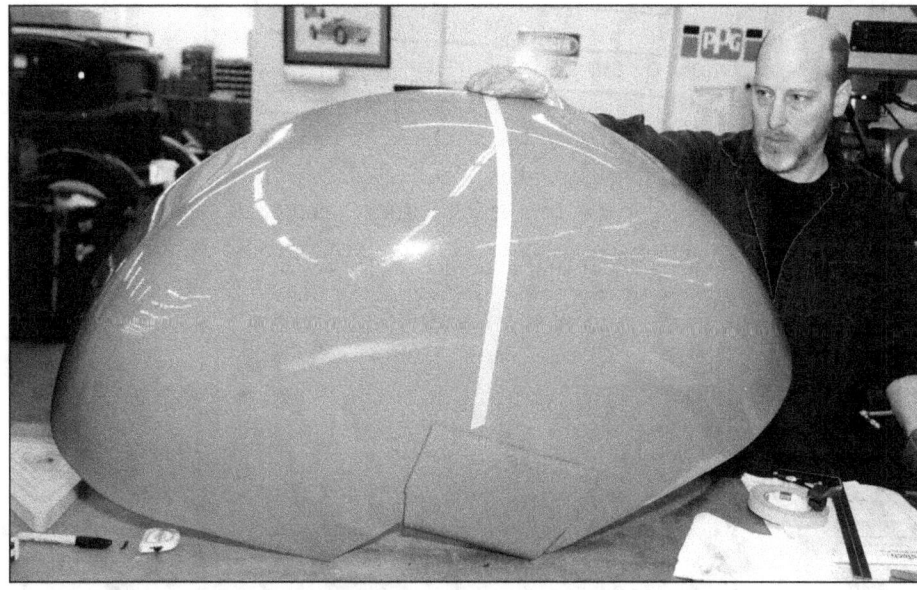

For several reasons, reproducing this John Deere orchard tractor fender was a very advanced sheet metal fabrication project. Note the fender's indexing tape mark for later use, its basic symmetry, and its heavy-gauge bottom bracket.

This is the inside of the John Deere fender. Note the blue tape indexing mark for patterning, the side fender braces, and the hefty bottom support brace. All braces are spot welded to the fender body. Note also the wire edging. All of these features were reproduced in this fabrication.

This profile template is one of many such patterns and templates that Wayne created to capture and transfer the dimensions and features of the original panel to his fabrication. Useful and accurate templates and patterns are one of the keys to getting this kind of work right.

braces from 14-gauge material. This was still extremely thick panel material to work into complex shapes. Making these parts in their original gauges would have been possible, but very costly, due to the extra time required to form the thicker materials.

It may have been possible to hammer and wheel these fenders from flat stock without the use of advanced, modern metal forming machinery, but it would have taken legendary skill and epochal time to do this. Besides, there was no point in doing it that way. The original fenders were spun on a machine. It made perfect sense to form their replicas on modern machinery.

Planning and Patterning

The basic project plan was to form the fender's shape into sheet metal in two lengthwise (circumferential) sections and then to weld them together. A joint position in the middle of a highly crowned area was chosen for the seam, because it was a logical place in terms of forming each section. Specifically, it meant that major crown could be added at the edge of each of the two pieces, a far easier proposition than electing to add that crown in the middle of a panel. Making a joint where the flat fender side bent into the crowned top area was not considered, because placing the seam adjacent to the flat side area might have made it more time consuming to deal with the inevitable welding distortion that would have occurred there. The chosen joint position was also optimal in terms of panel strength and for maximizing the effectiveness of the under fender braces. The bottom support bracket and side support braces were dealt with as later additions to the basic shape, just as the factory had treated them originally.

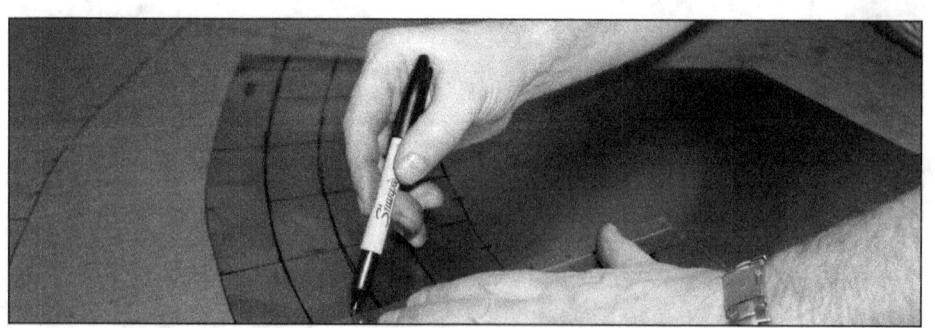

After cutting sheet metal to dimensions that accommodate the side section of the fender, plus some extra trim metal, Wayne marks the working grid for the job onto the metal. The grid indicates position and depth for the basic shrinking operation. It will be used extensively to implement Wayne's plan.

LARGE DEMONSTRATION PROJECT: FENDER FABRICATION

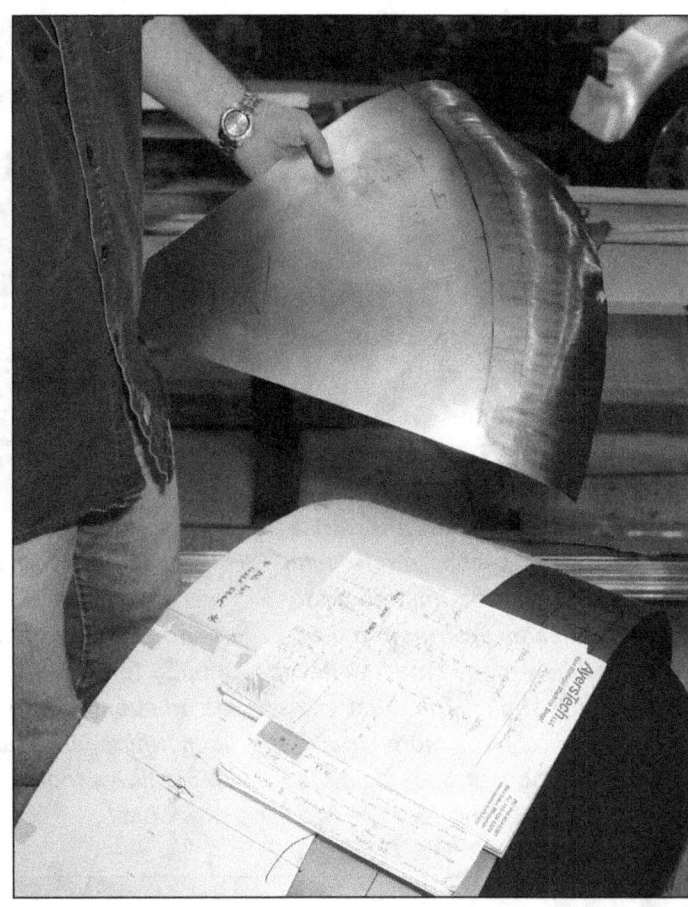

These paper flap patterns are the most important patterns for this job. Closing the flaps indicates the panels' contours in three dimensions. Such patterns guide good forming work. Note how they join at the welded seam.

In his left hand, Wayne holds a proof piece for the crown in the fender's side piece. He has successfully replicated this part of the fender and recorded his process on a tablet. It details exact sequences of shrinking die work, and other processes, that yielded the correct result.

An original, albeit substantially repaired, pair of fenders was available for measuring and recording gross dimensions and modeling contours. However, like the project described in Chapter 13, templates and patterns were still very necessary to translate the original fenders' dimensions and shapes into what were more useful representations for the purpose of duplicating them in metal. Wayne made numerous versions of these patterning and templating items. Mostly, they were variations of the two patterns shown above. That is, templates for checking profiles against the original in several places, and paper flap patterns for determining overall and specific contours in both particular areas, and generally, for the whole panel. In the left-hand photo on page 133, you see the two most crucial paper flap patterns, one for each of the fabricated pieces. These patterns are extensively indexed to the original fender and to each other. They were used to check and guide this fabrication throughout its construction. (See Chapter 4 for more on patterning and templating.)

Fabricating the Side Section

The photographs above reveal the very heart of planning for this kind of ambitious sheet metal fabrication project. There is no flame, smoke, violence, or tricks in it. What it does show are the key steps that should be taken before metal is moved. They are mostly derived from observation, analysis, and experimentation. The piece in Wayne's left hand is a proof piece for the side piece's crown. It replicates that section of the fender. It is not the first test piece that Wayne made, but rather, the one that got the fender's crown right. Sitting on top of a slip-rolled piece that approximates the top piece's contour, you can see Wayne's notes on fabricating the side piece. Those notes record the exact process that worked successfully on the proof piece to yield the correct contours for the finished fender side piece. They are expressed as a series of numbers that indicate where, at what depth, and how many times the flat sheet metal in the piece will be run through the Cook shrinking heads to achieve roughly the correct crown in the panel.

I cannot overemphasize the importance of this proofing process in fabrication work. In the immortal words of my high school chemistry

CHAPTER 14

This is Wayne's second run through the Cook heads. The marked grid pattern indicates how far into the panel and how many times he needs to take each stroke. The outer edge of the panel requires more shrinking and will get more strokes than the deeper parts of the grid.

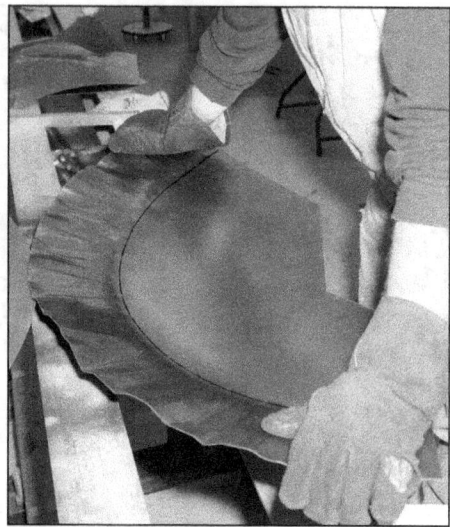

Throughout this fabrication, there were times when Wayne used his hands, and even his feet, to impart shape to his work. Sometimes there is no substitute for just bending something, emphasis on sometimes. Most times tools and machinery work best.

Eckold shrinking heads (shown) produce local shrinking and smooth the metal that was inevitably roughed up a bit in the Cook shrinking heads. Eckold heads gather metal very calmly. These two devices make a terrific one-two punch for forming metal.

Wayne used an English wheel to further smooth and form the fender side section. Running circumferentially through the wheel also added more crown to the piece, which was highly desirable at this point in this fabrication.

teacher, "The trouble you don't get into, you don't have to get out of." It would be folly to sally forth into a project of this complexity without a very clear and specific idea of and plan for how to successfully perform its most critical procedures. This job is just too complex to try to figure out how to do it on-the-fly.

The basic forming plan for the side piece was now transferred from recorded measurements to a grid drawn on the piece of stock from which this part of the fender would be formed. The piece of stock had been cut to a size and shape that would accommodate the formed piece, while allowing for some excess edge metal to trim after forming was complete. The grid would have to be redrawn on the piece from time to time, as work on it eradicated the original markings.

The photos on this page represent the central forming operations that were used in this fabrication, repeated over and over again. They are: radical shrinking in a Pullmax with Cook shrinking heads; non-machine manipulation with gloved hands, hammers, etc., shrinking and smoothing with Eckold heads, and smoothing and shaping with an English wheel. These repeated processes will now be discussed in more detail. (They are also covered in Chapter 11.)

About half a dozen runs through the Cook heads were needed to fully form this piece. These were interspersed between other operations that further shaped and smoothed it. Each run through the

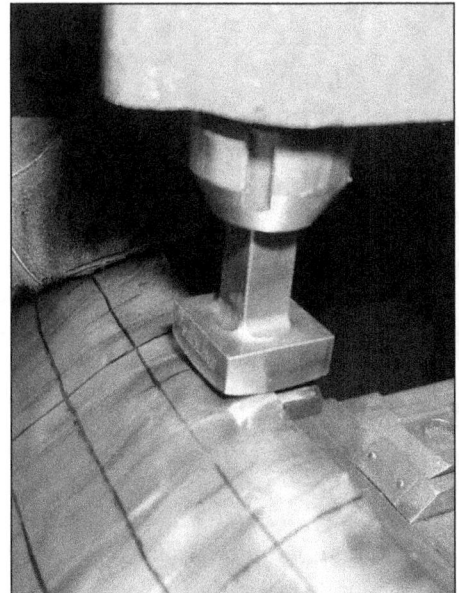  

There is no better way to move and shrink a lot of metal quickly than using this type of metal working head. It leaves the surface of your metal somewhat rough, but that is something that can easily be corrected later.

Eckold shrinking heads at work are wonderful to behold. They perform without drama, almost serenely. But for all of that peacefulness, they gather, shrink, and smooth metal with certainty and great precision.

The English wheel was used to smooth and shape the side panel. Note that the panel grid lines were getting erased, and would need redrawing. Also, note that the wheel was being used circumferentially. Later in this fabrication, it was used diagonally and laterally.

Cook heads brought it closer to its final shape. The Cook shrinking heads did enormous local shrinking, without permanently damaging metal. Performing this job without them would have been vastly more time consuming. The key to making this process work in a complex fabrication, like this one, was to predetermine the exact shrinking needed, and to follow the regimen that had already proven itself for the location and frequency of this operation on the proof piece.

The Eckold shrinking heads performed much less radical shrinks than the Cook heads; it was more of a fine-tuning operation. The Eckold heads also smoothed the metal, removing some of the inevitable roughness left by the Cook head operations. Like the Cook heads, the Eckold heads did their work without damaging the panel surface. The Eckold heads were also used to impart much more specific and local shrinking to the panel than was possible in the radical shrinking done with the Cook heads.

The final basic operation in this fabrication was to use an English wheel on the panel, again, to smooth and shape it. (Remember that English wheels are primarily controlled stretching devices that also tend to smooth surfaces rolled through them.) Both of the English wheel's capabilities were used in several stages of this fabrication, but primarily the wheel's smoothing capabilities. For that purpose, wheel pressure settings were kept relatively low much of the time.

At every stage of the forming process, pieces were checked against the templates and patterns that had been made before actual metal work began. Every contour, shape, and measurement was ruthlessly compared to the collected data. What was ruthless about it was that when deviations were noted, they weren't blamed on defective data—akin to claiming that "The dog ate my homework." Instead, the part was reformed and refined to what the data said it should be. This kind of discipline is critical to success in complex forming jobs.

At every point in this job, particularly at this final stage, the finished side piece was checked against its paper flap pattern for its outside contours and dimensions. Then, it was marked, taped, remarked, and trimmed, until the pattern indicated that the trimmed edge would fit perfectly to the top piece when they were welded together.

CHAPTER 14

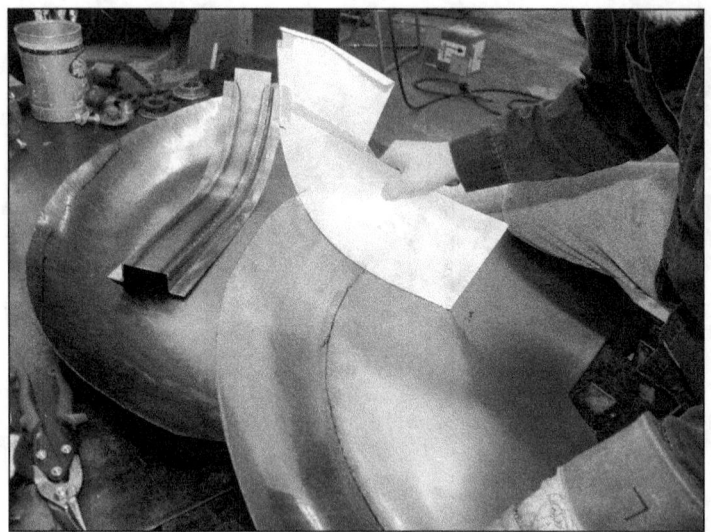

This simple-looking template is one of the most critical of dozens of templates used in this fabrication to verify the forming of its parts. The side brace (on the left) will also be checked against the fender panel for fit.

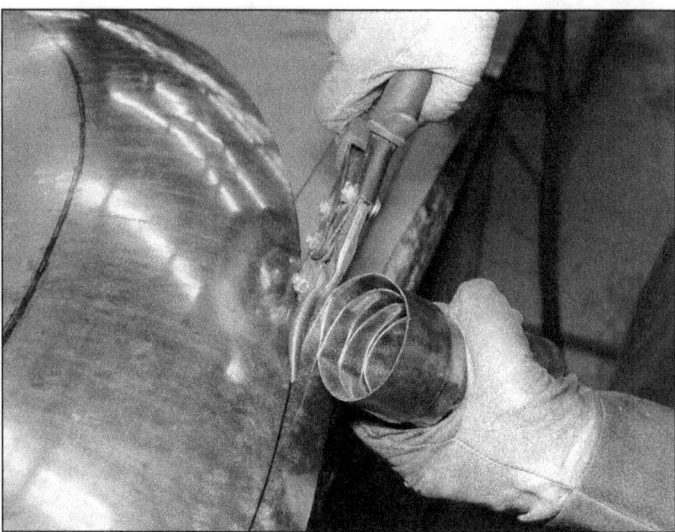

After confirming its correct contour and dimensions, Wayne trimmed the side panel's mating edge for an exact fit to the top panel. Note how he deals with the trim metal by rolling it into a neat coil as he shears the metal.

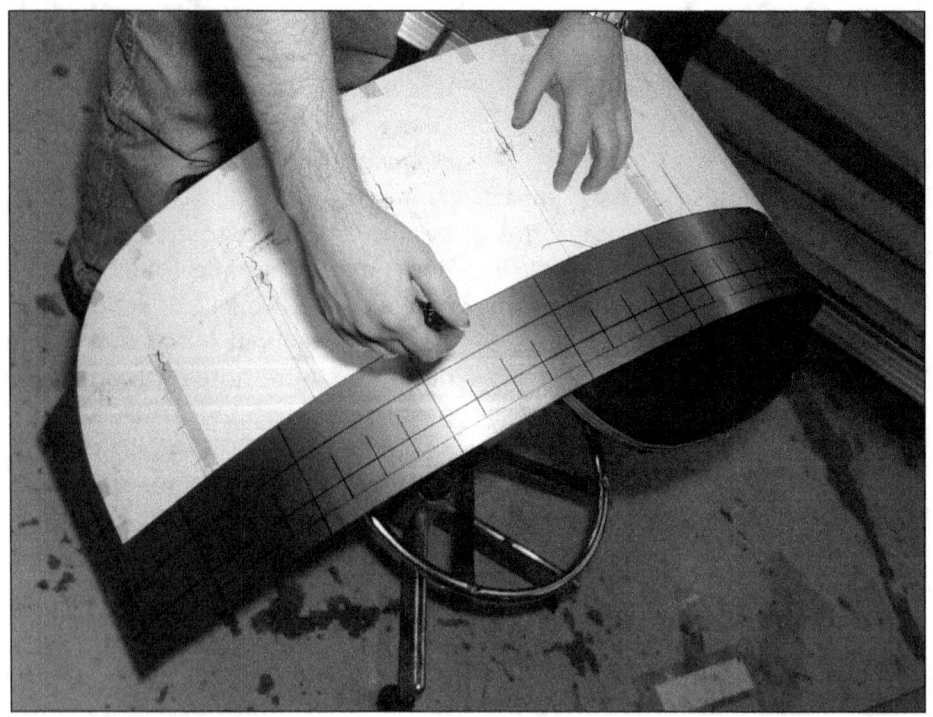

Wayne carefully marked additional grid intersects from his paper flap template onto the panel that would be formed into the fender's top piece. Each time that he made the top and side pieces he was able to slightly refine and improve his plan.

Fabricating the Top Section

The process and sequence for creating the top section of this fabrication was exactly the same as the process used for the side section. It involved careful planning, creating a proof piece, and forming the metal according to the plan. This part of the project presented a similar level of challenge to that of fabricating the side piece of the fender.

The first step was to transfer the markings from a proof piece work-up to the metal to be formed. In this case, the metal had been slip rolled into roughly the arc of the finished piece, before crown was added to it.

The rest of the steps in forming the top piece will be familiar to you from the description of how the side piece was formed: repetitions of radical shrinking with the Cook heads, followed by manual adjustments by hand and by hammer, leading to work between the Eckold shrinking heads, and last, smoothing and contouring on the English wheel. Amazingly quickly, each application at each stage of this work brought the top piece closer and closer to perfectly fitting the patterns that guided its fabrication.

LARGE DEMONSTRATION PROJECT: FENDER FABRICATION

This was the second or third pass through the Cook shrinking heads. Each position on the grid indicates where passes will be applied, and how deeply into the panel, according to the initial plan for this piece.

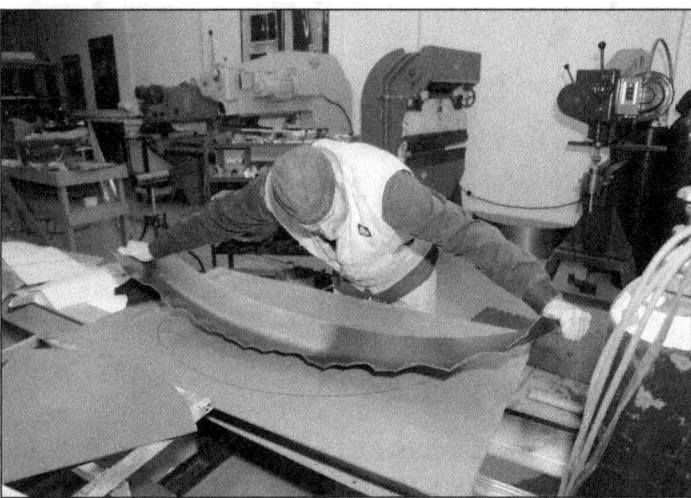

At this stage of shrinking its edge, some manual bending helped Wayne bring the top piece into its correct arc. Note the drawn cardboard pattern under it for comparison of the mating edges of the two pieces.

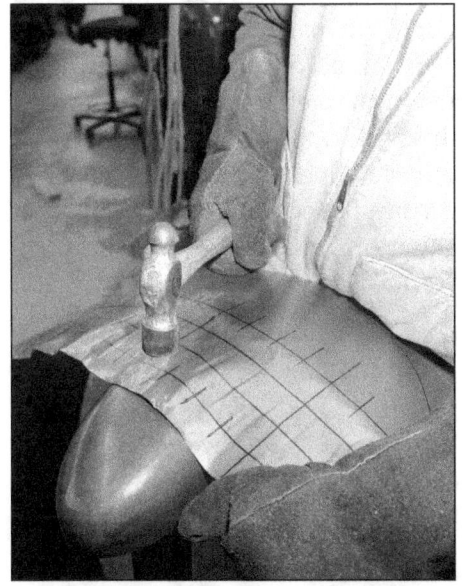

As this fabrication progressed, some hand hammering was necessary to smooth the panel before other smoothing measures could be applied. Specifically, the worked part of the panel wasn't flat enough to use the Eckold heads or the English wheel.

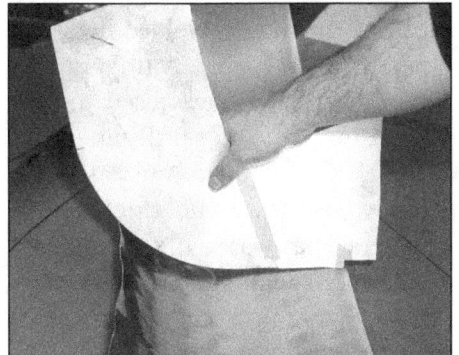

This all-important side template check revealed that much shaping remained to be done, and, more significantly, roughly where it was needed. Constant checking greatly reduced the possibility of overworking any panel area and having to come back and undo what had been done.

With the piece smoothed out a bit, the Eckold shrinking heads were applied to further smooth the metal, and to work some more local shrinking into the edge of the piece.

Wheeling provided more smoothing and shaping. The cross-work maneuver (shown) provided a little needed stretch to one small area and a lot of smoothing to the whole worked area of the panel.

AUTOMOTIVE SHEET METAL FORMING & FABRICATION

CHAPTER 14

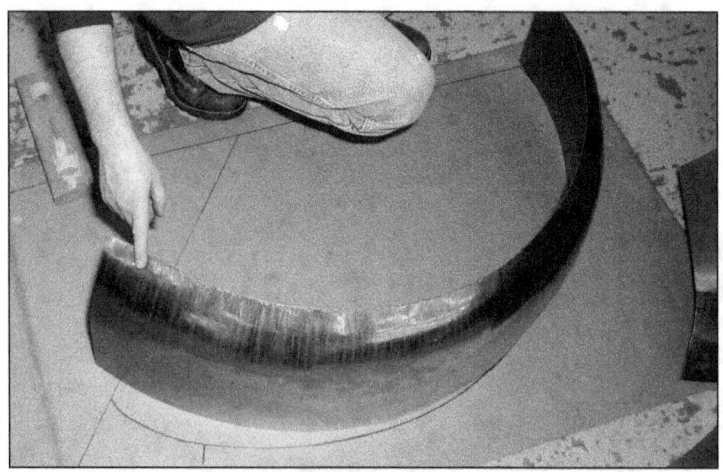

Making the outer edge of the top piece fit this cardboard pattern was critical. This check indicates that more work was still needed to make it fit the side piece.

The accuracy of this fabrication is indicated and confirmed by how closely the mating areas of the top and side pieces fit. The top piece was now marked for exact edge match to the side piece.

The top piece's mating edge to the side piece was taped along the marked cut line, remarked, and trimmed. After the top and side pieces of the fender were joined, trims along lines like the visible curve marked on the metal would prepare the fender for wire edging.

Joining the Two Pieces

With the two fender sheet metal pieces completed with outstanding accuracy, it was time to join them into one panel. The precision of the work done on each piece was verified by the near perfection of how accurately their mating edges met. These edges were now loosely clamped together and tack welded to each other in a butt weld configuration. Since TIG welding was used to join them, almost no fit-up distance was necessary, and little was allowed, actually less than the thickness of the metal that was being welded.

The first tack welds were widely spaced, working from the center of the panels to their edges. Then, tack welds were added between them, and the panel's mating edges were fine tuned for fit. Next, more tack welds were added between the existing ones, and more minor adjustments were made, not just to the mating edges of the joint, but also to the metal that flowed into them. This attended to overall shape of the panel in the joint area, not just the actual seam.

When the tack welds reached a spacing of about 3/4 inch, a continuous seam weld was applied over them. By the time that the seam weld was made, the shape of the panel had been almost completely perfected, and the TIG welded seam did little to change or distort it.

Now, the weld seam was ground flat to the panel on both of its sides. This was accomplished with two different-diameter pneumatic sanding discs. Because the TIG weld bead was relatively flat, this step was accomplished very quickly. In most situations, only the outer aspect of a seam weld is visible, but in this case,

The top and side pieces were loosely clamped together at their mating edges and tack welded into position. Tacks were applied from the center of the seam out to its ends at wide intervals, with position checks and adjustments after every tack weld was made.

LARGE DEMONSTRATION PROJECT: FENDER FABRICATION

As tack welds were added between existing tack welds, the positions of the edges were adjusted to keep everything in proper alignment. If you were wondering, this is how you accomplish a perfect seam area.

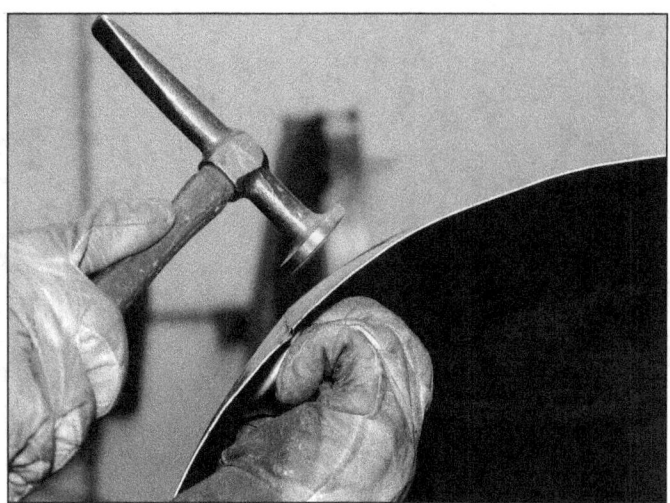

By working and refining the metal for several inches on either edge of the welded seam, the shape of the entire panel was made to flow properly and accurately into the joint. And that is how you create a perfect panel.

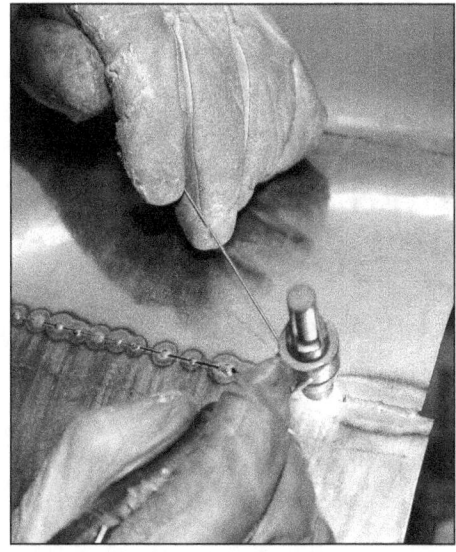

With the contour at the joint perfected and the tack weld density at about one per 3/4 inch, a seam weld was made over the tack welds. Note the use of filler rod to make the seam weld. Also, note the very minor fit-up distance between the panels being welded.

Two different disc sanders were used to level and finish the seam weld. This is the smaller of the two. It was used after the larger one. This photo shows finishing the underside of the fender seam.

both sides of the weld would be highly visible after the fender was mounted.

At this point in this fabrication, Wayne tried a very unusual experimental step. It was a step that couldn't harm anything, but that had a considerable potential for verifying and improving the job. (I like those odds, and so did Wayne.) A set of heavy water jet cut dies that had been developed to fabricate the fender support brackets was available. They perfectly represented most of the radial format of the fender. (These dies are seen on page 140 in the context of their primary purpose, forming the sides of the fender side brackets.)

What enabled this step was that the bracket format exactly matched the radial cross section of the fender panel. It was a terrifically imaginative use of resources to employ these dies to verify and true most of the fender's high crown formed area. To do this, the dies were welded to mountings and attached to the Pullmax. The fender was then fed through them. They actually made some minor improvements to the shape of the fender. I consider this a brilliant use of resources to improve the quality of a job. More to the point, it worked.

The final step in forming the sheet metal in the fender top section was to apply careful English wheel work to it. This was done in a diagonal cross pattern that is designed to create and leave a perfectly smooth and uniform surface.

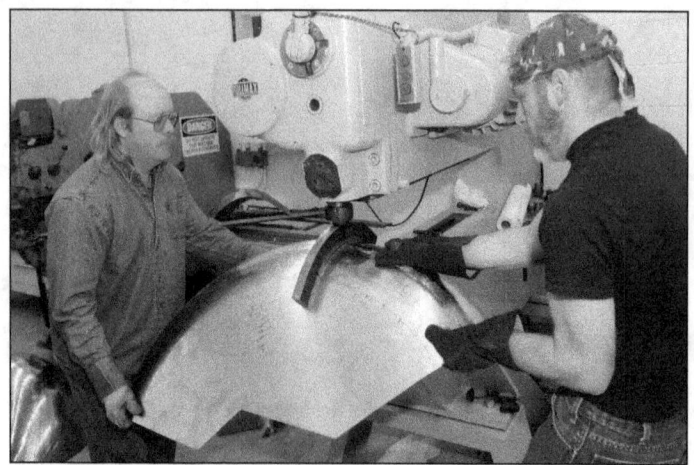

The step shown here is experimental and very unorthodox. Dies that had been cut to fabricate the fender's side brackets were used in a Pullmax to check and uniform the panel's shape. This step was experimental, and it worked.

Final smoothing and shaping of the welded fender was done on the indispensable English wheel. Note the radial marks on the metal, made by the bracket dies used in the previous uniforming operation. Wheeling almost completely eliminated these marks, leaving a surface requiring only light sanding before it was painted.

Wire Edging the Fender Panel

Wire edging is a difficult operation. With a panel this thick, this large, and with these curves, it would be nearly impossible to do it without a Magee wire edging machine. With the Magee, it took about five minutes to wire edge each fender to near perfection. (I am told that speaking nicely to the Magee as it wraps the panel edge around the wire helps.)

Even with the Magee's precision, some manual adjustments to the Magee wire edge were necessary. A wooden mallet and some hammer and dolly work accomplished this. It is interesting to note that the Magee left some gaps and roughnesses in the wire wrap in areas where the wired edge made sharp radius bends. It is even more interesting to consider that some similar gaps and roughnesses are visible in the wire edge of the original fender. That is because that fender probably was also wire edged on a Magee. Far from being a defect, this turns out to be a detail of authenticity.

After a final edge trim, the fender was wire edged with the rare and wonderful Magee wire edging machine. Matt fed the 1/4-inch wire while Wayne guided the fender through the machine's roll formers. This operation would be difficult, or impossible, to accomplish without the Magee.

After trimming the wire, there was one more refreshingly manual operation to perform. Wayne compared the new fender to the original with depth measurements to the floor, and crosswise. Then he applied his hands and feet to bring the panel into perfect dimensional condition. This may seem crude by comparison to most of the work that preceded it, but it was necessary to correct some distortion introduced by the welding and wire edging procedures. At this point, the wire reinforced edge helped the fender keep its proper shape.

Further refinement of the wire edged area was accomplished with the English wheel. It was lightly applied to the wire edge's bead, and to the areas near its bead, to level and uniform them. Very light pressure was used with relatively flat wheels. This was very precise work that allowed for little error. In some places, hammer-on and hammer-off

LARGE DEMONSTRATION PROJECT: FENDER FABRICATION

After the fender was wire edged, there was still need for some manual adjustments to its edge. This was done with various hammers. Here, a wooden mallet was used to perfect the wire wrap.

Even with the accuracy that has accompanied this job, the final step in shaping this panel was good old human grunt force. With the wire installed, the panel was now rigid enough to hold its final shape in service. Note the cardboard protecting the fender's surface as Wayne bends it.

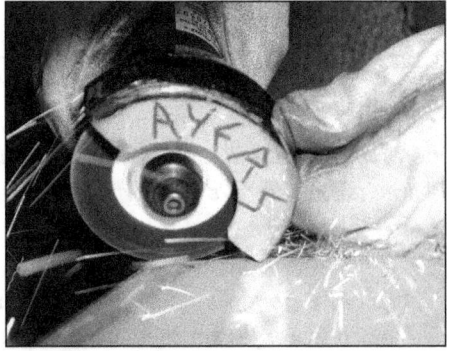

The extra wire was now trimmed to length with a small air disc grinder, leaving it flush with the panel edge. Note the smoothness of the panel, as indicated by the reflection of the grinder.

dolly work was required to bring these areas to exact final contours.

When the new and original fenders were laid side-to-side for comparison, it was clear that this fabrication was a success. All critical dimensions were accurate, and the new panel was regular and smooth to a degree that equaled, or surpassed, those factors in the original.

Making Support and Base Brackets

The final step in this project was to fabricate and mount the fender's side support brackets and base bracket. The side support brackets were particularly important, because they help to stabilize and strengthen the fender's shape. They must perfectly match its contour, or they will pull it out of shape. While the original brackets were die stamped, the new ones were custom fabricated from three pieces of stock. Visually, they were indistinguishable.

The fender side support fabrication was accomplished using a set of 1-inch-thick water jet formed dies, cut from a pattern that perfectly captured the fender's radial profile for the length of its side brackets. 14-gauge mild steel was then clamped between the dies and its extending top edge was bent over the inner die's edge with an industrial strength pneumatic hammer. This not only formed the metal, it also shrunk it by compacting it. The result was a very strong, work-hardened piece that serves well as one of this fender's side brace's sides.

The center piece, between the two air hammered side pieces, was now formed and checked against a plywood template (not shown). It was then tack welded to the side pieces, as it was hammered into final shape.

The fender side supports were tack welded together and then seam welded over the tack welds to finish the side brace fabrication.

The fabricated side braces were now fitted to the fenders, using paper templates that had been made specifically to locate them. This is an example of a situation where having the original fender doesn't help anywhere near as much as having useful templates made from it for specific purposes.

Making the spot welds to join 14-gauge support brace metal to the 18-gauge fender metal required an industrial spot welder and was done in another shop. It was even harder to spot weld the really thick, 3/8-inch bottom brace metal to the fender's 18-gauge material, but that was how John Deere had done it; so that was how Wayne at L'Cars did it.

Fabricating the bottom brace could have been accomplished with sheet metal equipment, but would have been time consuming and difficult. This was really a job for a full-service machine shop. Just cutting its shape on a band saw would have taken a long time. Then it would have required heating and bending. This would have compromised both its strength and its appearance.

CHAPTER 14

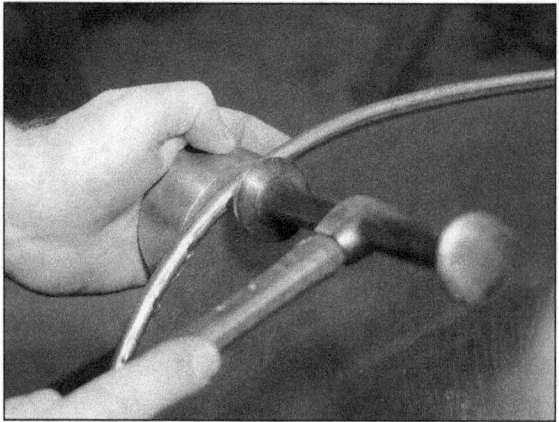

The wire edge was further repaired with a little hammer on-dolly work. This was done to improve the visible smoothness of this area and to make its curve more uniform. The visible gaps in the wire edging are characteristic of Magee forming with very thick metal around tight radii.

Wheeling the bead, and the area next to it, repaired the minor deformation produced there by the Magee wire edger. This kind of slight damage is inevitable when you deform metal as severely as wire edging does.

A strip of 14-gauge mild steel was clamped between two water jet cut dies, with one edge extended beyond them. Then, that edge was air hammered flat over the inside die. It looks rough here, but this process yielded a smooth and very strong side section for the fender brace.

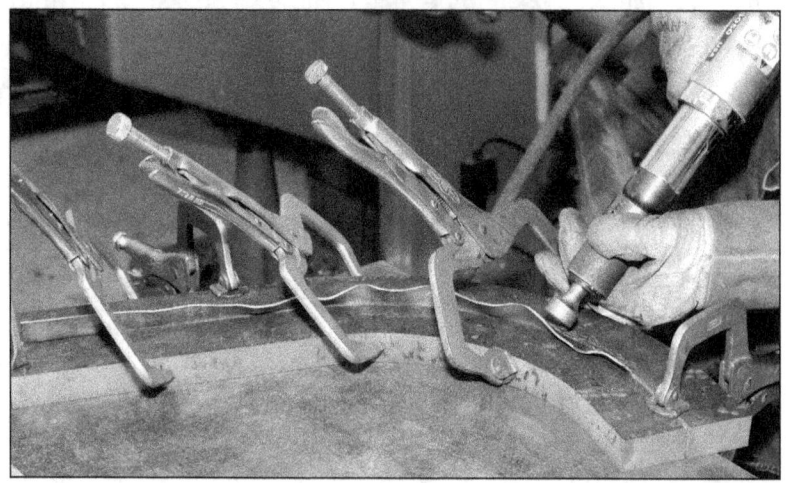

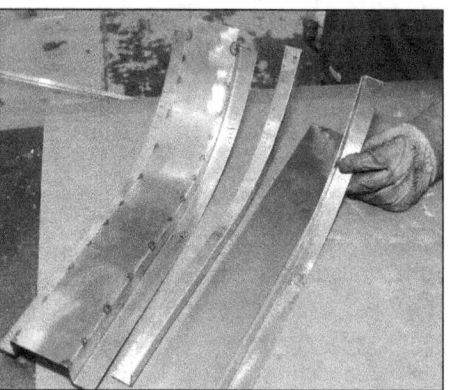

Laying the old and new fenders side-by-side on the floor allowed comparison of their depth and contours. Note that the new fender's surface is much more accurate than the original. (The newly fabricated fender had not yet received its final wire trim or wheel and hammer work.)

As promised, the air hammered side piece of the bracket was pounded smooth and made very strong. Your average air muffler gun won't work for a job like this. It lacks sufficient power. This job took a very-heavy-duty industrial air hammer.

Left: a formed, tack-welded fender side brace, awaiting final seam welding. Right: the parts used to fabricate the brace. Note that the brace's strength is in its side pieces, specifically in their inner, air hammer formed edges. The center piece between them is mostly there to keep them apart.

LARGE DEMONSTRATION PROJECT: FENDER FABRICATION

Assembling the center part of the fender side brace to its formed sides was relatively easy. The center was roughly formed to shape, and then hammered and tack welded into its final position. Placing it in minor dynamic tension against the side pieces increased the strength of the entire assembly.

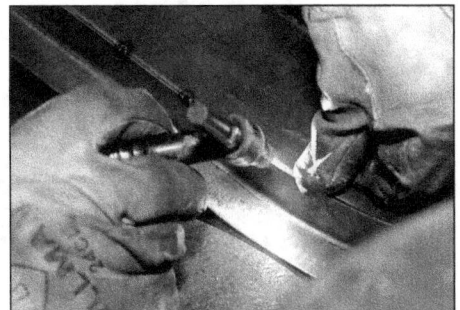

After the tack welds were completed, the side pieces were TIG seamed to the center piece of the fender side brace for a strong joint and a very strong brace. It was easy to finish these welds to give the reproduced braces the look of the stamped originals.

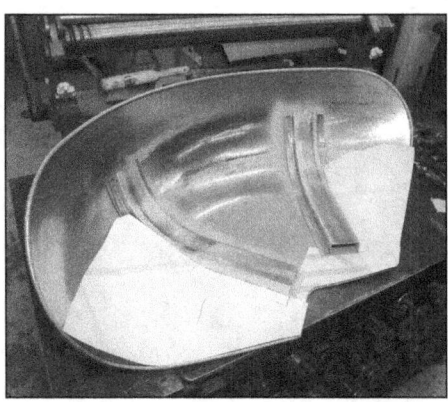

Here are the finished side braces with their positions on the fender indicated by three paper templates—ready for spot welding to the fender. The spot welding was done off-premises with a water-cooled industrial spot welder. Note the weld-through primer, applied where the fender will be welded to its braces.

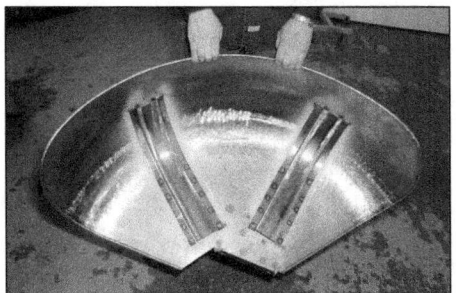

Here is the fender with its spot welded side and bottom braces. The stick welds that join the side brace tops to the fender duplicate how the factory originally made this joint (see the top left-hand photo on page 132). The bottom brace welds are visible through the fender sheet metal.

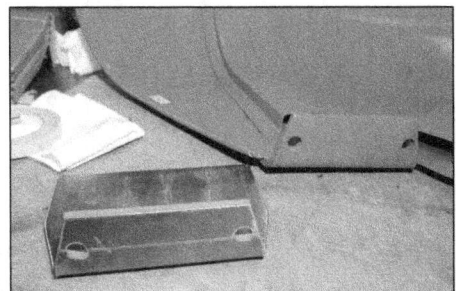

Here is a new bottom brace, next to an original bottom brace on an original fender. Fabricating material this thick is beyond the capabilities of most sheet metal fabrication shops, but can be done easily by shops equipped for this kind of thick section work.

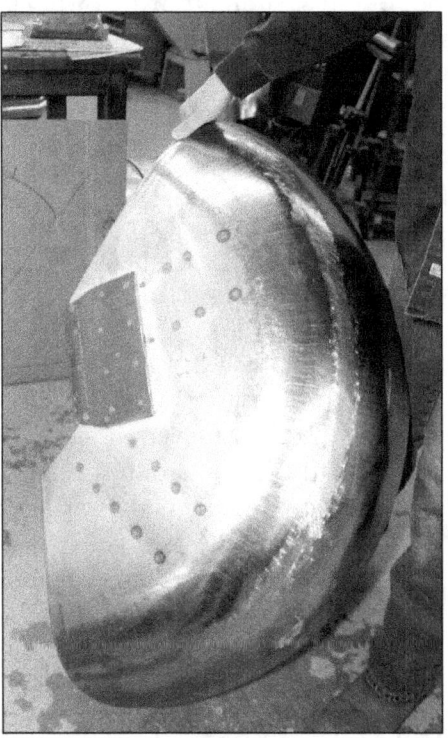

Here is the outside of the finished fender. You can see the central role of the bottom brace in positioning and strengthening it. The spot welds that secure the side braces to the sheet metal will require some finishing work to complete this fabrication.

Instead of all that fuss, the piece was sent to a shop that had water jet cutting capability and hydraulic press brake facilities. It was a small matter for them to make this piece. Note the perfection of the piece's edges and holes that were cut by the water jet method. It is the better part of wisdom to know what you can do well and what is best left others who specialize in doing what you can only accomplish with considerable difficulty and at the cost of excessive time, and probably quality.

As sheet metal fabrication projects go, this would be among the more difficult that I have ever seen. The size and crown of the panel, and thickness of the metal, make this a difficult project. Maybe its saving grace is its symmetry, which makes it relatively easy to pattern and verify. Still, given the ambitious nature of this project and the dimensional accuracy of its result, it remains about as impressive as sheet metal fabrication work gets.

APPENDIX

Radiated Colors

The chart below indicates the radiated colors from steel at various elevated temperatures. Below the barely visible red at 752 degrees F there are various tones of non-radiated browns, dark blues, and very dark blues. These are scaling colors, literally the formation of oxides on the steel at these temperatures.

Radiated colors are actually generated by the metal. If they are important to making temperature determinations, they are best viewed in dark conditions, certainly out of direct sunlight, which will largely hide the colors in the lower radiated ranges.

The most important radiated colors for sheet metal fabrication are the ones in the cherry-red to bright cherry-red range.

Degrees F	Color
752	Red, visible in dark
885	Red, visible in twilight
975	Red, visible in daylight
1,077	Red, visible in sunlight
1,292	Dark Red
1,472	Dull Cherry-Red
1,652	Cherry-Red
1,832	Bright Cherry-Red
2,012	Orange-Red
2,192	Orange-Yellow
2,372	Yellow-White
2,552	White Welding Heat
2,732	Brilliant White
2,912	Dazzling White (Bluish)

Gauge Specifications

The thickness, "gauge," specifications for sheet steel are based on one of several scales for metal thickness that are presently in use around the world. The thicknesses shown below represent the range for most automotive panels.

The gauge numbers below represent the most widely accepted thickness scale for mild steel in the United States. Different metals, such as steel and aluminum, are rated on slightly different gauge scales, usually for arcane purposes, to account for differences in the weights of cubic measures of those metals. Thus, 22-gauge aluminum is not the same actual thickness as 22-gauge steel.

There are also differences in the gauge scales used in different countries, and different parts of the world, again, for arcane reasons.

Consider the manufacturers' gauge numbers below to be a rough description of the thickness of steel panel material. It is always best to specify steel thickness by actual dimension, in either English or metric measurements. That avoids any potential confusion.

Gauge	Thickness
18-gage	.0478 inch
19-gage	.0418 inch
20-gage	.0359 inch
21-gage	.0329 inch
22-gage	.0299 inch
23-gage	.0269 inch
24-gage	.0239 inch

www.ingramcontent.com/pod-product-compliance
Lightning Source LLC
Chambersburg PA
CBHW051413070526
44584CB00023B/3412